**Paradoxes
of Rationality:
Theory of
Metagames
and Political
Behavior**

The MIT Press
Cambridge,
Massachusetts,
and London,
England

The Peace Research
Studies Series
Edited by Walter Isard
1. Paradoxes of Rationality:
Theory of Metagames and
Political Behavior—
Nigel Howard

Paradoxes of Rationality: Theory of Metagames and Political Behavior

Nigel Howard

Copyright © 1971 by The Massachusetts Institute of Technology

This book was designed by The MIT Press Design Department. It was set in Monotype Times Roman, printed on Mohawk Neotext Offset by Vail-Ballou Press, Inc., and bound by Vail-Ballou Press, Inc. in the United States of America.

ISBN 0 262 08046 X (hardcover)
Library of Congress catalog card number: 70-148964

To Marilyn

Foreword

This book on games, metagames, and rationality by Nigel Howard is the first study in The Peace Research Studies Series to be published by The M. I. T. Press. It reflects the urgent need for an approach to the problems of conflict management and resolution that is more rigorous than has generally characterized past studies of international relations, labor-management bargaining, and religious and ethnic group struggles.

The establishment of The Peace Research Studies Series parallels the formation and the successful growth of the Peace Research Society (International) and the publication of research findings of its members in *Papers*, Peace Research Society (International). The Studies Series has the same objective, namely, to foster exchange of ideas and promote studies focusing on peace analysis and utilizing tools, methods, and theoretical frameworks specifically designed for peace research as well as concepts, procedures, and analytical techniques of the various social and natural sciences, law, engineering, and other disciplines and professions. The Studies Series shall also serve as an outlet for quality research manuscripts written by doctoral and postdoctoral scholars associated with major graduate programs in peace research (such as at the University of Pennsylvania) and related fields at all universities of the world.

The particular contribution of Nigel Howard's book lies in its development of the metagame approach and in its new ideas concerning rationality. In developing the metagame framework, Nigel Howard pursues an exploration that was first recommended by von Neumann and Morgenstern. His approach is neither formal nor normative, but rather positive—positive in the sense that the assertions about the behavior of players can be tested under so-called controlled conditions and can be rejected if their consequences fail to pass appropriate tests.

Howard's approach is also nonquantitative. He is able to avoid numerical utilities, which have so often characterized the work of game theorists, and which have very rarely been successfully estimated in the real world. Howard is also able to develop new concepts of rationality, for example, metarationality, which in many ways enable the game-theoretic approach to be of greater application to problems of the real world. His development of illustrations based on simplified models of real conflict, such as the Cuban missile crisis, the U.S.–Soviet confrontation, make possible a better appreciation of the possibilities of the metagame approach.

While the Nigel Howard approach will undoubtedly be sharply criticized by many in peace research and related fields, there is no question whatsoever that this approach has much to add to the effective analysis of real world problems—especially when contrasted with the highly abstract, formal models with which the literature abounds.

Walter Isard

Preface

The theory presented in this book is for the most part quite new. The most primitive ideas of mathematical game theory—the extensive and normal forms, and the equilibrium point—are developed in a new way so as to build a positive theory applicable to the "real world."

The history of these developments is as follows. In 1965, Russell L. Ackoff invited the author to join the Management Science Center, University of Pennsylvania, which at that time had an unclassified contract with the United States Arms Control and Disarmament Agency to develop methods of analyzing the escalation and de-escalation of conflict. The principal investigator was Ackoff himself. The sponsor at A.C.D.A. was Thomas L. Saaty, whose emphasis on the need to develop analytic methods for the understanding of real-world conflict problems had inspired the agency to support research in this area (see Saaty 1964).

The author was asked to work on the A.C.D.A. contract, and it was in this encouraging milieu that metagame theory was born. One can safely say that had it not been for the efforts of Saaty and Ackoff the work presented here would not now exist. Saaty in particular proved an ideal sponsor.

Others have contributed this and other kinds of help. Anatol Rapoport became keenly interested in the ideas at an early stage, arranging for their early publication in the *General Systems Yearbook* (Howard 1966, 1970). Walter Isard arranged for the publication of this book and in other ways disinterestedly "pushed" the approach. Meanwhile, the interest shown by Herbert Scoville, Jr., then at the U.S. Arms Control Agency, encouraged experimental applications to realistic problems as in the case of the Vietnam analysis described in Section 5.3. P. J. Long was among other members of the Agency who (actively persuaded by Dr. Saaty) cooperated in these applications. On a technical level, André Ducamp, Jeffrey Smith, and John Hall worked with me at the Management Science Center for various periods during the growth of these ideas and contributed much during many hours of ardent discussion. Finally, in 1969, the National Research Council of Canada contributed research funds and H. K. Kesavan found a place in the Department of Systems Design at the University of Waterloo for the continuing development of metagame theory and the writing of the final version of this book. An earlier version was accepted as an external Ph.D. thesis by the University of London (1968), and I am grateful to Drs. George Morton and Ailsa Land of the London School of Economics, who supervised my Ph.D. work, for their interest, inevitably "long-distance" though it was.

I shall now attempt to elucidate the connections between this work and the work of other game theorists. What follows will therefore assume a knowledge both of their work and the contents of this book; but those who know only the work of other game theorists may nevertheless profit by skimming through this first.

EXTENSIVE AND NORMAL FORMS. We build the extensive form in much the same way as other game theorists (which is essentially the way laid down by von Neumann) except for one difference. Preferences, or utilities, are not introduced at this stage.

The game tree is merely a structure in which particular strategies chosen by the players and by "chance" lead to particular *time-paths of the system*, or "scenarios." Hence when the normal form is constructed, a particular strategy n-tuple—choice of one strategy by each player—leads to a probability distribution over various possible time-paths, or a probabilistic spectrum of "scenarios." Preferences of a *nonquantitative* kind are now introduced; that is, for each player a preference *relation* of a general kind is assumed over the various strategy n-tuples (now called "outcomes"). The reason for this different treatment is to carry through a nonquantitative approach to preferences. We end up with a normal form differing from the usual one only in that it is more general: general preference relations take the place of numerical utility functions.

EQUILIBRIUM POINTS AND RATIONAL OUTCOMES. Within this framework, equilibrium points are defined as usual. Much use is made, however, of the concept of a "rational outcome for player i" (a point at which player i is optimizing his preferences). This is done to bring out a point that is often overlooked—that the arguments for "stability" of an equilibrium point actually do not depend on players knowing each other's preferences. This is mathematically trivial but carries with it a considerable reinterpretation of applied game theory.

MIXED STRATEGIES. Most game theorists, after some examination of the general case, proceed to further consideration of only a certain type of normal-form game—that which is a *mixed extension* of (another) normal-form game. We do not specialize in this way. Of course, we consider mixed extensions, these being seen as a particular kind of normal-form game in which each player has an infinite set of strategies (his so-called mixed strategies) and a numerical utility function. But we do not consider only these—we consider all normal forms, even ones in which players have a finite number of strategies and their preferences need not even be ordinal. We do not take advantage of the special structure possessed by mixed extensions.

CORRELATED MIXED STRATEGIES. Since we consider all normal forms, we consider also games in which players may *correlate* their mixed strategies (Luce and Raiffa 1957, p. 116) provided that this situation is first represented in normal form—a prior step omitted by most authors. For instance, a normal-form representation might allow each player i to choose a strategy consisting of a 3-tuple

$$(C, \sigma_C, \sigma_i),$$

in which C is his choice of a *coalition*, σ_C his choice of a *coalition correlated mixed strategy*, and σ_i his choice of an *individual mixed strategy*. The choice σ_C is carried out if and only if each player in C chooses C and also σ_C; otherwise, the choice σ_i is carried out. Numerical payoff functions are defined in the obvious way.

In order to refer to this normal form later on, we may call it a *correlated mixed extension*. We remark that unless some normal-form representation of a game is given, the game cannot be run experimentally. The universality of the normal form (or of the extensive form from which a normal form can be derived) consists in the fact that giving any well-defined set of rules for actually playing a game amounts to specifying the game in this form. Of course, in experiments the players' final choices may or may not be preceded by a period of communication—the normal form says nothing about this.

Unfortunately the normal form suggested here—the correlated mixed extension—does more than allow correlated mixed strategies. It also allows the individual players to choose "threat" strategies similar to (though not the same as) the threat strategies defined by Nash (1953) in his "bargaining solution" to a game. These are the individual strategies σ_i that are implemented in case the coalition fails to agree. They can be used as "threats" against the other members of the coalition. It does not seem possible to avoid adding this feature if we wish to construct a normal form allowing correlated mixed strategies. This is unfortunate because, if we consider a game without correlated mixed strategies, the metagame approach makes "threat" strategies in the normal form superfluous; whatever can be achieved by them can be achieved more naturally by using metagame "policies"; and if despite this we allow "threats" to appear in the normal form, we obliterate a very meaningful distinction between "basic" equilibria (equilibria in the original game) and "nonbasic" ones (which are equilibria only by a process of derivation from some metagame).

TRANSFERABLE UTILITIES. Our approach also covers the case of numerical utilities freely transferable between players, provided again that this is represented in normal form. This can be done by allowing each player, in addition to making his "ordinary" strategy choice (pure or mixed or correlated as above) to choose the proportions in which he will distribute his utility payoff among all the players.

α- AND β-EFFECTIVENESS. Generally speaking, the notion of α-*effectiveness* (Aumann 1961) corresponds to the metagame notion of *general metarationality*, while β-*effectiveness* corresponds to *symmetric metarationality*. To make this precise, however, we must first note that α- and β-effectiveness are defined (Aumann 1961) only for a limited class of games—those which are correlated mixed extensions.

But if in a correlated mixed extension with numerical payoff functions M_i we let "s_K" stand for a joint strategy of the coalition K and "N" for the set of all players, the coalition C is said to be α-effective for the payoff vector x if

$$\exists s_C \; \forall s_{N-C} : \forall (i \in C) : M_i(s_C, s_{N-C}) \geq x_i,$$

and it is β-effective for x if

$$\forall s_{N-C} \, \exists s_C : \forall (i \in C) : M_i(s_C, s_{N-C}) \geqslant x_i.$$

On the other hand, we find that an outcome $\tilde{s}$ (a strategy n-tuple) fails to be general metarational for C if

$$\exists s_C \, \forall s_{N-C} : \forall (i \in C) : M_i(s_C, s_{N-C}) > M_i \tilde{s},$$

and it fails to be symmetric metarational for C if

$$\forall s_{N-C} \, \exists s_C : \forall (i \in C) : M_i(s_C, s_{N-C}) > M_i \tilde{s}.$$

The similarity can be seen. The real difference is that between strict and nonstrict inequalities. A coalition C is α-effective for x if C can guarantee each of its members i at least x_i; an outcome yielding the payoff vector x fails to be metarational for C if C can guarantee each of its members i more than x_i. A coalition C fails to be β-effective for x if $N-C$ can guarantee that some member i of C will receive less than x_i; an outcome yielding x is symmetric metarational for C if $N-C$ can guarantee that some member i of C will receive no more than x_i.

α- AND β-DOMINATION. Based on the above two concepts of effectiveness, Aumann (1961) forms two concepts of *domination*, saying that a payoff vector x α-*dominates* (respectively β-*dominates*) y *through* the coalition C if $x_i > y_i$ for all $i \in C$, and C is α-(respectively β-)effective for x.

The result, at least in "well-behaved" games, is that the set of general (respectively symmetric) metarational outcomes for C is precisely the set of outcomes yielding payoff vectors α-(respectively β-) *undominated* through C.

Finally, the "α-core" and "β-core" being defined as the sets of payoff vectors not α-(respectively not β-)dominated through any coalition C, we find that the sets of outcomes that are general (respectively symmetric) metarational for all coalitions are just those that yield payoffs in the α- and β-core. Hence in this book we have called these sets (though they are sets of strategy n-tuples, not payoff vectors) the α-core and β-core, respectively.

We remark again that general and symmetric metarationality are defined for far wider classes of games than correlated mixed extensions, being defined for all normal-form games, even ones with "general" preferences that are not even ordinal. But corresponding generalizations of the notions of effectiveness and domination present no difficulty. With general preferences, one can no longer speak of numerical payoff vectors. The simplest way around this seems to be to define outcomes as *strategy n-tuples*, as we do in this book, rather than as *payoff n-tuples*. We may then form general preference relations over the set of outcomes (strategy *n*-tuples). The alternative chosen by Peleg (1966), which is to define a function leading from strategy *n*-tuples to a set of nonnumerical "payoffs," over which, finally, preference relations are formed, seems clumsier, introducing as it does an unnecessary concept in between strategy *n*-tuples and preferences.

GAMES IN CHARACTERISTIC FUNCTION FORM. If a game is given in characteristic function form, we must put it in normal form before we can apply metagame theory. That this can be done is well known. It is also well known that if a game is transformed from normal form to characteristic function form and then back again, much detail is lost. Accordingly, many distinctions made in metagame theory are obliterated. The sets of general and symmetric metarational outcomes remain the same, but there is no longer any distinction between different types of metarationality within these broad categories.

These remarks apply not only to the von Neumann–Morgenstern characteristic function form (derived from a numerical correlated mixed extension with transferable utilities), in which symmetric and general metarationality coincide, but also to the corresponding form for games without side payments in Stearns (1964) and Aumann and Peleg (1960) and to the game in partition function form (Thrall and Lucas 1963).

BARGAINING SOLUTIONS. Following Nash (1950, 1953), Harsanyi (1959, 1963, 1966) has developed a "bargaining solution." Aumann and Maschler (1964) have investigated the "bargaining set." Maschler and Peleg (1966) have developed the idea of the "kernel"; and we know of the "Shapley value" (Shapley 1953). These concepts, unlike the ones discussed so far, presuppose players who know each other's preferences. But a metagame approach to such players is at present very underdeveloped; the last chapter of this book merely sets out some simple notions on the subject. Hence no real connection yet exists between metagame theory and these approaches.

GENERAL DISCUSSION. There are three main points to be made about the approach taken in this book.

a. The approach is *positive*. It is neither purely formal, nor is it normative. This means that assertions about the behavior of "players" in a "game" are to be interpreted as empirical statements and their consequences tested under controlled conditions if possible. The assertions are to be rejected if their consequences fail to pass such tests. It also means that to us a "game" is not only a mathematical object but also and simultaneously an *experimental* object. Hence our insistence on the normal-form (or extensive-form) representation, without which it is not clear under what experimental conditions any assertions are to be tested.

b. The approach is *nonquantitative*. Numbers are not used. Our motive is not only mathematical generality but also real-world applicability. Numerical utilities, even if they are well founded theoretically, cannot be reliably estimated in the real world.

The result, mathematically, is an extremely general approach— so much so that mathematically this is really a book about abstract set theory à la Cantor. Fraenkel (1953) is a good book to read to see how the subject appears from this viewpoint. But for this generality we pay a price. Cold winds blow through unstructured sets! Existence theorems in particular are hard to find. Thus the papers (e.g., Aumann 1961) to which we have referred earlier, and concerning which we have had to remark that the corresponding metagame concepts are more general, usually contain delicate and interesting existence theorems that we lose entirely.

c. The approach is *based on the metagame tree*. This is a separate point from the two preceding ones. We could have constructed a *formal* (nonempirical) or a *normative* theory based on the metagame tree; moreover, this theory could have been *quantitative*. Instead, we have a positive, nonquantitative metagame approach.

The metagame idea is that to analyze a game we should analyze the n metagames based on it. This was first recommended by von Neumann and Morgenstern (1953, section 14.2) in the context of the two-person zero-sum game. However, they failed to follow it through. They did not see that the recommendation is recursive, and hence they did not analyze the metagames based on the metagames (the "minorant" and "majorant" games) that they did analyze. Clearly, to follow the idea through we must analyze the whole infinite tree of metagames. Also, they did not extend the idea beyond two-person zero-sum games.

Thus von Neumann and Morgenstern may be said to have originated the metagame approach. In other respects also our approach is based on theirs. Thus, the von Neumann–Morgenstern approach is, in contrast to later approaches, thoroughly positive. True, they did not experiment, but their approach was neither normative nor purely formal. In drawing an analogy with the development of physical theory, they compare themselves (1953, section 1) to theoretical, in contrast to experimental, physicists. Second, von Neumann and Morgenstern looked forward (1953, section 66) to a nonquantitative generalization of game theory. This suggestion has not of course been so thoroughly neglected as the metagame suggestion; our work is merely the least quantitative of all that has been done so far (see, for example, Peleg 1966).

Finally, von Neumann and Morgenstern (1953, section 66.4) look forward to a unification of their rather separate theories of the two-person zero-sum game and the n-person variable-sum game. Such a unification has probably been delayed by the distinction introduced later between "noncooperative" and "cooperative" theories of games —a distinction that clearly has its genesis in von Neumann and Morgenstern's two approaches. Their plea for unity is, however, answered by metagame theory. There is no need in metagame theory for different approaches or different "solution concepts." We have a unified treatment applied to all games and based on

1. The normal form.
2. The concept of the equilibrium point as an intersection of rational outcomes.
3. The metagame tree.

Within this framework we find that the outcomes *undominated through C* (which in the von Neumann–Morgenstern treatment are the outcomes at which C receives at least the characteristic function value $v(C)$) are *derived*. They are just the outcomes metarational for C from *some* metagame in the infinite tree. Hence this set of outcomes —and similarly the sets of α- and β-undominated outcomes—is inevitably singled out by our approach.

We start, in other words, by looking for rational outcomes: an approach that is definitely "two-person zero-sum" and "non-cooperative." We apply this to the metagame tree. And we obtain the "many-person variable sum" and "cooperative" concept of the set of outcomes undominated through C. Meanwhile, what has happened to the noncooperative solution? Has it disappeared? Not at all. The outcomes rational for C (corresponding to the noncooperative solution) are those which are metarational for C from *every* metagame in the infinite tree. The distinction previously embodied in separate theories is now simply that between different classes of metarational outcomes in the metagame tree.

Traditionally, game theorists have used an arbitrary and ad hoc procedure that consists in first proposing a "solution concept" and then investigating its properties. Because this in effect means that the disunity of the field is continually increased by the laying down of new sets of basic definitions, it has been abandoned. We lay down no new basic definitions except the definition of a metagame. With this one exception, our definitions are not proposed as basic concepts but as tools with which to explore the structure of the metagame tree, a distinction that, though it may be somewhat cloudy, embodies an essential difference. New tools with which to explore a given structure may create unity; the continual creation of new structures to be explored has the opposite effect.

THE EXISTENTIALIST AXIOM, THE FREE WILL ARGUMENT, AND THE AXIOM OF CHOICE. As we have said, the one new basic definition introduced is that of a metagame; and we have therefore gone to some trouble to interpret and justify this concept. In so doing we have used two arguments that may interest philosophers and one that may interest students of the foundations of mathematics. In Section 3.3

we argue that if a person comes to "know" a theory about his behavior, he is no longer bound by it but becomes free to disobey it. This is the "existentialist axiom." In the same section is the "free will argument," which points out that it is harder to believe that one's free choice will be as predicted by another than to believe that one can predict his (the other's) free choice; yet such a bias is illogical. Finally, in Section 4.3 we propose an interpretation of the axiom of choice based on the consideration of an imaginary experiment (which could actually be performed) in which to *reject* the axiom of choice is to assert that a certain player cannot choose certain strategies.

THE BREAKDOWN OF RATIONALITY. We not only discover facts about the metagame tree, we try to interpret these facts. And in so doing we accept the discipline of experiment: if it predicts wrongly, it is wrong. This enables us to proceed without appealing, as other game theorists have done, to arguments based on elaborate concepts of "rationality." Instead we find a use for the simplest and most straightforward definition of "rational behavior" (namely, *optimizing behavior*) as a building block in our theory. We say that *rational* behavior consists in choosing the alternative one prefers.

Adherence to this simple definition leads us, however, to point out that people are not rational. First, sometimes two people cannot both be rational (our first breakdown). Second, sometimes both are better off if they are both irrational (our second breakdown). These facts are well known to game theorists—who, however, have generally preferred to change the definition of rationality, often making it abstruse and hard to accept, rather than admit that the concept has "broken down."

Our third breakdown, however, appears not to have been noticed before. It is described in Section 6.4, where a theorem is proved (Theorem 9) to the effect that to be rational in two-person games is usually to be a sucker. It is suggested that this is the reason why, even when they are rational, people such as political leaders, businessmen, and those involved in the battle of the sexes seldom talk as if they are.

Why has Theorem 9 been overlooked? It is a very simple theorem.

The reason may lie in the attitude adopted by most game theorists toward so-called sure-thing strategies—this being that a player lucky enough to have such a strategy should "obviously" pursue it. Theorem 9 flatly contradicts this, showing that sure-thing strategies are, in many realistic situations involving two players, incredibly silly.

THE ANALYSIS OF OPTIONS. This book is primarily about theory. But Section 5.3 sketches a method, called the "analysis of options," whereby our theory can be applied usefully to real-life political conflicts. The method, now under intensive further development at the University of Waterloo, is described more completely in Management Science Center (1969b). It takes full advantage of the non-quantitative approach to game theory.

As development has increased the scope and power of this method, it has been applied with increasing success to larger and more complex models. The first applications, starting in 1967 on a tentative experimental basis, were carried out in Washington with the cooperation of A.C.D.A. personnel and concerned such problems as the strategic arms race (the A.B.M. problem, etc.) and nuclear proliferation. In 1968 the Vietnam conflict was studied. As we have said, an excerpt from this analysis is given in Section 5.3. Later, T. L. Saaty and the author, at the Urban Institute in Washington, D.C., helped to analyze two urban conflict problems: one, a problem involving urban transportation systems, was analyzed in cooperation with Henry Bain; the other, a historical analysis of the New York school strike problem, was conducted with the help of Betsy Levin. But the most complex and thoroughgoing analysis so far (also the most sensitive) was an analysis of many aspects of the Arab–Israeli conflict, conducted in the spring of 1970 by T. L. Saaty and the author with a group of interested individuals in Beirut, Lebanon, under the auspices of the Royal Jordanian Institute. In all this, the extent of the author's indebtedness to Thomas L. Saaty cannot be overemphasized. Indeed, without his efforts no applications of the theory would have been made.

I believe that further development of this technique will significantly improve the methods presently used in international politics. This could be important for the future of mankind. For this reason, we should indicate the limitations of the game-theoretic approach.

There are two main causes of all the evil that exists in the world. One is that humans are very wicked; the other is that they are very stupid. Technocrats tend to underestimate the first factor and revolutionaries the second. But both are important.

Now there is no reason to hope that applied game theory will diminish human wickedness. It will not affect our preferences for killing, persecuting, and displacing one another. These can be affected only by changes in political consciousness and by the creation of *moral* theories, which to that extent are *not* scientific—though they may be based on scientific findings. To the extent that a theory is scientific, it is value-free and has no tendency to make people morally better or worse than they were before.

Nor will applied game theory diminish most kinds of human stupidity. Only certain kinds will be affected. Our approach is to take as given whatever misconceptions and delusions (or possibly sound information) decision-makers may have about the preferences and alternative courses of action open to the participants in a game situation. Having accepted these as premises, we can correct the stupid and illogical assertions (or possibly agree with the sound assessments) that the same decision-makers have derived from these premises. In other words, all we can say is "*If* your view of the world is correct, still this does not follow" (or possibly "then you are quite right for these reasons").

Even so, the area in which we *can* bring about improvements is quite significant. What we might call "game-theoretic" stupidity is both extremely pervasive and usually damaging to the interests of the "players." This, in any case, is the area which we have to explore.

THE NONMATHEMATICAL READER. This book is supposed to be mathematically self-contained, the required background being given in Appendix A. No mathematical knowledge is assumed beyond this, except in a few examples that may be skipped if necessary. If, however, I am lucky enough to attract a nonmathematical reader who really wishes to understand, he will have to work extremely hard. My advice to him would be to imagine continually that he is not *learning* from the book but is *teaching* from it, and to construct (a) examples to illustrate the material being taught and (b) exercises such as he would have to give to a class of students to test their understanding. Such examples and exercises will be far more valuable than any that I could give.

1
Introductory

1.1 The Nonquantitative Approach

(1) To make progress in the social sciences, we must give up the (often ridiculous) attempt to measure and quantify social phenomena. (2) To make progress in *game theory*, viewed generally as the study of interactions between conscious political beings, we must also give up the emphasis on rational behavior. These are important propositions that I hope are illustrated in this book.

In this section we discuss the first proposition. We distinguish between *quantitative* and *nonquantitative* models.

A *model*, as used in science, may be defined as a set of assumptions about a real-life phenomenon, from which conclusions are deduced. The deduction uses (a) logic and mathematics, (b) empirical generalizations such as "laws of nature."

For example, we may model the fall of a stone. We assume that the stone is at a height of 10 feet from the earth's surface and falling in a vacuum. According to the "law of nature" proposed by Galileo, the relation between distance fallen in feet and time elapsed in seconds is

$$d = 16t^2;$$

from which, using logic, we conclude that after one-half second the stone will be 6 feet from the ground.

Note that the model is incorrect if the stone is not in a vacuum. This often does not matter much—a model may be in error— provided the error is small enough not to affect the conclusions greatly. This is a matter of judgment. Errors in laws of nature are much more serious.

The preceding example is a quantitative model. Numerical assumption are made and numerical conclusions deduced. Quantitative models are less appropriate in the social sciences, where many phenomena are essentially nonquantitative, than in physics and the natural sciences. Hence very often, when a quantitative model is built, the social scientist will wave his hands and say "the actual numbers used in the mathematics do not matter. One has to apply this result in a general, qualitative kind of way."

Surely this is inadmissible. If actual numbers do not matter, the mathematics should not use numbers. If a general, qualitative insight is sought, the mathematics should be general and qualitative, not quantitative.

Nonmathematical readers may find this suggestion surprising. Nonmathematicians often think that mathematics is primarily concerned with numbers. That is not so today. In fact, while twentieth-century social scientists have tried desperately to become more quantitative in the belief that this would make them more mathematical, twentieth-century mathematicians have become increasingly nonquantitative. The subjects loosely called "modern mathematics" (say symbolic logic, topology, modern algebra, and, more than all, set theory) become less concerned each day with common-or-garden numbers. They discuss relations. The idea that mathematics is the science of quantity is a nineteenth-century notion, and social scientists who pursue it are immersing themselves in dead ideas.

But what of the idea that surely, in the end, motivates this pursuit of quantity and measurement—the idea that no subject is fully a science, no theory fully a theory, unless it is mathematical? With this idea we fully concur. A truly scientific theory is a structure containing a few very general assertions ("laws of nature") from which many particular conclusions can be deduced, and such structures, when perfected, are inevitably mathematical in nature.

Hence one aim of this book is to reconstruct game theory on a nonquantitative basis in the hope that thereby it will make more practical and intuitive sense. The mathematics required for this task is developed in Appendix A, where no prior knowledge is assumed. This development is condensed; applications and examples of concepts occur in the book itself. The nonmathematical reader who is ready to work hard should be able to read the book by looking things up in Appendix A when he is stuck.

1.2 The Nonrational Approach
The second main theme of this book is that the idea of "rational

behavior" breaks down when we investigate game-theoretic situations and has to be replaced.

Let us say that we feel this to be a shocking and philosophically upsetting notion, and the reader should be prepared to abandon certain deeply entrenched ideas if he is to understand fully what we have to say. To set this problem in the right context, let us compare two lengthy quotations—one from Dostoevski and one from Bertrand Russell.

Dostoevski's novel, *Letters from the Underworld*, is the journal of an introspective, alienated "outsider"; it contains the following attack on the idea of rationality.

Yet *I* tell *you* (and for about the hundredth time), that there is one occasion, and one occasion only, when man can wilfully, consciously desiderate for himself what is foolish and harmful. This is the occasion when he yearns to *have the right* to desiderate for himself what is foolish and harmful, and to be bound by no obligation whatsoever to desiderate anything that is sensible. It is his crowning folly; it is wherein we see his ineradicable waywardness. Yet such folly may also be the best thing in the world for him, even though it work him harm, and contradict our soundest conclusions on the subject of interests. . . . Of course, he *may* make his volition march with reason, and the more so if the former does not abuse the latter, but uses it with moderation. Such a proceeding is expedient, and may, at times, even be praiseworthy; but only too often do we see volition clashing with reason, and— and— Yet, do you know, gentlemen, *this too*, at times, may be both expedient and praiseworthy.[1]

Earlier, the underground man anticipates the objection that what one desires *is* one's interest—that is, may be made so by definition.

"Ah well, there are interests and interests," you might interrupt me at this point. Pardon me, gentlemen, but I ought to make it clear that, not to juggle with words, this interest of which I am speaking is a notable one, and escapes all classification, and shatters every system which has ever been established by lovers of the human race for that race's improvement. In short, let it be understood that it is an interest which introduces general confusion into everything.[2]

Now in this quotation it is clear that Dostoevski has in mind a specific definition of rationality. The same definition is stated as

1. Fyodor Dostoevski, *Letters from the Underworld*, translated by C. J. Hogarth (London: Everyman's Library, J. M. Dent, 1913, reprinted 1957), pp. 34–35.
2. Ibid., p. 27.

follows by Russell in the preface to his book, *Human Society in Ethics and Politics*:

"Reason" has a perfectly clear and precise meaning. It signifies the choice of the right means to an end that you wish to achieve. It has nothing whatever to do with the choice of ends. But opponents of reason do not realize this, and think that advocates of rationality want reason to dictate ends as well as means. They have no excuse for this view in the writings of rationalists. There is a famous sentence: "Reason is and ought only to be, the slave of the passions." This sentence does not come from the works of Rousseau or Dostoevsky or Sartre. It comes from David Hume. It expresses a view to which I, like every man who attempts to be reasonable, fully subscribe. When I am told, as I frequently am, that I "almost entirely discount the part played by the emotions in human affairs," I wonder what motive-force the critic supposes me to regard as dominant. Desires, emotions, passions (you can choose whichever word you will), are the only possible causes of action. Reason is not a cause of action but only a regulator. If I wish to travel by plane to New York, reason tells me that it is better to take a plane which is going to New York than one which is going to Constantinople. I suppose that those who think me unduly rational, consider that I ought to become so agitated at the airport as to jump into the first plane that I see, and when it lands me in Constantinople I ought to curse the people among whom I find myself for being Turks and not Americans. This would be a fine, full-blooded way of behaving, and would, I suppose, meet with the commendation of my critics.[3]

Clearly, Dostoevski and Russell are at odds. They adopt the same definition of rational behavior, but Dostoevski attacks it while Russell defends it. We shall adopt this same definition also. But we shall see that, "especially in certain cases," the caprice of "jumping into the first plane that I see" may be the only course that reason, albeit shakily, can advocate. In other cases it is "expedient, and may, at times, even be praiseworthy" for choice to be "wilfully" and "consciously" opposed to reason. That is, I should deliberately get on the plane to Constantinople.

Thus we shall agree with Dostoevski and not Russell. This does not mean that Dostoevski had the better argument of the two. One can give bad arguments and be right, just as one can give good arguments and be wrong. Dostoevski's arguments were in fact very intuitive and therefore diluted with irrelevancies and misconceptions.

We should say too that it is only this concept of rationality—

3. Bertrand Russell, *Human Society in Ethics and Politics* (London: George Allen and Unwin, 1954), pp. 8–9.

"the choice of the right means to an end that you wish to achieve"—that we shall attack. We are not discussing "rationality" in the sense of logical consistency, or facing up realistically to the true facts of a situation, or conformity with ethical norms considered "rational" by some philosophers. These are other, distinct meanings of the term "rationality"—and we certainly do not wish to be thought of as denying the validity of the first two, at any rate.

2
The
Breakdown of
Rationality

2.1 The First Breakdown

The idea of rationality is a basic one in Western culture. Like other basic ideas, for example, "nature" and "God," it has had a variety of meanings. We shall address ourselves to the idea of "rational behavior," meaning "optimizing behavior." That is, we shall say that a decision d_i is rational if there are a number of alternative decisions $d_1, \ldots, d_m$ with foreseeable results $r_1, \ldots, r_m$ none of which is preferred by the decision-maker to the result r_i of the decision d_i. The rational decision-maker chooses the decision that yields him the most preferred result.

Thus rationality has nothing to do with what the decision-maker "ought" to do in a moral sense. It has to do with satisfying his preferences, which morally may be good, bad, or indifferent. If Hitler preferred to exterminate the Jews, his rational course of action was one he thought would bring about their extermination, whether or not we, or they, or even he, thought he "should" do this.

Nor does rationality demand that we make a distinction between means and ends. If preferences attach to the decision d_i as well as to its result, we can simply include d_i in the result r_i.

It would seem, therefore, that rationality is a "good thing" provided only that the decision-maker is good (has good preferences). This view underlies utilitarian ethics as expounded by Bentham and, in this century, Russell, who says explicitly, "Men's actions are harmful either from ignorance or from bad desires."[1]

The great contribution of game theory is that it shows this view to be misleading. What happens in game theory is that the very concept of rationality, applied to interaction between conscious beings, breaks down and disintegrates. It will not bear the constructions we try to place on it. Quite new modes of thought are required.

1. Bertrand Russell, *What I Believe*, reprinted in *The Basic Writings of Bertrand Russell* (New York: Simon and Schuster, 1967), p. 384.

We shall distinguish three different ways in which rationality "breaks down." The first will be described in this section; the second, at the end of this chapter. The third and final breakdown will be discussed in the last chapter of this book.

To begin with, rationality makes perfect sense in a "one-person game" or "game against nature." This means a situation in which there is only one decision-maker. He has alternatives $d_1, \ldots, d_m$ with results $r_1, \ldots, r_m$, and rationally he chooses the d_i with the most preferred r_i.

This seems simple, but can be quite complicated. For one thing, r_i may be a probability distribution over various possible states of nature, as in the famous case of Pascal's wager.

In Figure 2.1, Pascal's problem is posed as a decision problem. The rows represent alternative decisions, one of which has to be made. The columns represent alternative "states of nature." A decision together with a state of nature yield a "result," represented by a cell of the matrix. The decision-maker does not know the state of nature; he only knows the probability that each state is the actual one. Thus his decision gives rise to a "probability mixture" of results, that is, to a certain probability that each of a number of results will occur. The difficulty is to decide preferences between these alternative probability mixtures.

Pascal argued that it was "rational" to believe in God if there was any probability greater than zero that God existed. For in the decision problem of Figure 2.1, Pascal argued that the probability mixture

STATES OF NATURE

		GOD EXISTS p	GOD DOES NOT EXIST $1-p$
PASCAL'S DECISION	BELIEVE IN GOD	ETERNAL REWARD	PIOUS LIFE ONLY
	NOT BELIEVE	ETERNAL PUNISHMENT	IMPIOUS LIFE ONLY

Figure 2.1. Pascal's Wager. Here p is the probability that God exists; that is, the probability that "Nature" will choose the first column.

"eternal reward" with probability p;
"pious life only" with probability $(1-p)$
should be preferred to
"eternal punishment" with probability p;
"impious life only" with probability $(1-p)$,
because of the infinite rewards and punishments associated with the first term in each case. Only if $p = 0$, so that there is no possibility of these rewards and punishments, could the second alternative be preferable, no matter how much one might prefer an impious life.

What is introduced here is the complication of "states of nature" that are probabilistic rather than deterministic.

Apart from the problem of estimating preferences between probabilistic results, there may be great mathematical difficulties in calculating results even when these are deterministic. The so-called traveling salesman problem is a case in point. This salesman wishes to choose a route between a number of cities that will pass through each city just once and, subject to this, will be as short as possible. The d_i are the various possible ways of ordering the cities and the r_i are the resulting route lengths. We are given the distances between all pairs of cities. No general method of solving this decision problem for a moderately large number of cities is known.

This illustrates the possibility that, in general, any kind of mathematical or scientific problem may be involved in calculating the result r_i that will arise from a course of action d_i.

From a mathematical point of view there is still another problem if the number of decisions is infinite. Suppose I prefer more money to less and can have any sum I care to name! No rational decision exists, since whatever sum I name I could have got more by naming a larger sum. But for practical purposes our world is finite, and this "breakdown" of the rationality concept is really a technical problem which may be left to mathematicians to resolve. In any practical context it can in fact be resolved technically.

For a practical example of the breakdown of rationality we turn now to a true game, not a "one-person" game. The term "game," as used in game theory, properly denotes a situation in which two or more decision-makers (called "players") each has two or more

WARSHIP'S
STRATEGIES

		NORTH	SOUTH
MERCHANT SHIP'S STRATEGIES	NORTH	I, 2	2, I
	SOUTH	2, I	I, 2

Figure 2.2. Game with No Equilibrium (that is, no way for both players to be rational). Numbers represent preference orderings for the players, a larger number being more preferred.

alternative decisions (called "strategies"), and for each player the result he will experience depends on the decisions of all the players.

To illustrate how rationality may collapse in this kind of situation, suppose as in Figure 2.2 that a merchant ship and an enemy warship must each choose the northern or southern route around an island lying between them. If they meet, the warship will destroy the merchant ship, so that the preferred outcomes for the merchant will be those in which the ships take opposite routes. But for the warship the preferred outcomes are those in which the two take the same route. These preferences are shown by numbers in Figure 2.2, the first number referring to row-chooser's preferences. Note that these numbers have only ordinal significance. They do not represent quantities of anything. A larger number for a player represents a preferred outcome.

It is clear that in this game one of the players must make the wrong decision. Now of course this can easily happen to a rational decision-maker that is misinformed or simply lacks relevant information. For this reason the *rational* thing to do is to get as much relevant information as possible before making a decision[2]—trusting and

2. Provided it can be got cheaply enough so that the cost of getting it remains negligible in comparison with the costs and benefits resulting from the decision.

believing, no doubt, that if one had all the relevant information there would exist a way of handling it so that one could choose correctly. The distinction between "subjective" rationality (based on the decision-maker's possibly erroneous information) and "objective" rationality (based on the actual state of affairs) is thus of considerable importance. To get on the plane to Constantinople having been misdirected at the ticket counter may be subjectively rational, but objectively, if one wants to get to New York, it is not. And although a rational decision-maker can only ever be subjectively rational, he is aiming at objective rationality. Indeed, if, as economists do, one defines a *stable* decision as one that would not be affected by additional information, then only an objectively rational decision will be a stable one for a rational decision-maker.

The first breakdown of rationality may now be stated in reference to Figure 2.2. *It is impossible for both players to be objectively rational.* Indeed, "relevant information" for each certainly includes knowledge of the other's strategy choice. But given this knowledge, the merchant will choose the opposite route to the warship, and the warship the same route as the merchant. This is absurd.

NOTE ON ORDINAL PREFERENCES. Throughout our discussion so far we have made an implicit assumption that we should state explicitly. This is that the decision-makers we are concerned with have *ordinal preferences*. This means roughly that they can rank the outcomes in a certain order reflecting their preferences, though there may be "ties" so that two or more outcomes occupy the same position in the preference ordering. We shall formalize this assumption later on. For the moment we point out that we are making this assumption solely in order to attack the concept of rationality, on the grounds that one would not in any case expect rationality from a decision-maker with nonordinal preferences. One would simply say that such a decision-maker does not have consistent preferences; for example, he prefers a to b and b to c, and yet prefers c to a. Therefore, it is not surprising if his behavior is odd. Later, however, when we construct a theory that does not in any case use accepted ideas of rationality, we shall be more general in our assumptions. We shall not assume then that preferences are ordinal.

2.2 Extensive and Normal Forms of a Game

The first to analyze the flaw in the architecture of Western thought discussed in the previous section was apparently Borel (1953; first published in the early twenties). Von Neumann (1959; first published in 1928, 1937) gave complete answers to some of the questions raised and created the general theory of games with more than two players. Later, von Neumann and Morgenstern (1953; first edition 1944), in the first book on game theory, approached our first breakdown of rationality by means of what we shall call the "metagame" idea.

To appreciate this, however, we must first go into the complex considerations that lie behind the apparently simple definition of a "game" given earlier. We defined a game as a situation in which there are $n \geq 2$ *players*, each having two or more *strategies*, and each having *preferences* among the various possible outcomes that may result from each player choosing a strategy.

If there are in fact only two players ($n = 2$), and if each player has a finite number of strategies, then we may represent this situation as in Figure 2.2 by a matrix whose rows are one player's strategies and whose columns are the other player's strategies. An *outcome* is then a cell of the matrix, and in each cell we may write ordinal numbers indicating the preferences of the two players.[3]

The above actually defines what is called a *game in normal form*. The game in normal form is, however, really a summing-up of an apparently far more general and complex underlying structure.

The structure that underlies the game in normal form is the *game in extensive form*. We introduce this with an example.

EXAMPLE. Suppose we have the following situation. Ford and General Motors are developing competitive models of a new type of car. Design decisions have been made, but price decisions have not. The GM model will, however, reach the market first, so that Ford will be able to make their price decision in knowledge of the GM price. See Figure 2.3.

3. It is more usual in game theory to use the word "outcome" for a pair of *numerical utilities* rather than for a pair of strategies. Since, however, we shall not in general assume numerical utilities, it is more convenient for us to discuss "outcomes" that are pairs of strategies, as here. We reemphasize that the numbers we place in the cells are not quantities of anything—they have only ordinal significance.

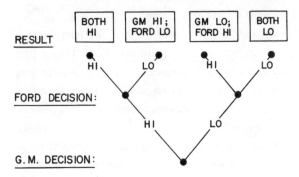

Figure 2.3. A Game Tree. "Hi" and "Lo" mean decisions to set high and low prices for the new model. We have not assigned preferences.

FORD

		HI/HI	HI/LO	LO/HI	LO/LO
GM	HI	BOTH HI	BOTH HI	GM HI; FORD LO	GM HI; FORD LO
	LO	GM LO; FORD HI	BOTH LO	GM LO; FORD HI	BOTH LO

Figure 2.4. Normal Form of the Extensive Form of Figure 2.3. Preferences have not been assigned.

At first glance this is not a game in normal form, since to give both Ford and GM the "strategies" Hi and Lo would be to ignore the asymmetry that exists because the GM decision comes first. But we can "reduce" it to a game in normal form.

To do this we define a *strategy* as a complete plan of action covering all contingencies. Then GM does indeed have the two strategies Hi and Lo. Ford, however, has four strategies. They are Hi/Hi, Hi/Lo, Lo/Hi, and Lo/Lo, defined by

$$X/Y = \begin{cases} X \text{ if GM chooses Hi,} \\ Y \text{ if GM chooses Lo,} \end{cases}$$

and we obtain the normal form shown in Figure 2.4, which has eight outcomes.

Why are there eight outcomes? The situation still, of course, has only four possible results, as in Figure 2.3. But an *outcome*, being a pair of *strategies*, now specifies not only the result but the complete plan of action by both players, covering all contingencies and including many that never in fact arose, by which the result was achieved. The outcome (Hi, Lo/Hi), for example, says that GM chose Hi while the Ford strategy was to choose Lo if GM chose Hi and Hi if GM chose Lo. The result was therefore (GM Hi, Ford Lo), but from this result GM is not able to deduce what the *outcome* was. It could have been either (Hi, Lo/Hi) or (Hi, Lo/Lo). The question as to what Ford would have done had GM chosen differently cannot be answered by GM.

We see, then, that the "extensive-form" game of Figure 2.3 can indeed be reduced to normal form. By giving Ford a choice between all *strategies* defined as complete contingent plans of action, we obviously give them exactly the same opportunities as in the original formulation. But the effect of this is that an outcome is not a simple thing: neither player may ever know the outcome because neither may ever know the other's strategy choice.

In order to complete the picture given in Figure 2.4, we would assign preferences to the outcomes; that is, for each player we would assign an ordinal number to each outcome so that larger numbers are assigned to preferred outcomes.

Let us now pause for a moment to see where we are going.

Already we see that when we define a "game in normal form" by assigning "strategies" to the players and then looking at the "outcomes" with a view to assigning preferences between them—when we do this relatively simple thing we do *not* have to make the "strategies" correspond to simple physical decisions by the players. They can be complex plans of action. Just how complex they can be is what we propose to show in the rest of this section.

We shall see that the *extensive form* or "game tree" (see Figure 2.3) can encompass a bewilderingly rich wealth of phenomena, and do it rigorously. But we shall also see that this rigor is not in practice of any use to us. Somehow the complex extensive-form models that theoretically can be built are not practical. We do not find that we can model real-life situations with them, not because they are too simple (they are not!) but because they are too specific. Detailed assumptions have to be piled up till the whole structure loses credibility.

Consequently, instead we have to try to go straight to the normal form, saying something like: "The broad strategies which these players actually see as their options are much simpler than this; and after all, it is the way the players see the game, not the game in some objective sense, that matters. So I will go ahead with a normal form defined in broad terms, and not get tied up in trying to build a detailed extensive form."

The point, therefore, of seeing how rich the extensive form can be is conceptual, not practical. Above all, the point is to get rid of any inhibitions we may feel about defining complex strategies and outcomes. We shall see that theoretically a whole essay should be inadequate to describe a "strategy," while an "outcome" generally is best described as a spectrum of scenarios stretching into the future and having different probabilities of being realized.

With this motivation, let us go on. The game tree illustrated in Figure 2.3 is the extensive form behind the normal form of Figure 2.4. But an extensive form can be considerably more complicated than this.

In the first place, there may be more than two players. It is easy to see how to take care of this. If we have players $P_1, \ldots, P_n$, decision nodes in the tree will be assigned to each of these players. Figure 2.5 shows how a part of the tree might then look.

Next, there may be a probabilistic element in the game in the sense that it is not certain what point in the tree a certain decision by a player may lead to, or even (as in the case of a card game when

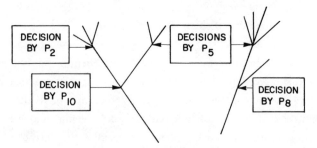

Figure 2.5. Excerpt from a Many-Person Game Tree.

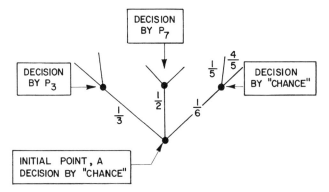

Figure 2.6. Beginning of a Game with Chance Moves. Numbers represent probabilities.

the first thing that happens is that the cards are shuffled and dealt) it may be uncertain at what point the game will start. We take care of this by assigning selected decision nodes to a fictitious player called "chance," whose decision is determined by a probability distribution. We obtain the kind of configuration shown in Figure 2.6.

In Figure 2.6 there is initially a $\frac{1}{3}$ probability that the game will go in one direction, a probability of $\frac{1}{2}$ that it will go in another direction, and a probability of $\frac{1}{6}$ that it will go in a third direction. Each of these possibilities gives rise to another situation: one in which player 3 has to make a choice, another in which player 7 has to make a choice, and a third situation which may develop in either of two ways with probabilities of $\frac{1}{5}$ and $\frac{4}{5}$, respectively. Thus the extensive form models all the different "time-paths" the system may take, depending on chance as well as on decisions by the players.

So far we have been assuming that when a player makes a decision he is "perfectly informed" of the whole past history of the game; for he knows exactly which decision node he is at. Suppose he does not know this. In poker, for example, "chance" makes an initial move when the cards are dealt out, but none of the players knows exactly where this move has put them. Each player knows only his own hand.

We deal with this possibility by partitioning each player's set of decision nodes into disjoint and exhaustive subsets called *information sets*. These are shown in Figure 2.7 by dotted lines. When a player

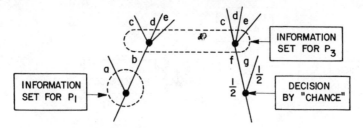

Figure 2.7. Excerpt from a Game with Imperfect Information.

makes a decision, we say that he knows only *what information set* his decision node is in; he has no idea which node *within that information set* he is at.

This does require that each node in a particular information set must have decision arcs leading out of it which "correspond" to those leading out of any other node in the set. We show this by attaching *labels* to arcs so that the arcs leading from each node have the same labels as the arcs leading from any node in the same information set. Thus in Figure 2.7 the labels "c, d, e" are attached to the arcs leading from each node in P_3's information set.

If each information set contains just one decision node, this reduces to the previous case; that is, there is no need actually to draw dotted lines showing these one-element information sets. Each player knows exactly where he is at each decision, and the game is called one of *perfect information.*

Can a player's imperfect information arise through not knowing his own past decision? Such a case would arise as in Figure 2.8. But does it make sense? Yes, for a player may be a *team* of individuals that make separate decisions, as in bridge, where two partners form a team. A game where no such case occurs is called a game with *perfect recall*; each player is perfectly informed at least of his own past decisions.

The foregoing discussion has fulfilled our promise of bringing many complicated considerations into the extensive form of a game. Why did we emphasize the uselessness of it as a method of analyzing realistic conflict situations?

The answer is that usually the real situation is not sufficiently well defined to enable us to draw one complicated game tree rather than

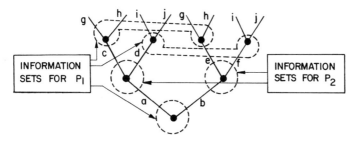

Figure 2.8. Game with Imperfect Recall.

another. If it is, as with parlor games, which do have well-defined rules, the game tree is simply too big to draw. In chess, for example, White has 20 possible first moves, giving an initial node with 20 decision arcs leading from it. Since Black then has 20 possible moves, White's second move is represented by 400 decision nodes!

Generally, games in extensive form can be analyzed only if they have some kind of "recursive" structure, that is, if a general formula will tell us the decisions existing at any and every node.

So our discussion is mainly of theoretical interest. This theoretical interest will be stressed later. Let us first bring our discussion to a general definition of the extensive form and the normal form that arises from it.

A game in extensive form consists of the following:

1. *A rooted tree T*. This, as in the figures we have shown, is a network of nodes and arcs (directed lines) having a particular node called the *root* such that there is one only directed path from the root to each node. The number of nodes may be finite or infinite; for a conflict (for example, between nations) may have no foreseeable end, so that it is best to regard it as going on forever. Likewise, we can allow the number of arcs leading from any node that is not a "chance" node to be infinite. (On the other hand, we shall require the number of arcs leading from any "chance" node to be finite, the reason for this being technical. This requirement can be circumvented if necessary. But we wish to avoid technicalities at this point.)

NOTE. Even if the game as a whole is infinite, it may have some *terminal* nodes—nodes from which no arcs lead. A node that is *not* terminal is naturally called a *decision* node, where someone has to make a decision.

2. *An assignment to each decision node of one of the numbers* 0, 1, . . ., *n*. The number 0 stands for the player "chance," and 1, . . ., *n* stand for the players $P_1, \ldots, P_n$. The number assigned to a node naturally says whose decision node it is.

3. *An assignment to each node labeled "0" of a probability distribution over the arcs leading from it.* The probability distribution will be an assignment to the arcs of numbers $0 \leqslant p_i \leqslant 1$ such that $\Sigma p_i = 1$. The probability distribution naturally says what chance there is of each decision arc being chosen if the particular "0" node is reached.

4. *For each i = 1, . . ., n, a partition of the nodes labeled "i" into disjoint and exhaustive subsets such that no directed path through the tree enters the same subset twice.* These are the "information sets." The reader may work out for himself the reasonableness of the condition that no path enter the same set twice.

5. *An assignment of labels to all arcs such that (a) different arcs leading from the same node have different labels; (b) if two nodes belong to one information set, the same set of labels is assigned to the arcs leading from each.* The interpretation is that two arcs leading from an information set belonging to player *i* are "indistinguishable" by player *i* if and only if they have the same label. It is obvious that for this condition to be fulfilled, the information sets created under condition 4 must be such that two nodes in the same information set have the same number of arcs leading out.

This is our definition of a game in extensive form. Note that preferences have not yet been assigned. We have merely constructed the possibilities that exist in the game, without saying anything about preferences between these possibilities. Before doing this, we first construct the normal form.[4] We begin with a formal definition of "strategy."

As we have said, a *strategy* for player *i* is a complete contingent plan of action for him. Formally, then, it is a rule s_i which assigns to

4. This procedure differs from the usual one in game theory. Our reason for adopting it is that the usual procedure requires the assignment of *numerical utilities* in the extensive form, which is something we avoid. We are from the beginning adopting a *nonquantitative* approach.

each of his information sets the label of some arc leading from that set. The rule s_i thus tells him what labeled arc to choose whatever the information set he is in. The usual terminology is as follows: s_i is a function from the set of all player i's information sets I to the set of all labels of arcs leading from those sets such that $s_i I$ (the label dictated by the rule s_i when P_i is in the information set I, or the value of s_i at the argument I^5) is the label of an arc leading from I.

Now write "S_i" for the set of *all* player i's strategies s_i. But S_i may be extremely large! Naturally, it will be infinite if P_i has an infinite number of information sets. In this case, it may be a very large infinite set.[6] But even in the finite case, numbers of strategies soon become astronomically large, far larger than the already astronomical numbers of decision nodes previously discussed.

Nevertheless we now have in theory a strategy set S_i for each player i. The set of all normal-form *outcomes* is now the set of all n-tuples $s = (s_1, \ldots, s_n)$ formed by selecting one element from each set S_i. Formally, the set S of outcomes is given by

$$S = S_1 \times S_2 \times \ldots \times S_n,$$

where "$\times$" represents the operation of forming the *Cartesian product* of sets, or the set of all n-tuples composed of one element from each set.

To illustrate:

EXAMPLE. In Figure 2.1 we have

$P_1 =$ Merchant; $P_2 =$ Warship;

$S_1 = S_2 = \{$North, South$\}$;

$S = S_1 \times S_2 = \{$(North, North), (North, South),

(South, North), (South, South)$\}$.

And so we have the normal form except for the preferences of the players. To obtain these, we must assign to each player a *preference ordering* among the outcomes. How shall we set about this?

We begin by constructing "strategies" for the fictitious player

5. We write "fx" for the value of a function f at an argument x instead of the usual "$f(x)$." We shall do this throughout the book, with some exceptions made to enhance clarity.
6. One infinite set is larger than another if we can find for each distinct element of the second set a corresponding distinct element of the first, but not vice versa. See Appendix A.

"chance" in the same way as we did for the other players. A "chance" strategy s_0 is thus a rule that says which arc "chance" will choose at each chance decision node (recall that chance has no information sets). In other words, s_0 is a function from the set of chance nodes N to the labels of arcs leading from these nodes such that s_0N is always the label of an arc leading from N.

Now since each label s_0N has a probability $p(s_0N)$ attached to it, the probability $P(s_0)$ that chance will choose the total strategy s_0 is naturally given by

$$P(s_0) = \prod_N p(s_0N),$$

that is, the product over all chance nodes N of the probabilities $p(s_0N)$ that chance at N will choose s_0N. (Note: It is correct, as here, to find the probability of a certain concurrence of independent chance events by multiplying together their separate probabilities of occurrence.)

For example, consider the game tree in Figure 2.9. Chance has four strategies; for chance must choose either a or b if the node N is reached; and if the node M is reached, chance must choose g or h. If we take the particular strategy s_0 defined by

$$s_0N = b, \qquad s_0M = h,$$

that is, the strategy "choose b if at N, and h if at M," then its probability $P(s_0)$ is equal to $p(b)p(h) = p(s_0N)p(s_0M)$.

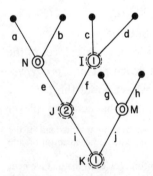

Figure 2.9. Illustrative Game Tree. Unlabeled nodes are terminal nodes.

Note too that if each player i chooses a strategy s_i and chance chooses a strategy s_0, a single *play of the game* is determined (that is, a single path through the game tree). For the strategy of the initial player (or of chance) will determine the first arc in this path. This arc will lead to a decision node for another player (or for chance); his strategy will determine the next arc; and so on. Thus, each pair (s_0, s), where s is an n-tuple $(s_1, \ldots, s_n)$ of players' strategies (that is, an outcome), determines a unique path $q = Q(s_0, s)$ through the tree, or in other words a unique *play of the game*. It follows that each outcome $\bar{s}$ determines that each play $\bar{q}$ will occur with probability

$$\Sigma P(s_0),$$

where the sum Σ is taken over all s_0 such that $\bar{q} = Q(s_0, \bar{s})$. (Note: To calculate the probability of an event that may occur in many different ways, we proceed as here to sum the probabilities that it will occur in each separate way.)

To illustrate this, we refer again to Figure 2.9. Suppose player 1 chooses the strategy $\bar{s}_1$ defined by

$$\bar{s}_1 K = i, \qquad \bar{s}_1 I = d,$$

while player 2 chooses $\bar{s}_2$ such that

$$\bar{s}_2 J = e;$$

then the outcome $\bar{s} = (\bar{s}_1, \bar{s}_2)$ determines that the play (i, e, a) will occur if chance chooses a strategy $\bar{s}_0$ such that $\bar{s}_0 N = a$. But chance has two strategies $\bar{s}_0$ obeying this condition. Their probabilities are $p(a)p(g)$ and $p(a)p(h)$. Hence, the strategy $\bar{s}$ determines that the play (i, e, a) will occur with probability

$$
\begin{aligned}
p(a)p(g) + p(a)p(h) &= p(a)(p(g) + p(h)) \\
&= p(a),
\end{aligned}
$$

since $p(g) + p(h) = 1$. Similarly, $\bar{s}$ determines a probability of $p(b)p(g) + p(b)p(h) = p(b)$ for the play (i, e, b), and determines a probability of zero for each other play.

Players obviously will have preferences over *plays of the game*, which represent alternative *scenarios* stretching, possibly, into the indefinite future. To find their preferences over outcomes, therefore,

we have to estimate their preferences over various probability mixtures of alternative scenarios, that is, prospects in which each of a
number of scenarios occurs with a certain probability.

Now this is conceptually interesting. To evaluate "outcomes" of a
conflict as probability mixtures of various possible scenarios is in
principle realistic. For example, take a certain settlement of the
Vietnam conflict as evaluated, let us say, by the Saigon regime. They
are likely in fact to see it as introducing a number of possible developments with varying probabilities—for example, a Communist take-
over with high probability, an eventual non-Communist government
with less probability, and so on.

The lesson of this section, then, is that although we may have to
limit the vast number of strategies open to the players to the relatively
few strategies that we suppose they will actually consider, nevertheless
we should not hesitate to regard *strategies* as complex contingent
plans, contingent not only on other players' moves but on future

NATION 2

		S = "SOFT" STRATEGY OF GENERALLY COMPROMISING WITH THE OTHER, SEEING THEIR POINT OF VIEW, NOT BLUFFING THEM, ETC.	H ="HARD" STRATEGY OF TAKING ADVANTAGE OF THE OTHER, BLUFFING AND DENOUNCING THEM OVER ANY CONFLICT OF INTERESTS, ETC.
NATION I	S	GOOD RELATIONS, NEITHER NATION GENERALLY DOMINATING THE OTHER.	NATION 2 GENERALLY DOMINATES I.
	H	NATION I GENERALLY DOMINATES 2.	BAD RELATIONS, NEITHER NATION GENERALLY DOMINATING THE OTHER.

(a)

	S	H
S	3,3	1,4
H	4,1	2,2

(b)

Figure 2.10. General Game between Two Nations.

chance events, and *outcomes* as probability mixtures of possible future scenarios.

For example, between almost any two nations we could set up the normal-form game shown in Figure 2.10a.

If we assigned ordinal preferences over these outcomes we would in most cases obtain Figure 2.10b.

Actually Figure 2.10b is the game called "prisoner's dilemma," which we shall discuss when we come to our second breakdown of rationality. The point to be made here is that Figure 2.10 represents a fairly realistic, if rather simplified, model of a realistic situation. It is obtained by giving an *informal* description of complex contingent strategies such as are found in the extensive form of a game, rather than by attempting to formalize in detail these dynamic, conditional strategies.

2.3 The Metagame Approach: Rational Outcomes and Equilibria

Our main theme is still the first breakdown of rationality. In the previous section we examined the extensive form that underlies the normal form of a game, it being in the normal form that the "breakdown" occurs. The discussion showed that the normal form, regarded as a model of a general conflict situation, is not necessarily an "over-simplified" model. Theoretically, it may encompass an altogether excessive amount of detail.

Here, to examine the nature of the breakdown itself, we introduce some more normal-form concepts. These are also generally applicable. To illustrate them, we conclude the section with a number of examples. It will appear that the normal form covers many interesting phenomena.

Von Neumann and Morgenstern (1953) took the view that to analyze any normal-form game one should analyze the "metagames" based on it.[7] A *metagame* is the game that would exist if one of the players chose his strategy after the others, in knowledge of their choices.

---

7. Called by them the "minorant" and "majorant" games. Actually, they expressed this view only for the so-called two-person zero-sum games, which we shall define and discuss later. We shall use the metagame approach much more generally than they do.

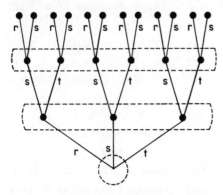

Figure 2.11. Extensive Form Corresponding to a Three-Person Normal Form
with $S_1 = \{r, s, t\}$, $S_2 = \{s, t\}$, $S_3 = \{r, s\}$.

From our discussion of the extensive form we know how to
construct such a game. First note that given an arbitrary normal form,
there is always at least one extensive form corresponding to it.[8]
This is found by supposing that the players make their strategy
choices in some fixed order, but that their information sets are such
that they are not informed of any strategy choices preceding their
own. Thus player 1, say, has a single decision node with one decision
arc for each of his strategies. Each decision arc leads to a decision
node for player 2, each of which has one decision arc for each of 2's
strategies.[9] And so on through to player n. At the same time, we
draw for each player a single information set containing all his
decison nodes. Figure 2.11 illustrates this.

From this we see at once how to construct a metagame. Suppose
player k is the one that is supposed to choose after the others, in
knowledge of their choices. Simply draw the extensive form as in
Figure 2.11 with player k coming last. Then delete k's information
set and give him one information set for each of his decision nodes.

8. We know already that there is a normal form corresponding to every extensive
form. The above is the converse statement. However, while a unique normal form
corresponds to a given extensive form, there will be many extensive forms
corresponding to a given normal form.
9. Until now we have used "P_i" or "player i" as alternative names for player i.
From now on we shall drop the first and use simply "i" instead. When it is
necessary to distinguish "i" as the name of a player from "i" as the name of a
positive integer, we shall say "player i." This seems to be the best way, as it is the
most usual.

Certainly this makes him choose last in knowledge of the other's choices, so we have constructed an extensive form for this metagame.

We remark that this particular metagame is called the "k-metagame"; clearly we have n metagames, one for each player, for we have the 1-metagame, 2-metagame, . . ., n-metagame.

What is the corresponding normal form? It is found as follows. Replace k's strategy set S_k with a set F containing all functions f from the joint strategy choices s_{N-k} of the other players to his own strategy choices s_k. We hasten to insert the following.

NOTATIONAL REMARK. We shall write "N" for the set $\{1, . . ., n\}$, that is, the set of players, identified as the set of positive integers up to and including n. If K is a subset of N, that is, a subset of players, we shall write "s_K" for a joint strategy choice by the players in the set K; that is, s_K is a list of strategies chosen by these players. Also to simplify the writing of sets as subscripts, we shall omit the curly brackets which should surround the one element of a singleton set, so that as above we write "s_{N-k}" instead of "$s_{N-\{k\}}$." The set of all joint strategy choices by the players in a set K will be written "S_K," so that S_{N-k} is the set of joint strategies of the players other than k. Hence we said that the normal form of the k-metagame is found by replacing S_k with the set F of all functions $f: S_{N-k} \rightarrow S_k$.

EXAMPLE. Consider the game of Figure 2.2, in which it was impossible for both players to be objectively rational. Write it as in Figure 2.12, so that we have

$$S_1 = S_2 = \{a, b\}, \qquad S = \{(a, a), (a, b), (b, a), (b, b)\}.$$

We have to construct the 2-metagame. There are four functions f from S_1 to S_2. Denote the function f such that $fa = x$, $fb = y$ by "x/y." Then the 2-metagame is as in Figure 2.13. The set F of 2's *metagame* strategies is $\{a/a, b/b, a/b, b/a\}$. The set of outcomes

		2	
		a	b
	a	1, 2	2, 1
1	b	2, 1	1, 2

Figure 2.12. Abstract Form of the Game between Merchant Ship and Warship.

		2			
		a/a	b/b	a/b	b/a
1	a	1,2	2,1	1,2	2,1
	b	2,1	1,2	1,2	2,1

Figure 2.13. 2-Metagame of the Game in Figure 2.12.

$S_1 \times F$ of the 2-metagame is $\{(a, a/a), (a, b/b), \ldots, (b, b/a)\}$. Generally, a typical outcome is an (s_1, f).

The *preferences* in Figure 2.13 have been determined in the obvious way. The metagame outcome (s_1, f) gives rise to a unique *basic outcome* (outcome of the original game); indeed, (s_1, f) gives rise to (s_1, fs_1). For example, $(b, a/b)$ gives rise to (b, b) because "$(b, a/b)$" means that player 1 has chosen b, while 2 has chosen to choose a if 1 chooses a, b if 1 chooses b. The preferences attached to (s_1, f) are then naturally those attached to the basic outcome (s_1, fs_1) that it yields.

So Figure 2.13 gives an example of a metagame. In general, the k-metagame will have as a typical outcome (f, s_{N-k}), preferences for which will be the same as for the corresponding *basic outcome* (fs_{N-k}, s_{N-k}).

FURTHER NOTATIONAL REMARK. Is it all right, in denoting an outcome, to mix up the order in which the strategies of the players are listed? For example, s is an n-tuple $(s_1, \ldots, s_n)$, s_{N-k} is an $(n-1)$-tuple $(s_1, \ldots, s_{k-1}, s_{k+1}, \ldots, s_n)$, and fs_{N-k} is a one-tuple s_k. If then we write "(fs_{N-k}, s_{N-k})," are we not writing "$(s_k, s_1, \ldots, s_{k-1}, s_{k+1}, \ldots, s_n)$," that is, mixing up the order in which strategies are listed? It is in fact all right to mix up the order in this way provided we continue to use subscripts to denote which player each strategy belongs to, and we shall do it freely. An n-tuple is in fact merely an *indexed set*, for which see the discussion in Appendix A.

Another difficulty arises concerning the use of *subsets* of players as subscripts. What does s_K denote when $K = \varnothing$ (the empty set)? We shall take s_K in this case as standing for a blank space on the page. All notations connected with s_K will likewise stand for blank spaces. Thus for example, if $K = \emptyset$, then (s_K, s_J, s_{N-K-J}) simply stands for $(s_J, s_{N-K-J}) = (s_J, s_{N-J})$. If this rule is consistently followed we shall encounter no problems.

We cannot usually draw the matrix of a metagame, as in Figure 2.13, even if we can draw the matrix of the original game. The number of functions from one set to another is too large if the sets themselves are even moderately large—in fact it is y^x, where x is the number of elements in the first set and y the number in the second. Nevertheless, the metagame is well defined, whether we can draw it or not.

Thus the metagames are defined. But we have not asked the question, Why do we accept the von Neumann–Morgenstern view that to analyze a game we must analyze the metagames based on it?

Quite simply, we are interested in objective rationality, that is, rational decision-making based on the relevant "objective" facts. As we have said, rational decision-makers can be only subjectively rational; but their aim is to be objectively rational, and their decisions will be *stable* only if they succeed.

Now objective rationality is achieved by having all relevant information. For each player k this includes knowing the decisions of the other. This is just the information he has in the k-metagame. Hence we study the k-metagame in order to study the objectively rational, stable behavior that "lies behind" k's actual behavior in this sense: k's actual behavior is arrived at in an attempt to achieve this behavior.

Now one case exists when k can certainly achieve objective rationality: when there is a strategy that is best for him whatever the others choose. The strategy H is such a "sure-thing" strategy for either player in the prisoner's dilemma game of Figure 2.10. More to the point, a/b is such a strategy for column-player in Figure 2.13. In fact, since we may construct a metagame strategy f by setting fs_{N-k} equal to k's "best reply" to s_{N-k} for each joint strategy s_{N-k} of the other players, it is clear that (at least in the finite case[10]) k always has a sure-thing, objectively rational metagame strategy. In the k-metagame k has no problem in achieving objective rationality.

10. Which here may be read "for all practical purposes."

The problem in the merchant ship–warship game is of course that the "sure-thing" metagame strategies for the two players do not intersect. That is, if f^* is the sure-thing strategy for player 1 and g^* the sure-thing strategy for 2, there is no basic outcome (s_1, s_2) such that $s_1 = f^*s_2$, $s_2 = g^*s_1$. Such an outcome if it exists is called an *equilibrium*. The problem is, the game has no equilibrium.

This can be put another way.

Call $\bar{s}$ a *rational outcome for* k if, given the strategies $\bar{s}_{N-k}$ of the other players, there is no outcome $(s_k, \bar{s}_{N-k})$ he prefers to $\bar{s}$. Write "R_k" for the set of all rational outcomes for k. Then we define $E = \cap_i R_i$ to be the set of equilibria of the game. In the merchant ship–warship game E is empty. No outcome is rational for all players.

We conclude this section by taking a deeper look at what we mean by "best reply," "sure-thing strategy," and "rational outcome" and following up with a number of examples.

So far we have talked of players' preferences without formalizing them. In our game matrices we have used payoff numbers to represent preferences, but we have stressed that these are not "really" numbers, they have merely ordinal significance. It is time now to introduce a formal notation to represent preferences, but we wish to do this without introducing numbers, the use of which might be misleading.

We proceed as follows. For each player k, let "M_k" stand for a function from the set S to the set of all subsets of S. (This includes $\varnothing$, the empty set, and also the set S itself; e.g., the set of all subsets of $\{a, b, c\}$ is $\{ \{a, b, c\}, \{a, b\}, \{a, c\}, \{b, c\}, \{a\}, \{b\}, \{c\}, \varnothing \}$.) Interpret $M_k s$ as the set of all outcomes not preferred to s by k. We may then call M_k player k's preference function.

Player k's preferences for the outcome s are then not represented by a number, but by a set: the set $M_k s$ of all outcomes not preferred by him to s. If now player k's preferences are ordinal, as we are at present assuming them to be, the result is that an outcome s is *not preferred* by k to an outcome t if and only if

$$M_k s \subseteq M_k t.$$

(Later on we shall say exactly what we mean by "ordinal," and then prove the above assertion rigorously.)

In particular, any outcome is "not preferred" to itself. Also, if s is *preferred* to t by player k, we shall have[11]

$$M_k s \supset M_k t.$$

This then gives us our nonquantitative notation for preferences. Using it, we can say that a *rational outcome for* k is an $\bar{s}$ such that

$$\forall s_k : M_k \bar{s} \supseteq M_k(s_k, \bar{s}_{N-k});$$

and a "sure-thing" metagame strategy is an $\bar{f}$ such that

$$\forall s_{N-k} : (\bar{f} s_{N-k}, s_{N-k}) \in R_k,$$

which is to say (on substituting), an $\bar{f}$ such that

$$\forall s : M_k(\bar{f} s_{N-k}, s_{N-k}) \supseteq M_k s.$$

FIRST EXAMPLE. In Figure 2.12 we have $M_1(a, b) = \{(a, a), (a, b), (b, a), (b, b)\} = S$, while $M_1(a, a) = \{(a, a), (b, b)\}$. Hence, $(a, a) \in M_1(a, b)$ and $M_1(a, a) \subseteq M_1(a, b)$—i.e., (a, a) is not preferred by 1 to (a, b). Of course, $R_1 = \{(a, b), (b, a)\}$—the outcomes in which the merchant avoids the warship.

SECOND EXAMPLE. A two-person "problem of coordination" may be described as a game in which there is a correspondence between 1's strategies and 2's strategies and the chief aim of each player is to make their strategies correspond. For example, the chief aim of two motorists approaching each other is to pass on opposite sides of the road. Each has two strategies, "left" and "right." As long as both choose the same strategy, all is well.

In such games, $R_1 = R_2$. Rational outcomes are the same for both players. "Sure-thing" metagame strategies intersect everywhere. The problem is not having too few equilibria; it is having too many.

Figure 2.14 gives some examples. Equilibria are circled, and off-diagonal cells are assumed to contain "0, 0".[12] Figure 2.14a is the game of motorists approaching each other as played in the United

11. We write "$A \subset B$": to mean "A is a proper subset of B," excluding the possibility that $A = B$. If A is a subset of B that may equal B, we write "$A \subseteq B$".
12. In these examples we shall continue to use payoff numbers as a succinct way of representing ordinal preferences. We have shown that their numerical character is inessential.

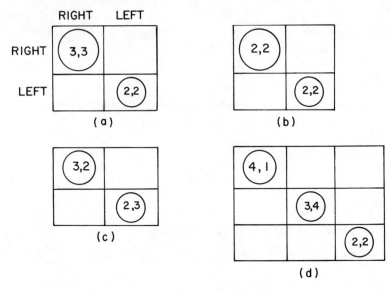

Figure 2.14. Some Games of Coordination. Equilibria are circled and off-diagonal cells are assumed to contain "0" for both players.

States, if we assume motorists prefer, other things being equal, to obey the law. Presumably it is not a problem provided players know each other's preferences. We shall return to this point. Figure 2.14b simply requires coordination. In Figure 2.14c there is the difficulty that while each player would rather coordinate, each prefers to coordinate at a different point. Figure 2.14d is a kind of mixture of Figure 2.14a and 2.14c. Can the (2, 2) outcome be dismissed if we assume that players know each other's preferences? Both would rather have (3, 4). But from (3, 4) player 1 would rather go to (4, 1), to which (2, 2) is preferred by player 2.

We shall encounter games such as Figure 2.14c and 2.14d when we discuss the third breakdown of rationality. But Figures 2.14a and 2.14b do not present any real crisis for rationality, though they do show that rationality is not enough. Figure 2.14b, for example, might represent two people in a corridor unable to pass each other, because, each being motivated only by rationality, they cannot decide which side to pass on.

"Games of coordination" may be regarded as opposite to "games without equilibria" (the games in which we find the first breakdown of rationality). In games of coordination

$$s \in R_1 \Leftrightarrow s \in R_2,$$

whereas in games without equilibria

$$s \in R_1 \Rightarrow s \notin R_2.$$

THIRD EXAMPLE.[13] A "continuous" game may be defined as one in which each player chooses a number in a closed interval of the real line as his strategy choice. By an appropriate transformation, each player may be regarded as choosing a number from the closed unit interval [0, 1]. Thus,

$$S_i = S_j = \{x \,|\, x \text{ real}, 0 \leqslant x \leqslant 1\}.$$

This is a game in which each player has an infinite number of strategies. We might be modeling an economic situation where each player chooses a price or a quantity. Or in a political situation, each might be choosing a level of armaments or a troop commitment. These are two examples of cases when it might be convenient to regard the number of strategies as infinite rather than considering a very large but finite number of possible "levels" of a single variable.

The name "continuous" comes about because a closed real interval is often called a "continuum." It does not imply continuity in any other sense. But continuous-game models are most useful if for each player i there exists a "well-behaved" function v_i from the set S of outcomes to the set of real numbers such that

$$M_i s \supseteq M_i t \Leftrightarrow v_i(s) \geqslant v_i(t),$$

in which case player i may be regarded as maximizing v_i. Hence, v_i is in some way a *measure of performance* for player i. For a firm in an economic game, v_i might be profit; for an army v_i might be the relative attrition rate.

In such cases calculus is useful to find R_i. Indeed, if the partial derivative of v_i with respect to s_i, which we write v_i', exists everywhere in S, then

$$R_i - B \subseteq \{s \,|\, v_i's = 0\},$$

13. This may be skipped by the reader unfamiliar with calculus.

where B is the boundary of S (the set of points such that some $s_j = 0$ or 1). The boundary must be investigated separately.

To illustrate, set $s_1 = x$, $s_2 = y$ and suppose that

$$v_1(x, y) = \tfrac{1}{2}x - \tfrac{1}{2}x^2 + \tfrac{1}{4}xy,$$

and

$$v_2(x, y) = x^2 y - \tfrac{1}{2}y^2.$$

Then

$$v_1'(x, y) = \tfrac{1}{2} - x + \tfrac{1}{4}y,$$

and

$$v_2'(x, y) = x^2 - y.$$

We then find

$$R_1 = \{x, y \,|\, x = \tfrac{1}{2} + \tfrac{1}{4}y\},$$

and

$$R_2 = \{x, y \,|\, y = x^2\},$$

so that eventually

$$E = R_1 \cap R_2 = \{x, y \,|\, x = 2 - 2/\sqrt{2} \text{ and } y = 6 - 8/\sqrt{2}\}.$$

The situation is illustrated in Figure 2.15.

FOURTH EXAMPLE. When dealing with finite games, particularly those having more than two players, an alternative representation to the

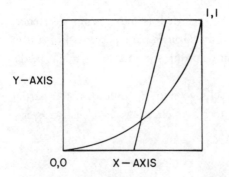

Figure 2.15. A Continuous Game. The straight line gives R_1, the curved line R_2.

U.S. PREFERENCES

STRATEGIES									
	U. S.	T	T	O	O	T	T	O	O
	SOVIET	O	O	O	O	T	T	T	T
	CHINESE	O	T	O	T	O	T	O	T

SOVIET PREFERENCES

STRATEGIES									
	U.S.	O	O	O	O	T	T	T	T
	SOVIET	T	T	O	O	T	T	O	O
	CHINESE	O	T	O	T	O	T	O	T

CHINESE PREFERENCES

STRATEGIES									
	U. S.	O	O	T	T	O	T	O	T
	SOVIET	O	T	O	T	O	O	T	T
	CHINESE	T	T	T	T	O	O	O	O

Figure 2.16. Nuclear Test Ban between U.S., U.S.S.R., and China. "T" is the strategy "Test," "0" is "Not Test." For any outcome s, $M_i s$ is the set of outcomes to the right of s together with s itself. For example, $M_{U.S.}(0T0) = \{0T0, 0TT\}$.

matrix representation is useful and instructive. In Figure 2.16, outcomes are written as columns of strategies. For each player i, the columns have been ordered from left to right in player i's preference ordering. (Some special device would have to be used to bracket together columns between which player i was "indifferent," that is, columns s and t such that $M_i s = M_i t$.)

In this representation, an outcome s is *rational for player i* if every outcome in which the others' strategies are s_{N-i} appears to the right of s (or is bracketed with s) in the table giving i's preferences. For example, $T00$ is rational for the United States while 000 is not. (To save space, we write a column such as T in the form "$T00$".)
$$0$$
$$0$$

On further examining Figure 2.16, we find

$R_{\text{U.S.}} = \{T00, T0T, TT0, TTT\}$,

$R_{\text{SOV}} = \{0T0, 0TT, TT0, TTT\}$,

and

$R_{\text{CHI}} = \{00T, 0TT, T0T, TTT\}$,

so that

$E = \{TTT\}$.

The only equilibrium occurs when all three nations are testing! This is a gloomy conclusion. Of course, the reader may disagree with our assumptions regarding preferences or with the simplifications used in this model. But let us accept these for the sake of argument. We will try an experiment. Fix the Chinese strategy at "*T*." This gives a "subgame" that is a two-person game between the United States and the Soviets. The reader should write this subgame in matrix form. He will find it is the same as the prisoner's dilemma game of Figure 2.10, in which the still-to-be-discussed second breakdown of rationality occurs. Thus we have not finished with our discussion of the nuclear test ban.

FIFTH EXAMPLE. The foregoing "tableau" representation of a game may be developed further. Often the most natural representation of a player's strategies is in terms of various "yes/no" alternatives we may call "options." The example in Figure 2.17 is based on a term paper submitted to the author by a student. Here we analyze a conflict taking place on the campus of a United States university by defining four players—militant students, campus authorities, legal authorities (that is, police, state government), and moderate students. Each player is given certain "yes/no" options as shown. The rule is that each option must be either taken or not taken.

If an option is taken, we write "1"; if it is not taken, we write "0." Hence an *outcome* is represented by a column of 1's and 0's, such as the first column in Figure 2.17, made up of sub-columns representing strategies for the individual players, a *strategy* being shown by a particular combination of 1's and 0's against the player's options. However, not every one of these possible combinations (2^m of them,

	A Particular Outcome	A Set of Infeasible Combinations
Militant Students:		
Violent Protest	0	1
Peaceful Protest	1	1
Request Negotiations	1	–
Campus Authorities:		
Call in Legal Authorities	0	–
Make Verbal Threats, etc.	0	–
Request Negotiations	0	–
Legal Authorities:		
Participate If Called	1	–
Participate Whether Called or Not	0	–
Moderate Students:		
Attend Classes	1	–

Figure 2.17. A Campus Conflict. Players have "Yes/No" options: "1" means the option is taken, "0" means it is not taken, "–" means it may or may not be taken. A strategy is a feasible combination of one player's options.

if the player has m options) has to be seen as representing a feasible strategy for that player. Some may be deemed "infeasible"; for example, it is deemed infeasible for militant students to protest both violently and peacefully. A combination may be called "infeasible" because it is physically impossible, or because it is hard to interpret, or merely to simplify the model. The *feasible* combinations of a player's options are the ones that are truly that player's strategies. The second column in Figure 2.17 shows a set of outcomes we have set aside as infeasible, a *set* of outcomes being represented by using *blanks* (the symbol "–") in a column to stand for "either/or"; the option may or may not be taken.

Note that the procedure is quite general in that if each player has a finite number of strategies these can always be represented as combinations of "yes/no" options (some of which may be infeasible), although unless this representation is a "natural" one there will not be much reason to use it. The fact is, though, that this often appears as a natural way of representing the strategies a real-life player seems to be faced with.

In Figure 2.17, we have described a very large game. Since there are nine options, there are altogether $2^9 = 512$ columns of 1's and 0's to be considered. To specify the game fully, we should have to consider each of these 512 columns. Some we would call "infeasible"; the rest would have to be ordered in four different ways corresponding to the preference orderings of the four players. After all this we would have fully defined the game, and could begin our formal analysis looking for rational outcomes and equilibria.

The trouble is that this would take a long time and would involve many detailed specific assumptions about the preferences of the players, assumptions about which we might not feel confident. And when we had made our analysis and drawn our conclusions, it would not be at all clear which assumptions were used and which were not used in reaching the conclusions.

So instead we proceed sequentially. We select a particular outcome (any outcome of interest) and ask whether it is rational for a particular player. For example, in Figure 2.18 we have selected the particular outcome already seen in Figure 2.17, and have asked if it is rational for the militant students. What assumptions are necessary to answer this question?

We wish to know whether

$$\forall s_i : (s_i, \bar{s}_{N-i}) \in M_i \bar{s},$$

where $\bar{s}$ is the particular outcome and i is the militant students. Hence we have to take each outcome of the form $(s_i, \bar{s}_{N-i})$ and decide whether it is "not preferred" to $\bar{s}$.

This is now a quite manageable task. In Figure 2.18 it is performed by assigning every column in which the other players' strategy choices are the same as in the particular outcome to one of three categories: "preferred" to the particular outcome, "not preferred" to it, or "infeasible." In this way we do make the minimum preference assumptions necessary to answer the question we have asked.

On our assumptions (Figure 2.18) the answer is that this outcome is not rational for the militant students and hence not an equilibrium.

	Preferred by Militant Students	Particular Outcome ӟ	Not Preferred		Infeasible
Militant Students:					
Violent Protest	1	0	0	0	1
Peaceful Protest	0	1	0	1	1
Request Negotiations	–	1	–	0	–
Campus Authorities:					
Call in Legal Authorities	0	0	0	0	0
Make Verbal Threats, etc.	0	0	0	0	0
Request Negotiations	0	0	0	0	0
Legal Authorities:					
Participate If Called	1	1	1	1	1
Participate Whether Called or Not	0	0	0	0	0
Moderate Students:					
Attend Classes	1	1	1	1	1

Figure 2.18. Analysis of Campus Conflict. A particular outcome is considered from the viewpoint of the militant students.

Violent protest, with or without a request for negotiations, is rational for them given the others' strategies.

The technique used here is called the "analysis of options." It provides a practical method of analyzing realistic conflicts and is investigated further in Section 5.3.

2.4 The Mixed-Strategy Solution

We now come to a section that is in a way a digression. We have to show that in a sense rationality can be "saved" from the first breakdown. But first, the rescue of rationality is only partially successful. The rationality concept that is rescued is a rather battered one. And second, we shall see that the method of saving rationality is useless against the second breakdown (next section). Therefore the concept does not finally survive, and we have in any case to reconstruct our ideas without it. In doing so, we shall not return at all to the "mixed-strategy" method we are about to discuss (although actually our later discussion will always contain it as a special case), our reason being that this method is essentially quantitative and numerical. As we have said, one of our basic aims is a nonquantitative reconstruction. We want to see how far we can go without resorting to the measurement of any numerical quantities.

Let us discuss the mixed-strategy method as it applies to a finite game in normal form.

The numerical quantities introduced in order to "save" rationality from the first breakdown are real-valued "utilities." These are real numbers that are assumed to express the "degree of preference" a player feels for an outcome.

The numbers express the degree of preference first in the obvious way: that is, for each player i a number $v_i(s)$ is attached to each outcome s in such a way that $v_i(s) > v_i(t)$ if i prefers s to t, while if i is indifferent between s and t then $v_i(s) = v_i(t)$.

Second, the v_i numbers are attached, not only to every outcome of the game, but to every *probability mixture* of outcomes; and this is done in such a way that if we write

$$(p_1, \ldots, p_m; s^1, \ldots, s^m)$$

for a probability mixture of outcomes, the outcomes being $s^1, \ldots, s^m$, with s^j having probability p_j of occurrence, then we always have

$$v_i(p_1, \ldots, p_m; s^1, \ldots, s^m) = p_1 v_i(s^1) + p_2 v_i(s^2) + \ldots + p_m v_i(s^m).$$

This statement says that the "utility" of a probability mixture of outcomes equals the *expected value* of the utility obtained from the component outcomes.

Now at least since the nineteenth century the following question has been debated. Is it valid, or meaningful, to attach real-valued utilities to outcomes of a situation? And if so, can it be assumed that a person confronted by two probability mixtures of outcomes will always prefer that with the higher expected value?

We see that the procedure of assigning v_i numbers answers "yes" to both these questions. Can the procedure be justified?

Von Neumann and Morgenstern (1953) argue that the procedure is in fact a mere matter of measuring a well-defined measurable quantity provided that the v_i numbers can be measured as follows. Assume that the quantity (whatever it is) to be measured by the numbers has an arbitrary origin and unit of measurement; and on this basis, arbitrarily set the value of the least-preferred outcome (chosen from the finite set of outcomes) at zero:

$v_i(s^0) = 0,$

where s^0 is least preferred.
Set the value of the most-preferred outcome at unity:

$v_i(s^1) = 1,$

where s^1 is most preferred.

Having done this, perform the following experiment with each other outcome s. Find a unique probability p which is such that the probability mixture

$(p, 1-p; s^1, s^0)$

is (for player i) indifferent to the outcome s; and then write the utility value of s as

$v_i(s) = p.$

EXAMPLE. To construct the v numbers representing the reader's preferences for coffee, tea, or chocolate, we would first find out in what order he preferred these drinks. If he preferred coffee to chocolate and chocolate to tea, we would write

v (coffee) $= 1,$
v (tea) $= 0.$

Then we would offer him various choices of different probabilities of tea or coffee until we found a probability p, say $p = \frac{1}{3}$, such that he would be indifferent between

$(\frac{1}{3}, \frac{2}{3};$ coffee, tea)

and chocolate. We would then write

v (chocolate) $= \frac{1}{3}.$

What does this procedure achieve? Having followed it, according to von Neumann and Morgenstern, we have done all that is needed. Provided that certain "consistency" assumptions about players' preferences are granted, they prove that by the above procedure we have measured a quantity which—call it "utility" or what you will— is such that player i always prefers greater amounts of it and always prefers to maximize its expected value.   Q.E.D.

But what are these consistency assumptions? Before describing them (without going into proofs at all) let us first discuss on what basis to criticize them. We are discussing the "mixed-strategy" concept as a means of "saving" rationality. As we have said before, rational behavior is only, after all, to be expected from a decision-maker with "rational" (consistent) preferences. Given strange (e.g., nonordinal) preferences, any kind of strange behavior will not be surprising. So the only basis on which to criticize the von Neumann–Morgenstern "consistency" assumptions must be this: Are they what one has a right to expect from a player one expects to exhibit rationality? This, moreover, is also the basis on which von Neumann and Morgenstern themselves justify the assumptions. Hence this seems to be fair to all concerned. And so we may also say beforehand that the consistency assumptions do seem, on this basis, perfectly acceptable.

The assumptions are

a. Players have ordinal preferences between all outcomes and probability mixtures of outcomes.

b. To the players, probability mixtures which are equivalent according to probability theory are in fact equivalent.

For example, the mixture

$$(p, 1-p; (q, 1-q; s, t), r),$$

which is a "compound" mixture in which the mixture $(q, 1-q; s, t)$ itself occurs with probability p, is equivalent to $(pq, p(1-q), (1-p);$ $s, t, r)$, which is the equivalent probability mixture of outcomes s, t, r.

c. A preferred (or indifferent) outcome, when substituted in a probability mixture, gives a preferred (or indifferent) mixture. For example, if s is preferred to t, then

$(p, 1-p; s, r)$

is preferred to

$(p, 1-p; t, r)$.

d. The procedure for assigning v numbers, after 0 has been assigned to the least-preferred outcome and 1 to the most-preferred, always gives a unique value $v(s)$ for every outcome s. (This may be shown to follow from the more basic assumption that "small" differences in probabilities make "small" differences in the utility value of a mixture.)

As we have said, these assumptions seem reasonable as what one might expect from a truly rational player. We can therefore proceed straight to the next step, which is to introduce "mixed strategies."

A *mixed strategy* for player i is a method of play whereby, instead of necessarily choosing a determinate strategy, he may choose any probability distribution over his determinate strategies and allow his actual strategy choice to be determined from this probability distribution. For example, in the merchant ship–warship game (Figure 2.2), instead of having to choose either north or south, the merchant ship might choose north with probability $\frac{1}{3}$, south with probability $\frac{2}{3}$.

Why? To this we answer, Why not? Allowing mixed strategies does not limit the merchant ship's choice of strategies, it extends it. The merchant ship can still choose either of its original strategies: the so-called pure, as distinct from "mixed" strategies. To choose a "pure" strategy is equivalent to choosing one pure strategy with probability 1 and the others with probability 0. So why not allow mixed strategies, say by allowing players to spin a coin or use some other random device?

Of course, to allow mixed strategies is to change the game, since it enlarges the strategy choices open to the players. It creates what is called a *mixed-strategy game* based on the original game.

But now we come to the point. If we allow the foregoing, the general result, due to Nash (1950), is that an equilibrium exists in any mixed-strategy game based on a finite game. This means that in any finite game (which is to say, for all practical purposes) it is always possible for all players to be rational—though for this they may have to employ mixed strategies.

And so we save rationality from the first breakdown. In the merchant ship–warship game, for example, the reader may check that if both players choose each of their strategies with probability $\frac{1}{2}$, then both are being objectively rational.

But surely a price has been paid! In Chapter 1 we quoted Russell giving as a prime example of irrationality "to become so agitated at the airport as to jump into the first plane that I see." This, however, is essentially the mixed-strategy version of rationality. (Russell apparently could not envisage the further step of deliberately getting on the wrong plane, a situation, however, that we shall come to in the next section.)

Indeed, to show the strict relevance of this, imagine that Russell knows that only two planes are leaving at a certain time—one bound for New York and one for Istanbul, that he must leave London immediately, and that he is being sought by police agents (for a political crime, no doubt) who themselves must choose whether to await him in New York or Istanbul. Then he is in a game similar to the merchant ship–warship game, and to jump into the first plane he sees may be the only recommendation with which "reason" can provide him.

But is the mixed-strategy game a good model?

As Luce and Raiffa (1957) point out, the commander of the warship, particularly if he missed his prey but even if he did not, might not receive a nation's gratitude for having chosen his strategy by tossing a coin! This can be put more generally. Let us grant that, for some purposes at least, we may wish to model a situation by assigning to each player the strategy choices that he himself sees as open to him. Then as a pure matter of fact it cannot be said that he must always be assigned, in addition to his strategies, all probability mixtures of them. Sometimes such an assignment will be indicated. More often, perhaps, it will not be.

This leads to the conclusion that there exist both games with mixed strategies and games without mixed strategies. Nash's theorem tells us that in the former category all games have equilibria. This is interesting. (In fact, the theorem applies more generally and can be stated, without referring to mixed strategies, so as to assert that equilibria exist in all games with a certain structure.) It does not however tell us that all games have equilibria.

But these objections, though they express the viewpoint we shall finally come to hold, are beside the point if we regard the mixed-strategy concept as a method of "saving" rationality. For then the fact that players may not wish to use mixed strategies does not alter the fact that if they did so they could all be rational. Finally, therefore, we see that by this device rationality is saved from the first breakdown, at a price. The price is to reconcile oneself to the idea of a rational decision being made "at random," though in accordance with predetermined probabilities.

To show how high is this price, we add the following. There exists a theorem that says that in a sense no player ever has any reason to play a mixed strategy! Specifically, whatever strategies, mixed or "pure," the other players are choosing, player i can always do as well for himself by playing a pure strategy as he can by playing any mixed strategy.

At a mixed-strategy equilibrium, of course, player i cannot do better by shifting to a pure strategy. For by the definition of an equilibrium, he cannot in any way do better than by choosing the (mixed) strategy that is his contribution to the equilibrium. The point is, however, that by a pure-strategy choice he can always do just as well. This is what we mean by saying there is never any reason for him to choose a mixed strategy; though it may be the case (and at a mixed-strategy equilibrium it will be the case) that there is no reason for him not to choose a mixed strategy.

The point is illustrated again in the merchant ship–warship game, where the mixed-strategy equilibrium occurs when each player plays each strategy with probability $\frac{1}{2}$. The reader may check that, given that the other player is choosing this mixed strategy, neither player has any reason to choose any pure or mixed strategy in preference to any other. All yield him the same expected value.

To clarify this point further, Figure 2.19 shows how the same kind of situation can occur without the introduction of mixed strategies.

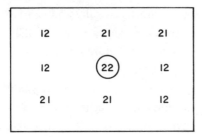

Figure 2.19. Game with a "Weak" Equilibrium. At the equilibrium, given the other player's strategy choice, neither player has reason to make any one choice rather than another.

The equilibrium outcome of this pure-strategy game is circled. But given that one player is choosing the strategy (the middle row or column) that is his contribution to this equilibrium, the other player has no reason to choose any particular strategy in preference to any other.

We now show, in the next section, how the mixed-strategy idea is in any case of no avail against the second breakdown of rationality.

2.5 The Second Breakdown of Rationality
In the game of Figure 2.20a, there is only one rational strategy for each player. The game is prisoner's dilemma. We have labeled the strategies "C" (for "cooperate") and "D" (for "defect").

The only rational strategy is D; for D is a "sure-thing" strategy: it emerges as the rational choice, whichever strategy the opponent chooses or is expected to choose. If he is going to defect, rationally one should defect. If he is going to cooperate, again one should defect.

From this it would seem there should be no game-theoretic problem. Game-theoretic problems arise from two or more decision-makers with differing preferences each able to influence the result. This leads to the problem we called the first breakdown of rationality, that there may be no outcome rational for both players, that is, no equilibrium. It also leads to the problem we discussed with "games of coordination," the problem that there may be more than one equilibrium. But these problems exist only when a player's

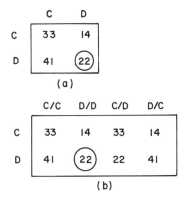

Figure 2.20. Prisoner's Dilemma and Its 2-Metagame. The symbol "X/Y" stands for the metagame strategy (or policy) of choosing *X* against *C*, *Y* against *D*.

rational decision hinges on the opponent's intentions. Here this is not so.

True, a player in this game would like the opponent to cooperate. The worst result (3) which he can get if the other cooperates is better than the best result (2) which is possible if the other defects. But the opponent's intentions are irrelevant in rationally deciding what to do oneself. If one does not defect, one must cooperate; but to cooperate is deliberately to minimize one's own payoff. It would be the sure-thing, only rational strategy for an enemy who, let us say, has managed to get into the position of deciding your strategy choice for you and who is a Count of Monte Cristo with the single aim of hurting you.

In this game *C* is, quite unambiguously, irrational. It is the one and only irrational choice just as *D* is the one and only rational one. It is, moreover, objectively irrational, just as *D* is objectively rational. The distinction we have drawn between objective and subjective rationality does not, in fact, arise here. Provided players know at least their own payoffs, the two kinds of rationality are the same.

Where, then, is the game-theoretic problem? Simply that if both players are irrational, they do better than if both are rational. Each obtains 3 instead of 2. If both minimize their own payoffs, do as badly for themselves as they can, each does better than if both do as well as they can.

To quote Dostoevski again: "Of course, he *may* make his volition march with reason. . . . Such a proceeding is expedient, and may, at times even be praiseworthy; but only too often do we see volition clashing with reason, and— and— Yet, do you know, gentlemen, *this too*, at times, may be both expedient and praiseworthy."

Dostoevski does not exaggerate the scope of his observation, for bear in mind that the prisoner's dilemma paradox is of wide application. We have seen it arise in the relations between two countries (Figure 2.10). In a general sense, it can arise in the same way between any two interdependent decision-makers, or (since the dilemma easily generalizes to any number of players) within any "social group" defined in the widest possible way.

Examples are two oligopolistic firms deciding whether to undercut each other; two opposed nations deciding whether to rearm; two men deciding whether to talk louder and drown the other's voice. It is easy to multiply examples. In the *n*-person case, phrases like "What would happen if everybody felt that way?" are used to persuade individuals to be irrational. The rational answer to this appeared in Joseph Heller's novel, *Catch-22*: "Then I'd certainly be a damned fool to feel any other way, wouldn't I?"[14] In prisoner's dilemma, if the other player does not defect, I am a fool not to, but what if he does defect? I am a fool not to.

The mixed-strategy concept is irrelevant, even if we succeed in measuring numerical utilities for the players. For suppose we do this, and obtain numerical utilities that order the outcomes in the "prisoner's dilemma" ordering; then the reader may check that, whatever "pure" or "mixed" strategy the other player chooses, the one rational choice is still D.

Also, the "sure-thing" metagame strategy found in either of the two first-level metagames (see Figure 2.20b) is not very informative. Since D was already a "sure-thing" strategy in the original game, the "sure-thing" metagame strategy is necessarily D/D—always play D.

When considering prisoner's dilemma, there is a temptation to assume the paradox away. One is tempted to say, "But in such a case

14. Joseph Heller, *Catch-22* (New York: Dell Publishing Co., 1962, reprinted by arrangement with Simon and Schuster, New York), p. 455.

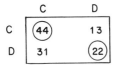

Figure 2.21. Coordination Game Obtained from Prisoner's Dilemma by Altering Players' Preferences. If the other player cooperates, each player now prefers to cooperate himself.

ethical motives, and so forth, will lead a player who expects the other to cooperate to prefer to cooperate himself." This is to change the assumed preference ordering. It is to say that the situation being studied is not prisoner's dilemma but the "coordination" game shown in Figure 2.21. It says that players faced with prisoner's dilemma will alter their preferences, so that in fact prisoner's dilemma will not occur. No doubt this will happen sometimes if the stakes are low enough. It is overoptimistic to assume that it will happen in "serious" games, played for high stakes, for example, in economics or politics.

There is also a tendency to lay the blame for the paradox on the game-theoretic model rather than on the real-world situation being modeled. This sometimes has the unfortunate effect of making it seem that game theory does not apply to the real world. One hears the paradox dismissed on the grounds that, after all, numerical utilities cannot be measured at all reliably. Our presentation makes it clear that this is irrelevant, since we do not use numerical utilities, only preference orderings. Again, it is often stressed that the game framework assumes that choices are made quite simultaneously and independently—which, it is pointed out, is not realistic. But if player 1 chooses first, so that player 2 chooses in knowledge of 1's choice, the dilemma is not solved, as we see in the 2-metagame (Figure 2.20b), which models precisely this situation. In the 2-metagame it is still the case that there is a nonequilibrium better for both players than any equilibrium; that is, both can do better by at least one being irrational than they can by both being rational. This preserves the essence of the dilemma, which is that *there seem to be reasons for being irrational.*

Note too that any communications, negotiations, and so on which may precede the actual choice of a strategy are irrelevant to rational players. We assume that such preliminaries leave each player a perfectly free choice of either strategy and do not affect preference orderings—otherwise they cannot be said to be preliminary to the game of prisoner's dilemma. But if that is so, then in the end our rational players are still faced with a prisoner's dilemma.

The existence of this practically important paradox seems to show that for man to be rational is something we cannot and should not expect. For in the course of evolution man must often have split into separate breeding groups. Consider two such groups. In one, men playing prisoner's dilemma with each other were instinctively rational, in the other, instinctively irrational. The second must have had more chances of survival. An argument along the same lines asks, If we wished to build groups of machines that would be viable, should we make them rational when playing prisoner's dilemma among themselves, or irrational?

We should perhaps reemphasize that rationality still means pursuing one's advantage as best one can, and objective rationality (as in prisoner's dilemma) means attaining it as best one can. The rational choice in prisoner's dilemma always pays better than the irrational one. Nevertheless, two irrational players do better than two rational ones. This is our second breakdown.

2.6 Discussion of Chapter 2
In this chapter we have discussed the concept of rationality and shown that it conceals paradoxes and dilemmas. But what is the point of such a discussion?

Let us accept the viewpoint, the chief progenitor of which is probably Hume, that there are just three modes of discourse: discourse about the empirical world (positive discourse), discourse about what is logically necessary (roughly the same as pure mathematics), and ethical or aesthetic discourse (discourse which makes value judgments). The first two discuss what is, the last discusses what ought to be; but from what is, with no assumptions about what ought to be, we cannot derive any propositions about what ought to be; and from what ought to be we can conclude nothing about what is. The third mode is therefore to be distinguished from the first two. But the first two must also be distinguished from each other; for no purely logical truth can tell us anything about the real world, nor can empirical facts yield logical truths. The three modes of discourse are therefore closed off from each other.

Of the three modes of discourse, science rejects the third entirely. It is not concerned with value judgments. It uses the second (logic) but only as a tool. Essentially it is concerned with the real world, although to discuss the real world it uses logic in order to deduce one empirical statement from another.

If now we ask what mode our discussion of rationality has been in, the answer is not clear. We have encountered difficulties (paradoxes, dilemmas). But in what do these difficulties consist? Are they empirical, logical, or ethical/aesthetic?

They seem to derive from the fact that we wish "rational behavior" to be simultaneously the way people *do* behave, the way that logically they *must* behave, and finally the way they *should* behave. But these are extraordinary demands, not fulfilled by any other science (though nearly all sciences in their early stages have tried to fulfill them). From this viewpoint it is not surprising that such an overloaded concept should break down.

The way out seems clear—to adopt a scientific approach. We shall not bother from now on with how decision-makers *should* behave, merely with how they *do* behave; and in discussing this, we shall resist the temptation to ignore experimental evidence and derive their behavior from logic alone, a sterile procedure that inevitably means defining the problem away by defining our terms so that, not only the behavior in question, but any behavior whatever would be consistent with our theory.

In the next chapter we start on the task of building a positive theory.

3
Metagames
and
Metarationality

3.1 The Positive Approach

We have said that the scientific approach may be called a "positive" one. Instead of asking what *should* happen in the world in accordance with some norm, which is ethical, aesthetic, or "rational" (in a wide sense), it asks what *does* happen. It seeks to predict what does happen by deducing this from as few axioms as possible. A science does not typically begin with this approach. Sciences have generally evolved the positive approach in a slow and often painful process of emancipation. Ethical, aesthetic, or "rational" norms embody deep value judgments that are hard to get rid of.

The accepted norm in game theory is the norm of "rational behavior" we have discussed above. The task of game theory is thought to be that of analyzing rational behavior.

At the same time, game theory is not (or not always) thought of as being "pure"—that is, telling us nothing about the world and dealing with mere abstract undefined entities in the manner of pure mathematics. This is possible only because it is believed that somehow actual behavior can be analyzed by analyzing rational behavior. The approach appears typical of a science that needs to be emancipated from an ethical or aesthetic norm.

Of course, if decision-makers were in actual fact rational, no emancipation would be required. In this case, the prisoner's dilemma paradox would show that the facts are surprising (why should they not be?) and regrettable. But despite such paradoxes, rationality would be not merely a norm, but a positive, empirical, predictive theory. On the other hand, if actual decision-makers are deliberately irrational, as we shall argue that they are, a positive theory requires other concepts to supplement or replace rationality.

Are decision-makers rational? We investigate this as follows. Call an outcome *actually stable* if it results from each player choosing his strategy on the assumption that the other players will choose the strategies they do choose. If now we find actual players who fully understand the game (not hard with simple games) and if these decision-makers are rational, only equilibria will be actually stable. This therefore gives us a means of testing whether decision-makers are rational. Used in the experiments discussed below and reported in Appendix B, it showed definitely that they were not.[1]

Many similar experiments (by other workers) have given the same result. Yet the question is still debated. It is still argued that only equilibria can be stable. Let us review some of these arguments.

To begin with, a distinction is made by game theorists between cooperative and noncooperative games. The distinction is not between games as mathematical entities but between the conditions under which they are played. In *cooperative* games players can make binding agreements of various kinds; in *noncooperative* games they cannot.

It is maintained—for example, by Harsanyi (1964)—that in noncooperative games only equilibria can be stable. A noncooperative theory must therefore confine its attention to equilibria.[2]

For cooperative games, however, we are advised to "give up" the equilibria. Many cooperative theories exist (e.g., those of von Neumann and Morgenstern (1953; first edition 1944); of Nash (1950), later generalized by Harsanyi (1959); and of Aumann (1959)). Applied to prisoner's dilemma, all would give (C, C) as a possible stable point.

This leaves us dissatisfied first on theoretical grounds. We would like to have a unified theory covering both cooperative and noncooperative games. We do not deny that external conditons must have an effect. But we would like them to behave like "initial conditions" inserted into a single theory. We feel it is presumptuous of them to determine the axioms of our theory.

Second, however, the experiments reported in Appendix B show that actual stability, as we have defined it, occurs very frequently at nonequilibria even under noncooperative conditions. For example, it occurs at (C, C) in prisoner's dilemma when players make simul-

1. We do not mean that the behavior of the experimental subjects was "wild" or "silly." We mean that in prisoner's dilemma, for example, they frequently chose to cooperate.
2. Harsanyi makes an exception that, however, does not affect our present argument.

taneous and independent choices with no communication, never see or hear each other, and have no chance of ever knowing each other's identity. Other experimenters[3] report similar findings—all leading to the conclusion that stability, defined operationally in any reasonable way, occurs frequently at (C, C) in prisoner's dilemma under non-cooperative conditions as well as cooperative ones.

It remains to go through the arguments against accepting this empirical evidence. We may note that some of these arguments are acceptable on their own terms. Our only objection to these will be that they envisage an aim for game theory which is not that of building a positive theory.

FIRST ARGUMENT. Even under noncooperative conditions, players may behave as if the game were a cooperative one.

OUR REPLY. We believe this to be so. But from the viewpoint of an empirical theory, it is surely an argument *against* distinguishing between cooperative and noncooperative conditions. We have already said that it is bad enough to have to live with two theories for the two sets of conditions. If, added to this, we are unable to distinguish between the empirical conditions under which the two theories should apply, the need for a unified theory is apparent.

SECOND ARGUMENT. Experiments have not falsified the noncooperative theory. If, for example, subjects in noncooperative prisoner's dilemma experiments (where D is optimal whatever the opponent's strategy may be) have often chosen C, their preferences must not have been those shown in the matrix, so that actually, unknown to the experimenter, player 1 preferred (C, C) to (D, C), or perhaps (C, D) to (D, D). We know this to be so because preferences are deducible from overt choices; the subject has made an overt choice; from this choice we can *deduce* that his preferences have changed.

OUR REPLY. Is the argument intended to prejudge the results of experiments? We must assume that it is, for I believe it has never been accompanied by a detailed examination of the evidence—and this is surely mandatory if the argument is not intended as a prejudgment. Also, the argument as we have stated it seems to be quite independent of any experimental results.

3. See, for example, Rapoport and Chammah (1965).

It follows that the argument is not empirical. The change in preference orderings which is said to take place must be taking place *by definition*. This makes the theory that equilibria are the only stable points a formal, purely logical theory.

Read in this sense, there can be no objection to the argument. In a formal theory, empirical games can well play the role that empirical space plays in geometry—that of aiding the intuition. For this purpose it is not necessary that space should obey the axioms imposed on it—only that it should be easy to imagine space doing so; and so long as it is easy to imagine players behaving in accordance with the noncooperative theory, the behavior of real players is irrelevant.

It is not, however, irrelevant to building an empirical, predictive theory. For this we need to ascertain players' preferences before the game is played, and use the information to predict their play.

THIRD ARGUMENT. Game theory is to be interpreted as a normative study, rather than a predictive one. It prescribes to players how they "should" behave if their aim is to maximize their utility (Luce and Raiffa 1957). A noncooperative theory prescribes to the individual player. Cooperative theories (all of which we recall give (C, C) as the solution to prisoner's dilemma) prescribe to all the players at once.

OUR REPLY. Again we have to say that we are interested in a predictive theory. Otherwise, as regards the cooperative game, we cannot object.

A difficulty for the noncooperative game is that a normative theory for the individual player, if based on the false assumption that the other player must act as the theory prescribes, may prescribe a strategy that is nonoptimal by its own definition of optimality. For example, in the game shown in Figure 3.1, where player 2's pay-offs are as in prisoner's dilemma, the prescription for player 1 is to

		2	
		C	D
1	C	4 , 3	2, 4
	D	1, 1	(3,2)

Figure 3.1. A One-Sided Prisoner's Dilemma.

choose D, since this leads to a unique equilibrium. But experimentally (C, C) is often stable, so that in fact player 2 is quite likely to act as he "should" not, choosing C in anticipation of player 1 doing likewise. If he does, the prescription for player 1 is nonoptimal.

Finally, then, we accept the empirical evidence. Players are not rational. This, in view of the two breakdowns of rationality discussed before, is not surprising. The task remains to build a positive theory.

3.2 Structure of the Theory of Metagames
The structure of our positive theory is briefly as follows. We have seen that an n-person game has n metagames based on it—the 1-, 2-, ..., n-metagames. Writing "G" for the original game, we write "kG" for the k-metagame. The k-metagame, as we have seen, is constructed by supposing that player k chooses his strategy after the others, in knowledge of their choices.

Our justification for constructing the k-metagame was that if player k is to attempt to be objectively rational, he must choose (and attempt to follow) a strategy in the k-metagame: for objective rationality generally requires knowledge of the other's choices—knowledge that is not available in the original game but is available in the k-metagame. But a more general reason for considering metagames is that we wish to build a theory of the "equilibrium" state—or rather the state of what we have called *actual stability*—meaning a state in which players guess correctly what strategies the others will choose. If they do not guess this, or guess incorrectly, they are in a "non-equilibrium" state, about which we make no predictions.

This procedure of building a theory just for certain states called "equilibrium"[4] states is quite usual in science, and we do not apologize for it. But obviously the "equilibrium" state we have called *actual stability* is particularly interesting, since an outcome that is not actually stable cannot result from honest agreement between the players, nor does it seem (though to justify this strictly requires a dynamic theory) that it can be expected to "last."

Thus we justify our consideration of the metagames based on G.

4. Here we are not using the word "equilibrium" for *equilibrium outcomes* as we have defined these but in a more general, nontechnical sense.

But now note that the metagame kG is itself a well-defined n-person game, and there is nothing to stop us from constructing n further metagames based on kG. We may call them the 1-k-, 2-k-, . . ., n-k-metagames.

We write "jkG" for the j-k-metagame. It is constructed by supposing that player j moves in knowledge of the others' choices in the k-metagame. We will soon construct an example.

We need not stop even here. Since jkG is a well-defined game too, we may construct n third-level metagames based on it. They are $1jkG$, . . ., $njkG$.

And so we can go on ad infinitum, so that if we are to consider the game G fully, we must consider all the games in the *infinite tree* shown in Figure 3.2. In this infinite tree we exhibit every game of the form $k_1 . . . k_r G$, where r is any nonnegative integer and each k_i is in $N = \{1, . . ., n\}$.

This infinite tree is the mathematical object studied by the theory of metagames. Thus this tree is the basic structure of the theory. The assertion is that behavior in G is to be interpreted as behavior in the infinite tree of metagames, because players will in one way or another think in terms of these metagames.

To show how this works, we consider prisoner's dilemma. Figure 2.20b shows the game $2G$. The game $1G$ is, of course, similar, with the roles of the players reversed.

In $2G$ (Figure 2.20b) the outcome $(D, D/D)$ is the only equilibrium.

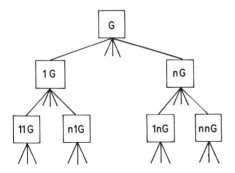

Figure 3.2. The Infinite Metagame Tree. Each game gives rise to n further metagames.

It yields the *basic* outcome (D, D). (Note: We shall always use the word "basic," as here, to refer to the game G as distinct from the metagames based on G.)

The way in which $(D, D/D)$ yields (D, D) is of course the same as the way in which every outcome of kG yields a unique outcome of G. That is, the game G (whether it be a "pure" or "mixed" strategy game) is an object

$$G = (S_1, \ldots, S_n; M_1, \ldots, M_n),$$

where each S_i is a set of strategies s_i for player i and M_i is i's preference function. We recall that M_i is actually a function from the set of all outcomes

$$s \in S = S_1 \times \ldots \times S_n$$

to the set of all subsets of S, and that

$$s \in M_i \bar{s}$$

means

i does not prefer s to $\bar{s}$.

Next, the game kG is formed from G by replacing k's strategy set S_k with the set F of all functions f from S_{N-k} to S_k. This gives outcomes (f, s_{N-k}) for the game kG, and each outcome (f, s_{N-k}) yields (fs_{N-k}, s_{N-k}).

We may define an operator[5] "β" by

$$\beta(f, s_{N-k}) \equiv (fs_{N-k}, s_{N-k})$$

and say that a metagame outcome x always yields a unique outcome βx. Now since $(D, D/D)$ is the only equilibrium of $2G$ in our game of prisoner's dilemma, we have that $(D, D) = \beta(D, D/D)$ is the only basic outcome yielded by an equilibrium of $2G$. We may say that (D, D) is the only *metaequilibrium* from $2G$, where the set of *metaequilibria* from kG is defined as the set

$$\beta E(kG),$$

---

5. An "operator" is a general type of function. The operator β is a function from the set of outcomes of any metagame kG to the set of outcomes of G.

that is, the set of outcomes of G yielded by equilibria of kG.

Note: As before, $E(H)$ is the set of equilibria of a game H. The operator "β" is extended to apply to sets of outcomes by defining

$$\beta T \equiv \{s|s = \beta x, x \in T\},$$

where T is a set.

To repeat what has been said using this new notation, we have

$$\beta E(2G) = E(G) = \{(D, D)\},$$

so that nothing is gained by going from the equilibria of G to the metaequilibria from $2G$. Nothing is gained because, of course, players' preferences for metagame outcomes x are the same as for the outcomes βx yielded by them. That is, the preference functions M_i' of the players in kG are defined by

$$x \in M_i'\bar{x} \Leftrightarrow \beta x \in M_i \beta \bar{x}.$$

However something is gained in terms of rational outcomes. A *rational outcome* for player i is, as before, one which is the best attainable for him given some joint strategy of the other players. A *metarational outcome for i from kG* may be defined as one yielded by a rational outcome for i in the game kG. That is,

$$\beta R_i(kG)$$

is the set of player i's metarational outcomes from kG.

Now we see that

$$\beta R_2(2G) = R_2(G) = \{(C, D), (D, D)\};$$

that is, 2's metarational outcomes are just his rational ones. But

$$\beta R_1(2G) = \beta\{(D, C/C), (D, D/D), (C, C/D), (D, D/C)\}$$
$$= \{(D, C), (D, D), (C, C)\}$$

so that 1's metarational outcomes include (C, C)!

This is because if 2 chooses C/D ("I'll cooperate if you will"), it is in 1's interests to cooperate. The problem remains that 1 cannot make it in 2's interests to choose C/D.

This problem is solved in the metagame $12G$ (Figure 3.3). This is formed from $2G$ as $2G$ was formed from G. Thus, since 2's strategy

	C/C	D/D	C/D	D/C
C/C/C/C	3,3	1,4	3,3	1,4
D/D/D/D	4,1	(2,2)	2,2	4,1
D/D/D/C	4,1	2,2	2,2	1,4
D/D/C/D	4,1	2,2	(3,3)	4,1
D/D/C/C	4,1	2,2	3,3	1,4
D/C/D/D	4,1	1,4	2,2	4,1
D/C/D/C	4,1	1,4	2,2	1,4
D/C/C/D	4,1	1,4	3,3	4,1
D/C/C/C	4,1	1,4	3,3	1,4
C/D/D/D	3,3	2,2	2,2	4,1
C/D/D/C	3,3	2,2	2,2	1,4
C/D/C/D	3,3	2,2	(3,3)	4,1
C/D/C/C	3,3	2,2	3,3	1,4
C/C/D/D	3,3	1,4	2,2	4,1
C/C/D/C	3,3	1,4	2,2	1,4
C/C/C/D	3,3	1,4	3,3	4,1

Figure 3.3. The 1-2-Metagame of Prisoner's Dilemma. The symbol "$W/X/Y/Z$" represents the policy "W against C/C, X against D/D, Y against C/D, Z against D/C." Equilibria are circled.

choice in $2G$ is a reaction to 1's basic strategy, 1's strategies in $12G$ are reactions to 2's reactions to 1's basic strategies. In general, a metagame jkG (where $j \neq k$) is constructed by replacing j's strategy set S_j by the set of all functions g from $S_{N-j-k} \times F$ to S_j (where F is of course the set of all functions f from S_{N-k} to S_k); that is, j's strategies become the functions from k's metagame strategies f *and* the others' basic strategies s_{N-j-k} to j's basic strategies. An outcome of jkG is thus a (g, f, s_{N-j-k}), and the basic outcome yielded by it is obtained by two applications of the β operator.

Thus

$$\beta^2(g, f, s_{N-j-k}) = \beta(g(f, s_{N-j-k}), f, s_{N-j-k})$$
$$= (g(f, s_{N-j-k}), f(g(f, s_{N-j-k}), s_{N-j-k}), s_{N-j-k}).$$

Meanwhile the preference functions M_i'' of the players in jkG are defined by

$$x \in M_i'' \bar{x} \Leftrightarrow \beta x \in M_i' \beta \bar{x}$$
$$\Leftrightarrow \beta^2 x \in M_i \beta^2 \bar{x}.$$

(Note: The case when $j = k$, so that the metagame is kkG, is trivial, but is included for completeness. The reader may work out how the metagame kkG is constructed and why it is trivial.)

The example of prisoner's dilemma (Figure 3.3) makes all this clear. Take, for instance, the outcome $(D/D/C/D, C/D)$, which is an equilibrium yielding (C, C). $D/D/C/D$ is a "policy" for player 1 that involves playing C if player 1 plays C/D. But player 1 has in fact played C/D, so 1's basic strategy is C. The "policy" C/D, however, involves 2 playing C if 1 plays C. Therefore player 2 also plays C, and the outcome is (C, C). (Note: We shall, as here, use the word "policy" to refer to metagame strategies that are not (as some are) basic strategies. It is an illuminating term for these "functional" strategies.)

We have

$$E(12G) = \{(D/D/D/D, D/D), (D/D/C/D, C/D), (C/D/C/D, C/D)\},$$

so that

$$\beta^2 E(12G) = \{(C, C), (D, D)\},$$

and (C, C) as well as (D, D) is a metaequilibrium from $12G$! For, of course, the set of *metaequilibria* from a general metagame $k_1 \ldots k_r G$ is defined to be the set

$$\beta^r E(k_1 \ldots k_r G),$$

while the set of *metarational outcomes for i from $k_1 \ldots k_r G$* is defined to be

$$\beta^r R_i(k_1 \ldots k_r G).$$

We find in fact that there are two ways in which (C, C) may become a metaequilibrium. The first, via the equilibrium $(D/D/C/D, C/D)$, is perhaps more convincing, and may be described as follows. Player 2 says "I'll cooperate if you will" (implying "not if you won't," i.e., the policy C/D), and 1 replies "In that case (meaning "if C/D is your policy") I'll cooperate too" (implying "not otherwise," i.e., the policy $D/D/C/D$).

This "agreement" between the players seems a reasonable model of the processes leading to cooperation. Our theoretical structure (the metagame tree) appears to work well in prisoner's dilemma. But many questions remain. Our approach needs more justification than we have given. For consider this. In appealing to metaequilibria and metarational outcomes we are appealing to rationality. But this leads us to give up rationality at least for the basic game G, since in this game (C, C) is definitely irrational for both players. How can rationality be turned against itself in this way? If it can be overthrown, it is overthrown and cannot logically be enthroned again at a later stage.

In the next section we attempt a justification by means of a discussion (not a formal axiomatization) of our basic premises. Meanwhile we should clear up some other doubts by mentioning now that (C, C) and (D, D) are the only metaequilibria from all higher-level metagames based on $12G$. They are also, by symmetry, the only metaequilibria from $21G$ and its descendants. And in fact they are the metaequilibria from every *complete* metagame—every metagame in which each player is named in the title at least once. Thus, having achieved (C, C) as a metaequilibrium, we do not lose it again nor obtain other embarrassing metaequilibria by going further down the infinite tree. These assertions will be proved later.

3.3 Basic Premises of Metagame Theory: The Free Will Paradox
As we have said, we are interested in the possible *stable* outcomes of a game. We do not hope to be able to assert unconditionally what outcome will occur. As game theorists we are satisfied if we can assert what *may* occur given that players can predict each other's strategy choices. Even in so simple a game as the "coordination" game of Figure 2.14a (for the analysis of which metagame theory is irrelevant), it is impossible for a game theorist to say what *will* happen. All he can say is that only the circled outcomes will ever be stable. Assuming, that is, that players can predict each other's choices, the outcome will be one of the circled ones (though we cannot say which).

It may be the case that no outcome of a certain game can possibly be stable because some player's prediction must necessarily be incorrect. We would expect this to be the case in the merchant ship–warship game discussed previously (Figure 2.2). On the other hand, consider a game in which no player prefers any outcome to any other.

In this game we would expect *every* outcome to be stable. In general, we hope to be able to find a *subset* of the outcomes such that we can predict that any stable outcome will lie in this subset.

This means that we consider a game played under stable conditions —conditions of mutual prediction. Thus we assume that each player can predict correctly. Assuming such mutual prediction conditions should enable us to determine the subset (possibly empty) of outcomes that may be stable.

To begin with, consider the rationality argument, according to which only equilibria can be stable. The argument runs as follows. Assume each player k can predict correctly. Then he knows beforehand the actual joint strategy $\bar{s}_{N-k}$ of the other players. Knowing this, and given his own preferences, he will optimize—that is, choose an $\bar{s}_k$ such that $\bar{s} = (\bar{s}_k, \bar{s}_{N-k})$ is rational for him. Applying the same argument to each player, the outcome $\bar{s}$ will be rational for all players—that is, an equilibrium.

We note that the rationality argument, while it finally produces a prediction concerning stable outcomes, does so by making a separate prediction for each player, as follows. Let us use the phrase *anticipated outcome* for the outcome determined by a player's own choice together with his prediction of the others' choices. Then the rationality argument predicts that each player's anticipated outcome will be rational for him. Since by definition a stable outcome is one anticipated by all players, the prediction concerning stable outcomes follows.

The rationality argument is perfectly valid under certain restrictive assumptions. It assumes that each player k himself chooses a basic strategy s_k and sees each other player i as choosing a basic strategy s_i. Since, however, it is assumed that before choosing an s_k player k obtains a correct prediction s_{N-k}, he could, before receiving this prediction, choose a metastrategy $f_k : S_{N-k} \to S_k$. He would then not choose an s_k at all. The strategy s_k that he would use would be determined by his previously chosen f_k. Similarly, player k could see any other player i as choosing an $f_i : S_{N-i} \to S_i$ instead of an $s_i \in S_i$. In general, player k could see any player j (where j may or may not be himself) as choosing a metastrategy $f_j : S_{N-j} \to S_j$.

Suppose player k does adopt such a viewpoint. He sees player j as choosing an f_j. If at the same time he continues to see every player $i \neq j$ as still choosing a basic strategy s_i, then he sees himself as playing in the j-metagame. His "subjective game," previously G, has become jG. Applying the theory of rationality to jG, we obtain the prediction for player k that his anticipated outcome will be metarational for him from jG, instead of, as before, rational for him.

Repetition of the argument leading us from G to jG will lead us from jG to ijG—a typical second-level metagame. Let us review this. Suppose jG is player k's subjective model of the situation. Then as k sees it, any player $i \neq j$ who is able to predict must do so by predicting the strategies s_{N-i-j} and also the "reaction" f_j of player j (or at least a part of this reaction). Hence as k sees it, any player that can predict does so by predicting the others' strategies in jG. Suppose then that player k comes to see some player i as able to predict. Then player k sees that player i may actually be choosing in ijG. If k then supposes that i is doing this, k's subjective model becomes ijG. And so on through the metagame tree.

The above argument justifying the metagame approach has been criticized on various grounds. We shall review these criticisms, not only in order to answer them for the critical reader, but also in order to bring out various facets of our approach.

FIRST OBJECTION. In replacing the game G with a game jG in which player j can predict the others' choices, you are changing the rules of the game. If j has a method of predicting the others' choices, then G is not in any case the correct normal form: jG is. Next, ijG is the correct normal form if and only if i can predict in jG. Thus you have not produced an analysis of the game G at all, but of various other games. As game theorists we must take care to construct a normal form which correctly models the actual situation. But if we find, let us say, that a prisoner's dilemma normal form is the correct model, we are not entitled to evade the problem thus posed by substituting another normal form.

OUR REPLY. A distinction must be made between conditions laid down by the rules of the game—that is, the actual "real-world" conditions that lead us to our choice of a particular normal form—

and stability conditions. The difference is that the latter do not restrict or affect the possible outcomes of the game at all; they are requirements laid down, not by the nature of the situation, but by the game theorist in order to single out certain actual outcomes in which he is interested. In our discussion G is assumed to be the correct normal form, modeling the actual conditions. The metagames based on G model various ways in which stability may occur when G is played. But there is nothing in the rules of the game that says that stability must occur. Hence it would be wrong to model the game by any normal form other than G.

SECOND OBJECTION. You state that the rationality argument assumes that player k does not choose an $f_k : S_{N-k} \to S_k$, he merely chooses an s_k. The point is, however, that the rationality argument first assumes what is the case—that k can choose any s_k. It then inquires what factors might allow us to predict his choice of an s_k, and it singles out his own prediction of s_{N-k} as such a factor. To assume after this that he can choose any function from S_{N-k} to S_k is thus equivalent to saying that he is not bound to obey the theory that predicts his behavior given certain factors but can choose how those factors will affect his behavior; that is, he can choose to obey or disobey the theory in any way he likes. Your approach, in other words, if correct, destroys any hope of constructing predictive theories in the social sciences. To show this, it is sufficient to point out that any theory predicting a conscious choice made by a subject must predict it from a knowledge of certain factors affecting the choice in question; such factors must be known at least unconsciously to the subject whose choice is being predicted, or they could not affect his conscious choice; yet if they are known to him then your principle dictates that he can choose the manner in which they will affect his behavior—he can choose whether or not to obey the theory! If this were accepted, no theory could ever predict choice. Your approach is thus self-defeating. Indeed, it negates itself as follows. You argue that player k may choose an $f_k : S_{N-k} \to S_k$ instead of an s_k, and thus put himself in the k-metagame. But in the k-metagame he is also able to predict! Hence, by your argument, he should choose an $f_k' : S_{N-k} \to F_k$, where F_k is the set of all f_k's. This puts him, I suppose, in the k-k-

metagame. But here too he can predict! So he chooses an f_k'' : S_{N-k} → F_k', putting himself in the k-k-k-metagame, and so ad infinitum. You are caught in an infinite regress.

OUR REPLY. The principle in question was proposed in Howard (1966a), under the name of the "existentialist axiom," and may be stated as follows: If certain factors affect a subject's choice behavior, and he is conscious of this, he may always choose to make his behavior obey any function from the set of possible values of those factors to the set of his alternative choices. It is true that this implies that a conscious decision-maker can always choose to disobey any theory predicting his behavior. We may say that he can always "transcend" such a theory. This indeed seems realistic. We suggest that among socioeconomic theories, Marxian theory, for example, failed at least partly because certain ruling class members, when they became aware of the theory, saw that it was in their interests to disobey it. The axiom does not, however, mean that prediction is impossible. It merely means that to each predictive theory there must correspond a metatheory (a theory about the first theory) predicting a subject's behavior when he "transcends" the first theory—that is, predicting what function f determining his own behavior he will then choose to follow.

Thus we need an infinite hierarchy of theories—each one being a metatheory relative to the preceding one.

Such an infinite hierarchy is easily constructed, though quite trivial, in the case of the one-person game, where we predict simply that given his alternatives a player will choose one that he most prefers. The hierarchy is in fact similar in this case to the equally trivial construction of the metagames $G, kG, kkG, \ldots$, discussed in the preceding objection. In the case of the one-person game, the prediction made of a subject's choice depends on the alternatives open to him—for the prediction is that he will choose from these one that he most prefers. If α is the set of alternatives open to him, we may imagine α as a member of a suitably formed set A of various sets of alternatives he may from time to time encounter, and we may assert, using the existentialist axiom, that the subject can choose any function f from A to $\cup_{\beta \in A} \beta$ provided only that $f(\beta) \in \beta$ for all β.

The obvious metatheory we now apply to his choice of an f is that, given any $\beta \in A$, he will choose f such that $f(\beta)$ is his most-preferred alternative in β. Next, the axiom says he may choose any function f' from A to F (the set of all f's). The metametatheory is that, given β, he will choose f' so that $f'(\beta)(\beta)$ is always his most-preferred alternative in β, and so on. The construction of the infinite hierarchy only in fact becomes interesting in two-or-more-person games, where it gives rise to the infinite metagame tree, having n branches at each node since each one of the n players may "transcend" the theory. In this hierarchy the metatheory appropriate to any particular metagame is, of course, simply the theory of rationality reapplied to that metagame.

THIRD OBJECTION. The conditions of the normal form specifically state that each player makes his strategy choice independently of the others. This does not preclude each player from making a choice that is a function of his prediction. And perhaps, as you say, he can choose the form of that function. But it clearly precludes player 1, say, from considering himself to be in the 2-metagame. This amounts to player 1 considering that 2's strategy choice is dependent on his, in violation of the conditions of the normal form. Normal-form conditions are satisfied experimentally if players make simultaneous independent choices while in separate booths isolated from each other. Under these circumstances, player 1 can have no reason to suppose that 2 will know what he has chosen, and cannot suppose himself to be in the 2-metagame.

OUR REPLY. It does seem more difficult for player 1, isolated in a separate booth, to imagine himself in the 2-metagame than for him to imagine himself in the 1-metagame—and this has an important consequence, as we shall see later. But after all, this is an illogical bias on the part of player 1. Each player has the same information about the rules of the game. Why then should player 1 tend toward one subjective view of the situation while 2 tends to the other? As a matter of fact, there is a kind of reason for this, but it has nothing to do with logic; it is merely that, of the n exclusive alternative ways of modeling the situation represented by the n first-level metagames, the most advantageous for player k is in general the k-metagame. This

we shall see later. In the meantime, we admit that the idea of 1 playing in the 2-metagame is counterintuitive. This is because the idea
of a person A being able to predict a free choice made by a person B—
particularly if B, though he does not yet know the prediction, knows
that it has been made and that it is correct—is inherently counterintuitive. It is in fact an old paradox, that of "free will." The nature
of this paradox is worth discussing.

In medieval times the paradox arose as a consequence of the
supposed omnipotence of God. God was supposed to have predetermined the course of all events and consequently could predict
them. Where then was man's free will, if God (person A) knew
beforehand what man (person B) would choose to do? Later the
position occupied by God was taken by the ideal physicist, able to
predict any event deterministically from a sufficient knowledge of
a prior state of the universe. The twentieth-century substitution of
probabilistic prediction for deterministic prediction has not, of
course, lessened the paradox; for if the present-day ideal physicist
(person A) can predict a probability distribution for B's choice, in
what sense is B free to make a certain choice with probability one?

But now let us point out that the paradox is not limited to scientific
or theological prediction. In ordinary life we constantly predict each
other's free choices; if we could not do so fairly confidently most of
the time, social life would indeed be impossible. Thus it is perfectly
possible, and indeed very common, for player 1's choice to be predictable by player 2; furthermore, we feel no misgivings about player 1
supposing himself able to predict player 2's choice; why then
should we find it so counterintuitive, paradoxical, and difficult to
imagine player 1 believing that whatever he chooses will be what 2
has predicted?

We have answered this by saying that it brings us up against the
paradox of free will. But if we grant that choice may be free and yet
predictable, it is only our intuition that is at fault here, and there is
no logical reason why player 1 should not imagine himself to be
playing in the 2-metagame.

FOURTH OBJECTION. Your approach suffers from the drawback that it
is essentially indeterminate. If we take the game G as being the

subjective model used by each player, then each player has the same unique subjective model. But the attempt to replace G with subjective models in which a player imagines one or the other player as able to predict encounters the problem that any such model favors one player over another and fails to treat them alike, even though in the nature of the situation there is no reason to treat any player differently from any other. Thus you suppose first that player k imagines j alone as able to predict. This leads to the j-metagame. Then he imagines i as able to predict in the j-metagame. But why should he not have considered i and j in the reverse order or considered some other player first? The fact that you can give no reason for proceeding along one path rather than another through the metagame tree makes the whole construction unsatisfactory.

OUR REPLY. It is unfortunately true that there seems to be no way of treating the players symmetrically in constructing mutual-prediction models. This appears most clearly in the dilemma of an experimenter that wishes to set up mutual-prediction conditions in the laboratory. Should he tell the players what each other has chosen? If so, he must then give each player an opportunity to change his choice, or effectively the players were not told each other's choice until the game was over; but then the players have not, after all, been told one another's final choice. And so the problem is insoluble if the experimenter insists on treating the subjects symmetrically. If we treat the subjects asymmetrically, however, we may build mutual-prediction models in a number of essentially different ways: each metagame in the infinite tree represents a model in which the players named in that metagame (i.e., the players whose names appear in the title of the metagame) are able to predict the others' basic strategy choices. Thus in any complete metagame (one in which all players are named) there is complete mutual prediction. The best we can do in the way of treating players symmetrically is thus to consider the whole of the metagame tree. Equilibria that are equilibria from every complete metagame in the tree (i.e., that are equilibria under complete mutual prediction, however this is modeled) are called *symmetric equilibria*, and are particularly important.

FIFTH OBJECTION. Your metagames are enormously complicated. It is too much to suppose that players will adopt them as subjective models in the sense required—that they will comprehend their choice of any metastrategy and apprehend the results of any combination of metastrategies.

OUR REPLY. We recognize the force of this. We must therefore make an explicit hypothesis. If players do not consciously comprehend all their metastrategies and apprehend the results of all the metagame outcomes, they do so unconsciously. This says that "choosing a metastrategy" will often mean "reacting in a certain way without being able to give adequate reasons." Reasons given will be rationalizations. The proof of this pudding must be in the eating. Our theory will simply have to survive all the empirical tests we can set.

We may add that later, in the mathematical development (Section 4.3), we shall find that a certain interpretation of a deep mathematical principle called the axiom of choice does to a large extent solve this problem for us. This will in fact throw further light on the interpretation of the metagame tree, and the reader may wish to reread the whole of the present section after reading Section 4.3. We do not mean that the above hypothesis of "unconscious" motivation is unnecessary, but it will turn out to be weaker than it appears.

To sum up: in this section we have shown that the various metagames model various alternative subjective situations of a player who becomes conscious that he and the other players can predict. The metagame approach is thus justified, since the players, who are conscious beings potentially on a level with the theorist, must be allowed to make any assumptions and draw any conclusions that he makes and draws; in particular, if he is entitled to assume mutual prediction, they may assume it also. When a player thus rises to the level of consciousness of the theorist, however, the theorist must retreat to a still higher level; and so we obtain an infinite hierarchy of theories represented by the infinite tree of metagames—the theory applied to each metagame in this tree being the ordinary theory of rationality.

3.4 Area of Application of the Theory
In order to overcome the second breakdown of rationality, it is clear now what we must do. We must substitute metarationality for

rationality. That is, given any game G, we adopt the rule that we must study the metagame descendants of G in order to understand behavior in G.

We shall find when we come to the third breakdown in Chapter 6 that this does not "save" rationality (or metarationality, which is of course merely rationality in a metagame). We shall find that complete rationality is stupid—one might even call it suicidal—even in (indeed, particularly in) a metagame.

But the substitution of metarationality for rationality does save us from the second breakdown.

Moreover, because our approach is positive, breakdowns of rationality are no longer quite so disturbing to us. After all, we have reconciled ourselves to making fewer demands on the concept. We no longer ask that it provide us with a normative standard of behavior—merely that it enable us in some way to predict behavior. This we shall find that it does do.

Our predictions of behavior at present derive from what we call the theory of metarational outcomes. This is developed in the next chapter. But before going on to this theory, we must develop and interpret certain general definitions.

Our interpretations will attempt to describe the area of application of the theory both in terms of experimental conditions which will test the theory and in terms of real-world situations to which the theory is applicable.

The definitions that are thus being interpreted are, of course, definitions of a *game in normal form*. We have already defined this as an object

$$(S_1, \ldots, S_n; M_1, \ldots, M_n),$$

where $n \geqslant 2$; each S_i is a set with at least two elements; each M_i is a function from $S = S_1 \times \ldots \times S_n$ to $\mathscr{B}(S)$ (the set of all subsets of S, called the "Boolean" of S); and finally, M_i is what we have informally described as an "ordinal" preference function.

What does "ordinal" mean? And does M_i really have to be ordinal?

Mathematical Development[6]

G is a game if each M_i obeys the *reflexive* condition

$$s \in M_i s, \quad \text{for all } s.$$

Discussion. Thus we allow G to be a "game"—it falls within our theory—provided only that preferences are "reflexive." But to obey this condition, players' preferences need not conform at all to our ideas of consistency and rationality. A player may prefer s to t and t to r, and yet prefer r to s! Worse still, he may prefer s to t and also prefer t to s! In fact, reflexivity would not be disobeyed if a player preferred every outcome in the game to every other!

Our interpretation of these possibilities is that preferences are defined operationally: to say that s is preferred to t is simply to say that if the decision-maker were at the outcome s and saw an opportunity to move to t, he would take it. It may still be the case that if he were at t and saw an opportunity to move to s, he would take that opportunity also! In that case, if he were able to move freely between s and t, he would move to and fro between them indefinitely. This might be the case (we do not suggest that it is) with a choice of an armaments level, for example: when armaments are high, disarmers become strong, and armaments are lowered; when armaments are low, rearmers gain influence, and armaments are raised again. An analysis of possible indecisiveness such as this on the part of a collective decision-maker has been pursued by Arrow (1963).

Our interpretation, in short, is that preferences may depend on the current outcome. To clarify this, a player's preferences may be displayed in a graph as in Figure 3.4a. Here outcomes are represented by points, and an arrow goes from t to s if s is preferred to t.

In terms of such a graph, the only restriction laid down is that no arrow may go from a point to itself. This restriction is very weak, as it seems that no meaning could in any case be attached to the statement "when he is at s, player i would rather be at s than at s."

Another way of putting it is this. For G to be a game, any particular outcome s and particular preference function M_i are required to

6. We shall sometimes use this subheading when we wish to state pure-mathematical definitions, theorems, and so on. To indicate the end of such an interlude, we shall use the subheading "Discussion."

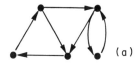

Figure 3.4. Graphs Representing a Player's Preferences.

determine a bipartition of all the outcomes into those "preferred" by i to s (the set $S - M_i s$) and those "not preferred" (the set $M_i s$). The latter set must always include s itself; but otherwise the sets may be chosen freely. The interpretation is that $S - M_i s$ is the set of outcomes to any of which player i would certainly move, starting from s, if he saw himself as able to do so.

Our answer, then, is that G definitely does not have to be "ordinal"; the theory applies provided only that it is reflexive. But stronger things can be said about G if it is ordinal. What then does "ordinal" mean?

Mathematical Development

Since for each outcome $s \in S$ the function M_i yields a unique subset $M_i s \subseteq S$, there exists also another function $\tilde{M}_i : S \to \mathscr{B}(S)$ defined by

$$\tilde{M}_i s \equiv S - M_i s.$$

This yields the outcomes *preferred* by i to s. We have, because of reflexivity,

$$s \notin \tilde{M}_i s.$$

Next, G will be called *partly ordinal* if (in addition to being reflexive) it satisfies

$$(s \in \tilde{M}_i t \quad \text{and} \quad t \in \tilde{M}_i r) \Rightarrow s \in \tilde{M}_i r.$$

This says that certain circularities of the kind discussed above cannot exist. A player cannot prefer s to t and t to r and also prefer *r* to *s*. This condition is called an assumption of *transitivity* for the relation "preferred." Taken together with reflexivity, it implies that no *cycles* exist in the preference graph—where a cycle is a path traced by preference arrows that, as in Figure 3.4a, returns into itself.

However, in a partly ordinal game it may still happen that though the relation "preferred" is transitive, the relation "not preferred" is intransitive; that is, we may have *s* not preferred to *t*, and *t* not preferred to *r*, while *s* is preferred to *r*. Figure 3.4b illustrates this.

This more subtle type of circularity is disallowed by adding a further condition. Adding this condition gives what we shall call an *ordinal* game. The condition is

$$(s \in M_i t \quad \text{and} \quad t \in M_i s) \Rightarrow M_i s = M_i t.$$

This says that if *s* and *t* are not preferred to each other, then they bipartition the outcomes into "preferred" and "not preferred" in precisely the same way.

Discussion. Thus we have three levels of generality: a (general) game; a partly ordinal game; and an ordinal game. All three are defined *qualitatively* (without the use of numbers).

These are the mathematical structures we use to model "reality." Let us see how we do this.

A simple example of a game that is not even partly ordinal is given in Figure 3.5. Here we look at the preferences of a certain nation *B*, which has to choose one of three possible weapons systems to

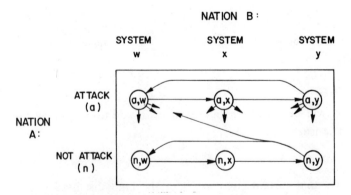

Figure 3.5. A Nonordinal Game. Arrows represent nation *B*'s preferences.

defend herself against possible attack by another nation A. For any given choice of nation A—that is, reading along any row of the figure—nation B prefers y to x and x to w but also prefers w to y. This might be because certain generals that strongly prefer w to both x and y would become powerful if y were adopted but would not control the decision if either w or x were adopted. Next, the preferences between rows are such that nation B strongly prefers not to be attacked; any outcome on the second row is preferred to any on the first. At the same time, however, the generals that obtain control of decisions when y is adopted believe strongly in the weapons system w—so strongly that they would prefer to adopt w and be attacked rather than adopt y and not be attacked.

Some equally simple examples of ordinal games have been given in Section 2.3. Examples of partly ordinal games arise most importantly in connection with coalition games, which will be discussed later. The point will then be made that ordinal players, when formed into coalitions, have only partly ordinal preferences.

What about the experiments used to test the theory? These have been of two kinds: so-called one-shot games and reaction games.

In the one-shot experiments players (who may be individual subjects or groups) are given a number of alternative choices and told the alternatives open to the other players. They then make simultaneous and independent choices. The experimenter must ensure, within the limits of experimental error, that the subjects
a. have the preferences required in the game that is being tested;
b. understand the game interaction between their choices and the other players' choices.

To make sure of the players' preferences in the case of an ordinal model, the players are usually given monetary payments that differ according to the outcome of the game. They should differ by large amounts—large by the subjects' reckoning, that is, so that it is a good idea to use poor subjects (e.g., students). Further, it should be arranged that the players never meet or see each other or know each other's identity, for this may contaminate preference orderings. If they know each other's preferences (it may or may not be necessary to tell them these, depending on the theory being tested) it is a good idea to tell them only the ordering of the others' monetary payoffs, not the exact amounts; this stops them from adding payoffs together or subtracting them, which are also possible sources of contamination. They should be aware that they will never play twice against the same opponent.

Prior to making their simultaneous independent choices the experimenter may wish to allow subjects to communicate, negotiate, and so forth; in this case communications must be controlled to stop players from making agreements to meet afterwards, which again would contaminate their preferences. Subjects should be told specifically that the experimenter wishes them to try to make as much money as possible, though of course the experimenter should not advise them as to how to achieve this aim.

To ensure that subjects understand the game interaction they should practice it beforehand several times until they and the referee are satisfied on this score.

Stability in these experiments is measured by obtaining every subject's predictions of the others' choices. An outcome is *stable for* a particular player if it is the outcome determined by his individual choice and individual prediction. An outcome is *stable* if it is stable for all subjects, in which case by definition it must be the actual outcome. To put it another way, each player who predicts will have an *anticipated* outcome, and this is *stable for* him by definition. A *stable* outcome is one that is stable for (anticipated by) all the players.

Except for the operational definition of stability, the above comments also apply to the reaction-game experiments. In these, the players start at a certain outcome of the game, and at any time during a certain period of time any player may change the current outcome by changing his strategy choice. When time is up, the subjects are paid according to the then current outcome. They do not know exactly when time will be up. Stability is measured by allowing players to indicate before time is up that they are willing to be paid off at the then current outcome, and this is done if all players agree. If a player is willing to be paid off at a current outcome prior to the final outcome, this current outcome is called *stable for* him. A *stable* outcome is again one that is stable for all players.

We should comment on many-shot experiments, where a normal-form game is repeatedly played between the same players with payoffs for each play. Many experiments of this type have been run in recent years. Game theory cannot be applied directly to them for the following reason. The correct normal form for such repeated games is not the normal form used in each separate iteration but a vastly more complicated one derived from the extensive form of this situation. To illustrate, Figure 3.6 shows the extensive form and Figure 3.7 the normal form for a twofold iteration of the prisoner's dilemma game of Figure 2.20. (In these figures we assume that a player is paid $1, $2, $3, or $4 at each iteration, and the total payoffs shown are the total payoffs in dollars.) What happens in Figure 3.7 is that all the ways in which a player may cause his choice at an iteration to depend on the outcomes of previous iterations are spelled out as separate strategies. Now it is obvious that a subject will not ignore the fact that he can choose this type of strategy; that is, he will not play with no memory of past iterations and no anticipation of future ones. On the other hand, neither is he likely to be able to comprehend his full choice of strategies of this type, and commit himself to a single one before the iterations begin, as the normal form would require. Indeed no one has suggested this. Thus his subjective model of the situation is not known to the experimenter. But game

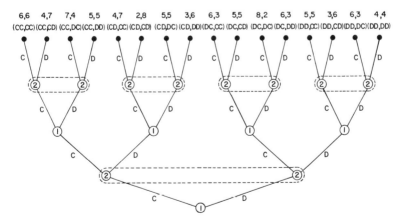

Figure 3.6. Twofold Iteration of Prisoner's Dilemma with Payoffs (in Dollars) of 1, 2, 3, and 4: The Extensive Form.

	C,C/C	C,D/D	C,C/D	C,D/C	D,C/C	D,D/D	D,C/D	D,D/C
C,C/C	(CC,CC) 6,6	(CC,CD) 4,7	(CC,CC) 6,6	(CC,CD) 4,7	(CD,CC) 4,7	(CD,CD) 2,8	(CD,CC) 4,7	(CD,CD) 2,8
C,D/D	(CC,DC) 7,4	(CC,DD) 5,5	(CC,DC) 7,4	(CC,DD) 5,5	(CD,DC) 5,5	(CD,DD) 3,6	(CD,DC) 5,5	(CD,DD) 3,6
C,C/D	(CC,CC) 6,6	(CC,CD) 4,7	(CC,CC) 6,6	(CC,CD) 4,7	(CD,DC) 5,5	(CD,DD) 3,6	(CD,DC) 5,5	(CD,DD) 3,6
C,D/C	(CC,DC) 7,4	(CC,DD) 5,5	(CC,DC) 7,4	(CC,DD) 5,5	(CD,CC) 4,7	(CD,CD) 2,8	(CD,CC) 4,7	(CD,CD) 2,8
D,C/C	(DC,CC) 6,3	(DC,CD) 5,5	(DC,CC) 5,5	(DC,CD) 6,3	(DD,CC) 5,5	(DD,CD) 3,6	(DD,CD) 3,6	(DD,CC) 5,5
D,D/D	(DC,DC) 8,2	(DC,DD) 6,3	(DC,DD) 6,3	(DC,DC) 8,2	(DD,DC) 6,3	(DD,DD) 4,4	(DD,DD) 4,4	(DD,DC) 6,3
D,C/D	(DC,CC) 6,3	(DC,CD) 5,5	(DC,CC) 5,5	(DC,CD) 6,3	(DD,DC) 6,3	(DD,DD) 4,4	(DD,DD) 4,4	(DD,DC) 6,3
D,D/C	(DC,DC) 8,2	(DC,DD) 6,3	(DC,DD) 6,3	(DC,DC) 8,2	(DD,CC) 5,5	(DD,CD) 3,6	(DD,CD) 3,6	(DD,CC) 5,5

Figure 3.7. Normal Form of Figure 3.6. Payoffs are total dollar payoffs. The strategy "$Z,X/Y$" consists of choosing Z on the first iteration, then X or Y on the second iteration according to whether the other's first choice was C or D.

theory can only be applied to a player's subjective model of a situation —this rule being equivalent, in fact, to the often-stated rule that game theory assumes players that understand the game.

We add that this requirement—that a game-theoretic model be each player's subjective model—though it creates difficulties in the laboratory, is an advantage in real-world applications. The reason is simple. In the laboratory we have a specific game we wish to test. We thus encounter difficulties in ensuring that this is the subjective game of every subject. But in real-world applications, we are not trying to test a specific game, we are trying to discover what (subjective) game is being played; and when we go to a real-world decision-maker the most readily available information is about his subjective game, not about any other. (It may not be the same as the subjective games of the players he is playing against, but that is another matter.) There is in fact no problem of preference "contamination," such as we find in the laboratory. For there is no such thing in the real world as a distinction between "prizes" offered by the referee and the players' actual preferences. The only preferences that exist reflect fully the influence of factors such as competitiveness or altruism, which create so many problems in the conduct of experiments.

The offsetting disadvantage is, of course, that we can never be sure that the model we use is the correct one. But this is always the case with applications of any theory. It is the main factor that distinguishes them from controlled laboratory tests, which enable us to test the theory because we control the correctness of the model.

We conclude with some more remarks about applying the game-theoretic model to real-world situations.

The n "players" are n decision-making parties—usually entities such as governments, firms, or interest groups. They are in a situation where each sees himself as having a number of alternative courses of action, and we include each such alternative in this player's strategy set. We note that in practice "real-world" players tend to simplify things, so that a president or prime minister and his immediate advisers in a crisis situation do not see themselves as faced with an inordinately complicated strategy set. Others have simplified the problem for them—perhaps oversimplified it—so as to present them with a set of alternatives they can comprehend; and what a man can comprehend is not much. This makes modeling a real-life situation easier than one might expect. However, it is not at all necessary from the theoretical point of view; we allow S_i to be any set with two or more elements, no matter how complex.

Infinite sets may arise because a quantity has to be chosen—for example, a price or a troop level—that is conveniently modeled as a real number chosen from a certain interval. Theoretically it could also be the case, as we have seen, that a player sees himself as choosing a probability distribution over a certain set of "pure" alternatives so that, after having chosen this probability distribution, his choice of a "pure" alternative will be decided by throwing dice or by some such random device. In this case S_i would be infinite because it would consist of the infinite set of alternative probability distributions. This is not common in real life, however, so that usually it will be wrong to use this "mixed-strategy" model.

Recall the extensive-form interpretation of a strategy as a complete plan of action that takes time to work itself out and the corresponding interpretation of an outcome as a spectrum of alternative scenarios each having a certain probability of occurrence. These interpretations are very relevant. Indeed, imagine our president selecting from his simple strategy set the alternative "invade." This is a highly complex plan of action, contingent on many future moves by others and many future chance events; and given the strategy choices of the others in the game, its only foreseeable result is indeed a probabilistic spectrum of alternative scenarios.

4
The Theory of
Metarational
Outcomes

4.1 The Theory of Rational Outcomes

Game theory is rich in simple, "obvious," intuitive theories that are, however, false.

We have encountered one such theory: the theory that only an outcome $\bar{s} \in R_i$ that is rational for i can be stable for him. This we may call the "theory of rational outcomes."

We remark that the definition

$$R_i = \{\bar{s} \,|\, (s_i, \bar{s}_{N-i}) \in M_i \bar{s}\}$$

applies just as well to general (reflexive) games as it does to ordinal games. Hence the theory of rational outcomes applies equally generally.

It follows from this (false) theory that only an equilibrium $\bar{s} \in E$ can be stable. Here again the definition

$$E = \bigcap_i R_i$$

applies just as well to general games as to ordinal ones.

Now the fact that game theory suggests simple, "obvious," false theories provides us with an approach to building true theories. This is to take such a false theory and apply it to the metagame tree— hoping that there it will "come true."

When we do this with the theory of rational outcomes, we obtain the Theory of Metarational Outcomes—the subject of this chapter. This theory therefore is that only an outcome that is *metarational* for player i can be stable for him.

But before we go on to this we must look a little more closely at the theory of rational outcomes on which we intend to build.

The main difficulty with this theory is no doubt that it is false. But this is not the difficulty that has been most discussed and felt.

The difficulty discussed by most authors is not that the theory goes too far and becomes false, but that apparently it does not go far enough. We may put it this way. The fact that the theory is false means that the equilibria are too few; there are stable outcomes that are nonequilibria. But the usual objection is that the equilibria are too many—that not all equilibria are possible stable outcomes. For instance, in the game of Figure 2.14a it is felt that only the (3, 3) outcome will ever be stable. The (2, 2) outcome, though an equilibrium, could never be so.

It is of course possible for both these objections to be sustained— for the equilibria to be too many as well as too few. But we shall argue that in fact they are not too many if we interpret the theory as we "should." In Figure 2.14a the (2, 2) outcome cannot be dismissed unless it is assumed that players know each other's preferences (and know that each other knows them, and so on). But the definition of the equilibria does not in any way incorporate such an assumption. The equilibria are the outcomes that happen to be rational for every player. But the set of outcomes that are rational for any player i depends only on his own preferences. Hence whatever each player's beliefs about the others' preferences, provided he knows his own preferences, he will perceive correctly his set of rational outcomes.

Consequently the theory asserting that only equilibria can be stable on the grounds that (a) only equilibria are rational for all players and (b) only an outcome rational for i will be stable for i "ought" to assert this regardless of the players' information or misinformation about each other's preferences. It ought to be a theory wide enough to cover all possible cases of such information or misinformation.

We assert therefore that the proper interpretation of the theory of rational outcomes is that it is a theory making no assumption about players' knowledge of each other's preference. Under this interpretation, the apparent examples of equilibria that could never be stable vanish. Any equilibrium in fact is such that we can find patterns of misinformation about others' preferences that make the equilibrium perfectly likely to be stable.

In the case of the game in Figure 2.14a, we could do this by supposing that players were misinformed as in Figure 4.1. This misinformation would certainly make the (2, 2) outcome of the actual game very

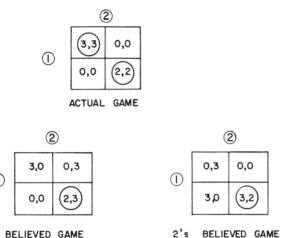

ACTUAL GAME

1's BELIEVED GAME   2's BELIEVED GAME

Figure 4.1. Game with Misinformation about Others' Preferences.

likely to be stable. And the method used in this case can be generalized.

We proceed in fact as follows. Let $\bar{s}$ be an equilibrium. Suppose
each player i is misinformed so that he supposes each player $j \in N - \{i\}$
to have preferences obeying

$$\forall(s, s') : (s_j = \bar{s}_j, s_j' \neq \bar{s}_j) \rightarrow s \in \tilde{M}_j s'.$$

Then i supposes that any outcome at which j chooses $\bar{s}_j$ is preferred
by j to any outcome at which he (j) does not. Clearly, believing this
about every player $j \neq i$, i will be convinced that the players $N - \{i\}$
will choose $\bar{s}_{N-j}$ whatever he chooses; hence, since $\bar{s}$ is rational for
him, he himself is perfectly likely to choose $\bar{s}_i$. Thus $\bar{s}$ will be stable
for him, and applying the same argument to each player, $\bar{s}$ is likely
to be stable.

This—together with the fact that because R_i is derived solely from
player i's preferences *only an equilibrium can appear to all players
to be an equilibrium, no matter what they believe about each other's
preferences*—convinces us that the theory of rational outcomes is
indeed best interpreted as a theory about players that know their
own preferences but may have any kind of beliefs about each other's
preferences. It is, in fact, best called a *theory of rational outcomes*,
as we are calling it, rather than a theory of equilibria, since essentially

it is a theory about the individual player's reaction to his own preferences and his beliefs about the others' strategies. It is not a theory about his reactions to the others' preferences.[1]

The difference is apparent in the running of experiments as described above (Section 3.4). Here when one runs an n-person game, one is in fact running n separate experiments simultaneously. The theory predicts for each separate player that an outcome stable for him must be rational for him. Hence each separate player can falsify the theory. What the actual outcome is, or whether it is stable, is of no interest experimentally.

The one-shot experiments reported in Appendix B make this clear and also show conclusively that the theory of rational outcomes is false. But the point to note here is that the theory of metarational outcomes, since it is based on the theory of rational outcomes, is also independent of any assumptions about the players' knowledge of each other's preferences.

Hence the theory we shall present is a theory about players who know their own preferences but may have any kind of beliefs about each other's preferences.

Before concluding this section we note some more facts about the theory of rational outcomes.

Mathematical Development

The set R_i is nonempty for all finite partly ordinal games. Hence, of course, R_i is nonempty for all finite ordinal games.

More than this can be said, in fact. In any finite partly ordinal game, player i has a "rational response" to each joint strategy of the other players in the following sense. Given any joint strategy s^*_{N-i} of the other players, there exists a rational outcome s for player i such that $s_{N-i} = s^*_{N-i}$. That is, we have

$$\forall s_{N-i}\, \exists s_i : s \in R_i(G).$$

1. This interpretation of the equilibria is actually implicit in the work of Harsanyi (1967–1968) on games with incomplete information (i.e., games in which players do not know the payoffs but have subjective probabilities concerning them). Harsanyi defines generalized equilibria for these games. It turns out (as it should) that in the special case when players know their own payoffs, these are the equilibria of the actual game being played and are therefore independent of the players' subjective probabilities concerning each other's payoffs.

But Figure 3.5 provides an example of a finite nonordinal game in which "nation B" has no rational outcomes.

Even in the finite ordinal case, moreover, the set E may be empty, as we have seen in the merchant ship–warship game. As noted, however, Nash has proved that E is nonempty for any mixed-strategy game derived from a finite game with numerical preferences.

Discussion. This means that "normally"—for example, in all finite games—an individual player or coalition of players with consistent, "reasonable" preferences is always able to respond rationally given his prediction of the others' strategies. We remark that the finite case may be regarded as "normal" and "typical" for questions of existence such as this. Investigation of these questions in the infinite case is mainly of technical interest.

4.2 The Characterization of Metarational Outcomes

We have already (Section 3.2) defined the infinite tree of metagames in the case of an ordinal game G. That description applies equally to a general game, so that we may take it that any metagame

$$H = k_1 \ldots k_r G$$

is well defined, where G is some given general game (called the *basic game*), r is a nonnegative integer, and each k_i is a player (an element of the set $N = \{1, \ldots, n\}$). Setting $r = 0$ we obtain the "zero-level metagame" G. If $r \neq 0$ we obtain what we may call a proper metagame.

Any metagame of the form $k_s k_{s+1} \ldots k_r G$ (where $s \geqslant 1$) is called an *ancestor* of H. In particular, H is an ancestor of itself. Next, $k_2 k_3 \ldots k_r G$ is called the *immediate* ancestor of H. G has no immediate ancestor. Any metagame of the form $j_1 \ldots j_s k_1 \ldots k_r G$ (where $s > 0$) is called a *descendant* of H, and any one of the form $j k_1 \ldots k_r G$ is called an *immediate* descendant of H. Note that H is *not* a descendant of itself. Any metagame has (an infinite set of) descendants. The descendants of G are just the proper metagames.

The metagame $k_1 \ldots k_r G$ is called an "rth-level" metagame. Thus there are n^r metagames at the rth level.

A metagame $k_1 \ldots k_r G$ is called *prime* if each player's name occurs at most once in the list $k_1 \ldots k_r$; it is called *complete* if each player's name occurs at least once in that list. Thus there are $n!$ *complete prime* metagames, corresponding to the different ways of ordering the set N.

Clearly every ancestor of a prime metagame is prime (including the zero-metagame, which is prime). There are $\sum_{r=0}^{n} n^{(r)}$ prime metagames. (Here "$n^{(r)}$" stands for $n(n-1) \ldots (n-r+1)$ if $r \neq 0$; if $r = 0$, "$n^{(r)}$" conventionally stands for 1.)

We have already defined the operator β, which takes any outcome (or set of outcomes) of a proper metagame H to a unique outcome (or set of outcomes) of the immediate ancestor of H. If H is an rth level metagame, clearly β^r (the operator β applied r times) yields a basic outcome (outcome of G) or, of course, a set of basic outcomes. If then, as a matter of notation, we write "$\beta*$" for the operation of applying β enough times to obtain a basic outcome (or set of basic outcomes), we may write

$$\beta* R_i(H)$$

for i's *metarational outcomes* from a metagame H. This merely saves us the trouble of specifying the level, r, of the metagame H.

This set $\beta* R_i(H)$ is, of course, a centrally important concept for our theory. We shall also write it "$\hat{R}_i(H)$."

Perhaps even more important is the set

$$\bigcup_H \hat{R}_i(H),$$

which we call the set of *general metarational outcomes for i* and write "Γ_i." For Γ_i is the set of all outcomes *metarational for i from some metagame*.

The importance of Γ_i is as follows. The empirical theory of metarational outcomes is a theory about the process whereby a player predicts or anticipates the outcome of a game G. The empirical theory is that if player i predicts the outcome s (i.e., if s is *stable for him*), then

i. i's subjective game must be some metagame H;

ii. i must predict some joint metastrategy x_{N-i} as the strategy choice of the other players (where "x" is an outcome of H);

iii. i's own choice must be an x_i such that $x \in R_i(H)$ and $\beta* x = s$.

It follows from this that s must be a general metarational outcome for player i. Hence one experimental prediction is that only outcomes that are general metarational for i will be stable for him.

This may be tested experimentally in either one-shot or reaction-game experiments by using the operational definitions of "stability" described previously, and the experiments reported in Appendix B show that when this is done the theory is vindicated.

But the theory asserts more than this. It asserts that player i will have a subjective metagame H in which he will "choose a meta-strategy x_i," and "predict an x_{N-i}," and that the x thus determined will be rational for him in his subjective game H. To test these assertions, more is required than an operational definition of stability.

The one-shot experiments with "certainty" described in Appendix B provide one approach, though its rationale is not entirely clear. In these experiments, based on a given game G, player 1 was required to state a *first-level policy*. He did this by filling in a form that ran "If you choose 0, I will choose . . .; if you choose 1, I will choose . . . ." (In these experiments, each player had two strategies, 0 and 1.) This first-level policy was then shown to player 2, who then made his choice of a strategy (0 or 1).

It was felt that this would ensure that player 2's subjective game would be $21G$. In fact, of course, the experimental procedure had the effect of making $21G$ the basic game: G ceased to be basic, since the player's predictions in G were now obtained, not "by prediction," but by the rules of the game. But this did not mean that $21G$ could not be 2's subjective game; and if the procedure in fact ensured this, our theory predicted that 2 would always optimize along 1's stated policy. This happened, providing a sort of conditional confirmation of the theory.

The empirical theory may be described as follows. It says that for any player only certain outcomes—that player's metarational outcomes—can be made to appear "best attainable" outcomes to him; and a particular metarational outcome from a metagame H will appear the "best attainable" to a player if his subjective game is H and he believes the others to be pursuing certain metastrategies in the game H.

But how are we to identify the outcomes that are metarational for a given player i from a given metagame H? That is, how can we identify which outcomes of G belong to $\hat{R}_i(H)$? Merely stating our theory brings us up against this mathematical problem.

Let us gain an intuitive "feel" for the problem by working out some examples. Let G be the "continuous" game on the unit square considered in Section 2.3.[2] Here $S_1 = S_2 = \{x \mid 0 \leqslant x \text{ real} \leqslant 1\}$, and player 1 has a numerical preference function v_1—that is, his preferences M_1 are such that $s \in M_1 t \Leftrightarrow v_1(s) \leqslant v_1(t)$, where v_1 is a real-valued function on S. The function v_1 is given by

$$v_1(s_1, s_2) = \tfrac{1}{2}s_1 - \tfrac{1}{2}s_1^2 + \tfrac{1}{4}s_1 s_2.$$

$\hat{R}_1(2G)$ is thus the set of all $\bar{s} = (\bar{s}_1, \bar{s}_2)$ such that for some function $f: S_1 \to S_2$ we have

$$f(\bar{s}_1) = \bar{s}_2,$$

and

$$v_1(\bar{s}_1, f(\bar{s}_1)) = \max_{s_1} v_1(s_1, f(s_1)).$$

That is,

$$f(\bar{s}_1) = \bar{s}_2,$$

and

$$\tfrac{1}{2}\bar{s}_1 - \tfrac{1}{2}\bar{s}_1^2 + \tfrac{1}{4}\bar{s}_1 f(\bar{s}_1) = \max_{s_1}\left[\tfrac{1}{2}s_1 - \tfrac{1}{2}s_1^2 + \tfrac{1}{4}s_1 f(s_1)\right].$$

At first it might seem that we would have to try each function $f: S_1 \to S_2$ to find the set of all $\bar{s}$ satisfying this condition. But this is not so. Let f^* be the function that, for each s_1, yields an $s_2 = f^*(s_1)$ that *minimizes* $v_1(s_1, s_2)$. Also let $f_{\bar{s}}^*$ be the function identical to f^* except that $f_{\bar{s}}^*(\bar{s}_1) = \bar{s}_2$. Then clearly the condition on $\bar{s}$ that for some f

$$f(\bar{s}_1) = \bar{s}_2,$$

and

$$v_1(\bar{s}_1, f(\bar{s}_1)) = \max_{s_1} v_1(s_1, f(s_1)),$$

2. This example may be skipped by the reader unfamiliar with calculus.

is satisfied if it is satisfied for $f_{\bar{s}}^*$. Vice versa, if it is not satisfied for $f_{\bar{s}}^*$, it is not satisfied for *any f*. Thus the condition is equivalent to

$$v_1(\bar{s}) = \max_{s_1} v_1(s_1, f_{\bar{s}}^*(s_1)),$$

which in turn is equivalent to

$$v_1(\bar{s}) \geqslant \max_{s_1} v_1(s_1, f^*(s_1)).$$

We can easily find an f^* as required. Since $\partial v_1(s)/\partial s_2 = \frac{1}{4}s_1 \geqslant 0$, an f^* such that $f^*(s_1) \equiv 0$ will do. The condition on $\bar{s}$ is thus

$$\tfrac{1}{2}\bar{s}_1 - \tfrac{1}{2}\bar{s}_1^2 + \tfrac{1}{4}\bar{s}_1\bar{s}_2 \geqslant \max_{s_1}[\tfrac{1}{2}s_1 - \tfrac{1}{2}s_1^2] = \tfrac{1}{8}.$$

The set $\hat{R}_1(2G)$ is therefore the set of points illustrated in Figure 4.2.

As our second example we consider the nonordinal game in Figure 3.5. How shall we find the set $\hat{R}_B(AG)$? It contains those outcomes $\bar{s}$ such that there is a function $f: \{w, x, y\} \rightarrow \{a, n\}$ such that

$$f(\bar{s}_B) = \bar{s}_A,$$

and

$$\forall s_B \in \{w, x, y\} : (f(s_B), s_B) \in M_B\bar{s}.$$

But the condition here that $f(\bar{s}_B) = \bar{s}_A$ is vacuous. For if an $f = f^*$ exists satisfying the second condition, the $f = f_{\bar{s}}^*$ that is identical to f^* except that $f_{\bar{s}}^*(\bar{s}_B) = \bar{s}_A$ will satisfy both conditions, since $\bar{s} \in M_i\bar{s}$ always. Hence the condition on $\bar{s}$ is simply

$$\exists f \forall s_B : (f(s_B), s_B) \in M_B\bar{s}.$$

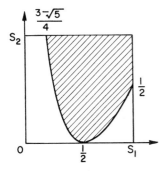

Figure 4.2. The Set $\hat{R}_1(2G)$ in a Continuous Game.

But to find an f such as is here required to exist we must, obviously, just find for each s_B an s_A such that $s \in M_B\bar{s}$. Thus the condition is

$$\forall s_B \, \exists s_A : s \in M_B\bar{s},$$

or equivalently

$$\sim \exists s_B \, \forall s_A : s \in \tilde{M}_B\bar{s}.$$

Therefore, we can find $\hat{R}_B(AG)$ by taking each outcome $\bar{s}$ in turn and asking whether there is a *column* in Figure 3.5 (i.e., an s_B) such that an arrow goes from $\bar{s}$ to every cell in this column. If such a column exists, $\bar{s} \notin \hat{R}_B(AG)$. If it does not exist, $\bar{s} \in \hat{R}_B(AG)$. Taking each outcome in turn, we find the following facts:

For (a, w), x is such a column.

For (a, x), y is such a column.

For (a, y), w is such a column.

For (n, w), no such column exists.

For (n, x), no such column exists.

For (n, y), w is such a column.

And therefore $\hat{R}_B(AG) = \{(n, w), (n, x)\}$.

(We may interpret this result. Nation B, because of divisions within itself, has conflicting and contradictory preferences, causing it to have no rational outcomes ($R_B(G) = \varnothing$). But nation A, by adopting certain metastrategies, or policies, in reaction to B's strategies, can resolve the conflict within B in favor of (n, w) or (n, x), these being metarational for B from the metagame AG.)

We shall now generalize the methods used in the above two examples in the proof of the *characterization theorem for metarational outcomes*. This theorem enables us to identify the set $\hat{R}_i(H)$ for any given i and H from an examination of the basic game G. It does this by characterizing $\hat{R}_i(H)$ in terms of basic outcomes—it gives what we may call a *basic characterization* of $\hat{R}_i(H)$. Basic characterizations are needed in metagame theory because the metagames themselves are generally "too large to look at."

To state the theorem we first need some definitions. A *prime* metagame, as noted, is one in which each player is *named* (i.e., his name occurs in the title of the metagame) at most once. Next, the *prime representative* of H is the prime metagame obtained by striking out all but the last occurrence (the one furthest to the right) of each player's name from the title of H. For example, the prime representative of $6362122G$ is $3612G$.

Next, the player k is said to *follow* player j in H if $k \neq j$ and some occurrence of k's name follows (is further to the right of) some occurrence of j's name in the title of H. For example, in the six-person game $6362122G$,

6 follows 3;

5 follows no one;

4 follows no one;

3 follows 6;

2 follows 6, 3, and 1;

1 follows 6, 3, and 2.

If k follows j in the *prime representative* of H or if k but not j is named in H, k is said to *follow j last*. Equivalently, k *follows j last* if every occurrence of j's name is followed by some occurrence of k's name or if the last occurrence of k's name follows the last occurrence (if any) of j's name. These conditions mean that there exists an ancestor of H in which k's metastrategy is a function from j's basic strategy, so that we may imagine that j makes his basic choice first, being "followed" by k who chooses his basic strategy in knowledge of j's basic strategy.

We can now state the theorem.

Theorem 1. (Characterization Theorem for Metarational Outcomes)
A basic outcome $\bar{s}$ is metarational for i from H if and only if

$$\exists s_P \, \forall s_i \, \exists s_F : (\bar{s}_U, s_{N-U}) \in M_i \bar{s},$$

where U is the set of players unnamed in H other than player i; F is the set of players who follow i last in H; $P = N - U - F - \{i\}$ is the set of players who "precede" i in the prime representative of H, that is, the players other than i who are named and do not follow i last in H.

Before proving this theorem we shall illustrate it, make some comments, and prove a lemma.

We have already discussed the convention that if K is the empty set, "s_K" shall stand for " "—a blank space on the page. Indeed, not only s_K, but also all symbols which depend on s_K for their meaning, were said to stand for blank spaces when $K = \varnothing$. Thus "$\exists s_K$" also stands for a blank space. Using this convention, the condition of the theorem for $H = G$ is

$$\forall s_i : (\bar{s}_{N-i}, s_i) \in M_i \bar{s},$$

which, as required, is simply the condition for $\bar{s}$ to be rational for i.

Next let us discuss the two cases we have considered in our examples. In these we set out to find $\hat{R}_1(2G)$. The condition of the theorem for $\bar{s} \in \hat{R}_1(2G)$ is

$$\forall s_1 \exists s_2 : (s_1, s_2) \in M_1 \bar{s}.$$

This is the formulation we arrived at in the second example. In the first example, where player 1 had a numerical preference function v_1, we obtained the condition

$$v_1(\bar{s}) \geqslant \max_{s_1} v_1(s_1, f^*(s_1)),$$

where f^* was a function such that $f^*(s_1)$ minimized $v_1(s_1, s_2)$ for each value of s_1. This is equivalent to

$$v_1(\bar{s}) \geqslant \max_{s_1} \min_{s_2} v_1(s_1, s_2),$$

which is the same as

$$\forall s_1 : [v_1(\bar{s}) \geqslant \min_{s_2} v_1(s_1, s_2)],$$

or equivalently,

$$\forall s_1 : [\exists s_2 : v_1(\bar{s}) \geqslant v_1(s_1, s_2)],$$

which is the same as the condition of the theorem.

Thus the theorem works in these cases. We note that in general in the case that player i's preferences are represented by a numerical preference function v_i, the condition of the theorem is equivalent to

$$v_i(\bar{s}) \geqslant \min_{s_P} \max_{s_i} \min_{s_F} v_i(\bar{s}_U, s_P, s_i, s_F)$$

provided this function is such that the "min max min" expression on the right-hand side exists.[3] This follows from the fact that in such

3. By our convention "$\min_{s_K}$" stands for a blank space when $K = \varnothing$.

cases the statement

$$v_i(\bar{s}) \geqslant \min_{s_K} v_i(s_K, \bar{s}_{N-K})$$

is equivalent to

$$\exists s_K : (s_K, \bar{s}_{N-K}) \in M_i\bar{s},$$

while the statement

$$v_i(\bar{s}) \geqslant \max_{s_K} v_i(s_K, \bar{s}_{N-K})$$

is simply

$$\forall s_K : (s_K, \bar{s}_{N-K}) \in M_i\bar{s}.$$

On the other hand, of course, these expressions involving quantifiers are more generally useful than the ones involving "max" and "min," since they are meaningful and may be applied even when max's and min's do not exist or are meaningless. This is the advantage of a nonquantitative approach.

We now lead up to our lemma (from which Theorem 1 follows directly) by discussing the procedure used above in the second example—the nonordinal game. Here we arrived at the condition of the theorem by arguing that the condition

$$\exists f \, \forall s_B : (fs_B, s_B) \in M_B\bar{s}$$

was equivalent to

$$\forall s_B \, \exists s_A : (s_A, s_B) \in M_B\bar{s}.$$

Generalizing this, let us consider for any given nonempty sets X, Y and given subset P of the Cartesian product $X \times Y$, the following statement (in which f is a function $f : X \to Y$ and x, y are elements of X and Y respectively):

$$\exists f \, \forall x : (x, fx) \in P.$$

We want to ask if this is in general equivalent to the statement

$$\forall x \, \exists y : (x, y) \in P.$$

To prove equivalence we would have to show that each statement implies the other.

Now clearly the first statement implies the second; for the y

required by the second statement to exist for each x can be taken as $y = fx$.

However, that the second statement implies the first is a fundamental unproved assumption of mathematics known as the "axiom of choice." We say "unproved" because though it can be stated in many equivalent forms, it has not been and perhaps cannot be derived from more fundamental considerations.

So we write without proof the following axiom:

Axiom of Choice

If X, Y are nonempty sets and $P \subseteq X \times Y$, then if we let f be any function $f: X \to Y$ and x, y be elements of X, Y respectively, we have

$$(\forall x \, \exists y : (x, y) \in P) \Rightarrow (\exists f \, \forall x : (x, fx) \in P).$$

We note that the axiom of choice is easy to prove if X and Y are finite; for then we may construct the f required to exist on the right-hand side by selecting, for each x, a $y = fx$ such that $(x, y) \in P$. The left-hand side guarantees us that for each x such a y will exist.

The problems that arise with the axiom when X and Y are infinite will be discussed after we have used the axiom to prove Theorem 1.

As we have noted, the right-hand side of the axiom implies the left-hand side, so that if the axiom is true, the statement

$$\forall x \, \exists y : (x, y) \in P \tag{1}$$

is equivalent to

$$\exists f \, \forall x : (x, fx) \in P. \tag{2}$$

Now clearly (1) can be written

$$\forall x \, \exists f : (x, fx) \in P,$$

so that comparing this with (2) we see that "$\exists f$" commutes with "$\forall x$" when followed by "$(x, fx) \in P$." Furthermore, "$\forall f$" commutes with "$\exists x$" when followed by the same statement. For the statement

$$\forall f \, \exists x : (x, fx) \in P \tag{3}$$

is the same as

$$\sim \exists f \, \forall x : (x, fx) \notin P,$$

which we have shown is equivalent to

$$\sim \forall x \; \exists f : (x, fx) \notin P$$

or

$$\exists x \; \forall f : (x, fx) \in P,$$

and comparing this with (3) shows that, indeed, "$\forall f$" does commute with "$\exists x$" when followed by "$(x, fx) \in P$." Meanwhile of course "$\exists x$" always commutes with "$\exists f$," and "$\forall x$" with "$\forall f$," when followed by anything whatever. So in general we can say that if Q^0, Q^1 are any two quantifiers, each equal to $\exists$ or $\forall$, then

$$Q^0 f \; Q^1 x : (x, fx) \in P$$

is equivalent to

$$Q^1 x \; Q^0 f : (x, fx) \in P$$

or to

$$Q^1 x \; Q^0 y : (x, y) \in P.$$

Obviously this can be extended to $r+1$ quantifiers, so we now state the following lemma.

Lemma 1

Let Q^0, Q^1, ..., Q^r be $r+1$ given quantifiers and Y, X_1, ..., X_r be $r+1$ nonempty sets. Then if y stands for an element of Y, x_i for an element of X_i, x for an element of $X = \Pi_{i=1}^r X_i$, and f for a function from X to Y, the statement

$$Q^1 x_1 \ldots Q^{k-1} x_{k-1} \; Q^0 f Q^k x_k \ldots Q^r x_r : (x, fx) \in P$$

is equivalent to

$$Q^1 x_1 \ldots Q^r x_r \; Q^0 f : (x, fx) \in P$$

or to

$$Q^1 x_1 \ldots Q^r x_r \; Q^0 y : (x, y) \in P.$$

We are now equipped for the proof of Theorem 1. It is essentially a simple induction on the level r of the metagame $H = k_1 \ldots k_r G$, the inductive step being essentially furnished by Lemma 1. The only complication arises from the fact that to show $\tilde{s}$ metarational for i from H, we have to show, not only that the other players have a policy f_{N-i} that always yields i a not-preferred result, but also that

f_{N-i} may yield $\bar{s}$. This extra condition is, however, always satisfied if the first condition is, because $\bar{s}$ is always not preferred to itself. Apart from this, the proof is just an application of the lemma to four possible cases.

Proof of Theorem 1: Let $H = k_1 \ldots k_r G$. The truth of the theorem for $r = 0$ has already been noted. Next we prove it for $r+1$, given that it is true for r.

The inductive assumption is that the condition for an outcome $\bar{s}$ of G to be in $\hat{R}_i(H) = \beta^r R_i(k_1 \ldots k_r G)$ is

$$\exists s_P \ \forall s_i \ \exists s_F : (\bar{s}_U, s_P, s_i, s_F) \in M_i \bar{s},$$

where the sets U, P, and F are obtained from the prime representative of H in the manner described in the theorem.

Now a metagame kG may if we like be regarded as a basic game. Hence, from the inductive assumption, the condition for an outcome $(\vec{f}, \bar{s}_{N-k})$ of the metagame kG to be in $\beta^r R_i(k_1 \ldots k_r(kG))$ is as follows, depending on whether $k \in U$, P, $\{i\}$, or F.

If $k \in U$,

$$\exists s_P \ \forall s_i \ \exists s_F : (\vec{f}, \bar{s}_{U-k}, s_P, s_i, s_F) \in M_i'(\vec{f}, \bar{s}_{N-k});$$

if $k \in P$,

$$\exists f \ \exists s_{P-k} \ \forall s_i \ \exists s_F : (\bar{s}_U, f, s_{P-k}, s_i, s_F) \in M_i'(\vec{f}, \bar{s}_{N-k});$$

if $k = i$,

$$\exists s_P \ \forall f \ \exists s_F : (\bar{s}_U, s_P, f, s_F) \in M_i'(\vec{f}, \bar{s}_{N-k});$$

if $k \in F$,

$$\exists s_p \ \forall s_i \ \exists f \ \exists s_{F-k} : (\bar{s}_U, s_P, s_i, f, s_{F-k}) \in M_i'(\vec{f}, \bar{s}_{N-k});$$

where the sets U, P, and F are defined from the list $k_1 \ldots k_r$, not from the list $k_1 \ldots k_r k$, and where M_i' is player i's preference function in the game kG, not in the game G; this being in fact the sense in which we have "regarded kG as a basic game."

But from the definition of M_i', these conditions assert the following necessary and sufficient conditions for $\bar{s} \in \beta^{r+1} R_i(k_1 \ldots k_r(kG))$.

If $k \in U$,

$$\exists \vec{f} \begin{cases} \exists s_P \ \forall s_i \ \exists s_F : \beta(\vec{f}, \bar{s}_{U-k}, s_P, s_i, s_F) \in M_i \bar{s}, \\ \vec{f}\bar{s}_{N-k} = \bar{s}_k; \end{cases} \tag{4}$$

if $k \in P$,

$$\exists \bar{f} \begin{cases} \exists f \, \exists s_{P-k} \, \forall s_i \, \exists s_F : \beta(\bar{s}_u, f, s_{P-k}, s_i, s_F) \in M_i \bar{s}, \\ \bar{f} \bar{s}_{N-k} = \bar{s}_k; \end{cases} \tag{5}$$

if $k = i$,

$$\exists \bar{f} \begin{cases} \exists s_P \, \forall f \, \exists s_F : \beta(\bar{s}_U, s_P, f, s_F) \in M_i \bar{s}, \\ \bar{f} \bar{s}_{N-k} = \bar{s}_k; \end{cases} \tag{6}$$

if $k \in F$,

$$\exists \bar{f} \begin{cases} \exists s_P \, \forall s_i \, \exists f \, \exists s_{F-k} : \beta(\bar{s}_U, s_P, s_i, f, s_{F-k}) \in M_i \bar{s}, \\ \bar{f} \bar{s}_{N-k} = \bar{s}_k; \end{cases} \tag{7}$$

where M_i of course stands for i's preferences in the game G.

Now although (4) requires an $\bar{f}$ to exist satisfying two conditions, in fact an $\bar{f}$ satisfying both conditions will exist if one exists satisfying the first condition. For if f^* satisfies the first condition, then consider the function $f^*_{\bar{s}}$ identical to f^* except that $f^*_{\bar{s}} \bar{s}_{N-k} = \bar{s}_k$. This will satisfy the second condition by definition and the first condition because $\bar{s} \in M_i \bar{s}$ always. Hence the second condition is redundant.

Deleting it, (4) becomes

$$\exists f \, \exists s_P \, \forall s_i \, \exists s_F : \beta(f, \bar{s}_{U-k}, s_P, s_i, s_F) \in M_i \bar{s}$$

and by Lemma 1 this is

$$\exists s_P \, \forall s_i \, \exists s_{F \cup k} : (\bar{s}_{U-k}, s_P, s_i, s_{F \cup k}) \in M_i \bar{s},$$

which is the required condition of the theorem for

$$\bar{s} \in \hat{R}_i(k_1 \ldots k_r(kG))$$

when k belongs to the set U obtained from the list $k_1 \ldots k_r$, and P and F are also obtained from this list.

Next, in (5), (6), and (7) there is only one condition on $\bar{f}$, which is easily satisfied by setting $\bar{f} \bar{s}_{N-k}$ identically equal to $\bar{s}_k$. Deleting this condition and also deleting "$\exists \bar{f}$," we obtain statements that by Lemma 1 are equivalent to the respective required conditions of the theorem for $\bar{s} \in R_i(k_1 \ldots k_r(kG))$. For example, (6) becomes

$$\exists s_P \, \forall f \, \exists s_F : \beta(\bar{s}_U, s_P, f, s_F) \in M_i \bar{s},$$

which by Lemma 1 is

$$\exists s_{P \cup F} \, \forall s_i : (\bar{s}_U, s_{P \cup F}, s_i) \in M_i \bar{s},$$

which is the required condition when $k = i$ and U, P, and F are obtained from the list $k_1 \ldots k_r$.

4.3 An Interpretation of the Axiom of Choice

The foregoing proof is rather abstract, and the nonmathematical reader may be feeling dizzy. The utility of the theorem will, we hope, have been established for him by its use in the two examples which preceded the proof: the theorem does enable us to find metarational outcomes and hence test our theory. But the reader may have been inclined to skip the proof itself.

This is understandable but not forgivable. In a mathematical subject the most rewarding objects of study are the proofs of theorems. In particular, if the subject is not "pure" mathematics but is interpreted to apply to the real world, it can be most rewarding to interpret proofs.

Now the axiom of choice plays an essential role in the proof of Theorem 1. In fact, the proof uses (a) this axiom, (b) the definition of a function, and (c) the reflexivity of preferences.

We have discussed the interpretation of (c) already. A *function*, as used in the theorem, of course describes a reaction pattern evoked in one player by the strategies (or metastrategies) chosen by the others. It remains to interpret the axiom of choice.

We have noted that the axiom is easy to prove if X and Y are finite sets. The argument then is that the function f required to exist on the right-hand side of the axiom may be constructed by selecting, for each x, a $y = fx$ such that $(x, y) \in P$. But when X and Y are infinite, this means constructing f by choosing one element from each of an infinite number of infinite sets!

This would still be all right if we could provide a rule stating how these selections are to be made. Otherwise it appears dubious. For example, suppose Y is the real-number interval $Y = \{y \mid 0 \leqslant y \leqslant 1\}$, suppose X is the set of all nonempty subsets of Y, and suppose P is the set of all pairs (x, y) such that $y \in x$. Then certainly the left-hand side of the axiom of choice is true by definition—but for the right-hand side, it appears impossible to state a rule for selecting an element from each nonempty subset of Y.

We cannot, for example, specify choosing the least or greatest element, for a subset such as $\{y|0 < y < \frac{1}{2}\}$ has neither a least nor a greatest element. Other attempts also fail.

The general conclusion reached by mathematicians is that the axiom of choice may be accepted provided we understand that to say, as we do on the right-hand side, that f exists is not to say that we can construct it. But in what sense, then, does it "exist"? This, for the pure mathematician, is a philosophical question concerning the interpretation of "mathematical existence." For him, the "choice" referred to in the phrase "axiom of choice" is regarded as a hypothetical choice made by a mathematician; and the philosophical question is, What does a mathematician mean when he says "we may choose ..."? Undoubtedly it is true that given any x, this mathematician can choose a y. But the axiom says that therefore he can "choose" an $f: X \to Y$. What does this mean?

On the other hand, in metagame theory, interpreted as being about actual players (e.g., experimental subjects) the choices in question are actual choices made by these players. These players choose strategies—and if they can predict, we would like to say that therefore they can "choose" metastrategies. For us, therefore, the axiom takes on a highly concrete meaning.

Let us, indeed, set up an experiment in which player 1 can choose any nonempty subset of the real unit interval and player 2 any point in this interval, and let us pay player 2 a sum of money if he chooses an $s_2 \in s_1$. We have not specified 1's payoffs, but these are not really relevant. Indeed, let 2 not be told 1's payoffs, but let him be told he will be allowed to negotiate with 1 before they choose. Clearly, 2's plan of action may be to try to find out 1's intentions so as to carry out a policy (metastrategy) $f: S_1 \to S_2$ such that $\forall s_1 : fs_1 \in s_1$. But he cannot state or specifically lay down such a policy! Were he to be called away and try to instruct a proxy unwilling to take any personal initiative, he could not do so!

What then do we mean by saying that he can "choose" such a policy? Of course one can argue that in the "real world" player 1, or the whole of mankind, is actually limited to a finite set of subsets of the unit interval, since only a finite set of subsets is specifiable in practice. But this "real" world is still not real enough for us! The fact is that here the theoretical problems connected with infinite sets correspond to practical problems connected with large sets, and the experimental player 1 can certainly choose from too many alternative subsets for the experimental player 2 to be able to instruct his proxy how to choose an element from each one.

Since therefore the question of "mathematical existence," and of interpreting the axiom of choice, has for us a concrete empirical meaning, we are only interested in finding an interpretation that will serve us in constructing an empirical theory. We lose interest in seeking the general philosophical interpretation but claim the right to adopt any consistent interpretation that works for the purpose we need it for. Our interpretation is therefore to be judged in this light only.

Our interpretation is this: To say player 2 has "chosen" a function $f: S_1 \to S_2$ means that his state of mind is such that he can answer any "yes/no" question that can be put to him as to how he will respond to player 1's strategies. Thus, for example, he can answer the questions, Will your s_2 necessarily be an element of s_1? Will s_2 be a rational number if s_1 contains rational numbers? Will s_2 be $\frac{1}{2}$ if $s_1 = \{x | 0 \leq x \leq \frac{1}{4}\}$? and so on. He must be able to answer, with a "yes" or "no," any such question that is put to him. If he cannot do so, or if his answers are inconsistent in that they imply that given some s_1 he has not prepared a unique response s_2, then by this operational test he must be judged not to have chosen a function f.

Thus the assertion "he has chosen an f" is generally in the class of nonverifiable but falsifiable empirical assertions. The point of course is that this way of putting the matter allows player 2 to have "chosen" an f (e.g., an f such that $fs_1 \in s_1$ for all s_1) without being able to specify (construct) this f. This is achieved by taking the burden of specifying and constructing away from player 2 himself and placing it on an *interrogator* who must ask player 2 specific questions. It is thus now impossible for the interrogator to ask player 2 whether his choice will obey such-and-such a specific function $f \in \{f | fs_1 \in s_1$ for all $s_1\}$, because the interrogator is unable to specify such a function. If we, as interrogators, were able to specify such a function, we could put the question to player 2. In the meantime, our interpretation is that we cannot deny that player 2 may have "chosen" (in the sense of being prepared to carry out) such a policy, even though he cannot specify it.

In the special case of a finite game our interrogation procedure is, of course, always capable in theory of completely determining a player's policy choice. This is as one would hope and expect. In the infinite case, the interrogation procedure may again be capable of completely determining a player's policy choice, for the policy may be a constructible function f and the interrogator may ask whether this f is or is not the player's policy. But in the infinite case this is not guaranteed, as it is not guaranteed that the policy choice will be constructible.

The above describes what is meant by a "choice" of a *first-level* policy $f: S_{N-i} \rightarrow S_i$. But the description applies to a policy choice at any level. For example, consider in our imaginary experiment how we would test player 1's second-level policy choice $g: F \rightarrow S_1$. (Here $F = \{f | f: S_1 \rightarrow S_2\}$.) We would ask player 1 questions such as If 2 chose an f such that $fs_1 \in s_1$ for all s_1, would your s_1 necessarily contain the point $\frac{1}{2}$? If f were such that fs_1 is a rational number whenever s_1 contains an irrational number, would s_1 necessarily be the entire interval $\{x | 0 \leqslant x \leqslant 1\}$? and so on. The procedure is simply that of asking any questions that can be asked. If the player can answer all that are put to him without contradicting himself, then operationally the procedure has not falsified the assumption that he has chosen a policy of the desired type. The definition of the player "having chosen a policy of this type" is that he is able to answer all such questions consistently.

The procedure also helps to determine which policy has been chosen. And from this fact we see that our interpretation of the axiom of choice naturally models the processes of bargaining and negotiation that actually occur between real-life players. Indeed, questions of the form we have described are important in real-life negotiations. They are put by one player to another, or a player may volunteer information—in effect he puts the question to himself and gives the answer. A player will say, for example, "If you will cease putting pressure on my client, I will consent to sign a nonprolifera-tion treaty," or "Will you call off the strike if we reinstate three men and raise wages by so much?" Such questions and answers as these concern first-level policies. More careful phraseology is needed to discuss second-level policies—for example, "If it were the case (I do not say it is) that my client could pay such and such damages, would you be willing to settle out of court?"

In such examples we see again that an important way in which players are often able to predict each other's strategies and policies is by asking each other what these will be or by being told without having to ask; though nothing in the rules of the game requires that they be told the truth or believe what they are told.

4.4 Corollaries of the Characterization Theorem

A number of corollaries follow from Theorem 1, which is really the fundamental theorem of the theory of metarational outcomes. The proofs of these corollaries are mostly quite easy.

The first thing to note is that metarational outcomes have a "descendance" property in the metagame tree; that is, an outcome that is metarational from H remains metarational from every descendant of H:

Corollary 1.1

If H' is a descendant of H, then $\hat{R}_i(H') \supseteq \hat{R}_i(H)$.

Proof: Let $\bar{s}$ be metarational for i from H. Then $\bar{s}$ obeys

$$\exists s_P \ \forall s_i \ \exists s_F : (\bar{s}_U, s_{N-U}) \in M_i \bar{s},$$

where U, P, and F are defined as in Theorem 1.

A fortiori, therefore, if A is any subset of U, $\bar{s}$ must obey

$$\exists s_A \ \exists s_P \ \forall s_i \ \exists s_F : (\bar{s}_{U-A}, s_A, s_{N-U}) \in M_i \bar{s},$$

since $\bar{s}_A$ is an s_A such as is here required to exist. But this implies, for any $B \subseteq A$:

$$\exists s_{A-B} \ \exists s_P \ \forall s_i \ \exists s_{FUB} : (\bar{s}_{U-A}, s_A, s_{N-U}) \in M_i \bar{s},$$

which (for some choice of $B \subseteq A \subseteq U$) will be the condition for $\bar{s}$ to be metarational from H' if H' is a descendant of H. Thus we have shown that $\bar{s} \in \hat{R}_i(H)$ implies $\bar{s} \in \hat{R}_i(H')$, Q.E.D.

In addition to the above "descendance" property of metarational outcomes, we also have a "finite convergence" property. Indeed, the condition of Theorem 1 is the same for any two metagames that have the same prime representative, so that we certainly have

Corollary 1.2

If H^* is the prime representative of H, then

$$\hat{R}_i(H) = \hat{R}_i(H^*).$$

And from this it is obvious that the prime metagames, of which there are $\sum_{r=0}^{n} n^{(r)}$, and which are all located at most n stages distant from the root of the tree, yield all the distinct sets of metarational outcomes that occur anywhere in the tree. Thus after n stages the metarational outcomes have "converged" in the sense that all metarational outcomes are already metarational from metagames at or before the nth level.

We may say that insofar as players are concerned with metarational outcomes, they "need not" think in terms of reactions to reactions to . . ., beyond the nth level: they may do so, but if they do, they will not find any further metarational outcomes. Indeed, the two corollaries taken together enable us to describe the situation as follows. Starting with the node G at the root of the tree, where $\hat{R}_i(H) = R_i(G)$, we may imagine ourselves proceeding downwards through the tree along some arbitrary path. As we do so, the set $\hat{R}_i(H)$ may expand when a new player's name is added to the title of the metagame H; otherwise this set remains the same. When all players have been named, so that H is *complete*, the set $\hat{R}_i(H)$ remains constant thereafter.

But what does this mean? We have three interpretations of "proceeding along a path through the metagame tree." In each case the "path through the tree" represents a sequence of reactions, reactions to reactions, and so forth. But the sequence may be traversed: (i) in the mental processes of a single player, as he reasons "if I do this, he will do that; but if he is going to react in that way, I should do this . . ."; (ii) in the process of bargaining and negotiation between players; (iii) in the process of making physical moves in a crisis situation (e.g., a postwar "Berlin crisis") with the object of conveying one's intentions to the other players.

In each case, the aforementioned rather general facts about such "reaction processes" are deemed to be applicable. For instance, our two corollaries imply that in any two-person situation reactions to reactions should be considered, but that for the purpose of determining "best attainable" outcomes for oneself or the other player reactions to reactions to reactions, or any other higher-level reactions, need not be considered. This is a general statement about empirical reaction processes of any of the three types (i), (ii), and (iii).

Mathematical Development

It follows at once from Theorem 1 that

Corollary 1.3

$$\hat{R}_i(iH) = \hat{R}_i(H).$$

Discussion. This tells us that in any game or metagame a player does not affect *his own* "best attainable" outcomes by electing to choose a policy (a pattern of reactions to the others' strategies) rather than just choosing a strategy. He only affects the others' "best attainable" outcomes.

Now he cannot affect these in the desired way unless the others know his policy choice. We conclude that one apparent hindrance to supposing that players can predict, does not exist. When it comes to predicting another's policy (as distinct from his basic strategy) the fact is that the other will often be anxious to communicate this. If, for example, in prisoner's dilemma (Figure 2.20) player 2's policy really is the "tit-for-tat" policy (C/D in Figure 2.20b) he will certainly wish to let player 1 know this, for otherwise there is no reason for him to choose it.

Note, however, that this does not work the other way. If his policy is the "sure-thing" policy D/D, he may wish to make the other think his policy is C/D in order to obtain (in an unstable manner) the outcome (C, D). Another point is that he may not wish all the players (only some) to know his policy. But in general, if there is no other player to whom he wishes to communicate his policy, we can say that this can only happen if his policy is a "sure-thing" policy.

In a two-person case, however, this is extremely strong. It is never too difficult to predict another's policy, for there are but two possibilities: either his policy is "sure-thing," or it is what he says it is. In particular, if he says nothing (and is able to communicate), his policy is "sure-thing."

Mathematical Development

The above corollaries give a general idea of the structure of the metagame tree. We note also that for any particular player i, there will be many metagames not having the same prime representative that nevertheless all yield the same metarational outcomes for this player i. Indeed, the metarational outcomes for player i yielded by a metagame depend only on the sets U and F of Theorem 1 (P being given when U, F, and i are given), which in general will be the same as between many different metagames with different prime representatives. For example, any two complete metagames of the form

$$k_1 \ldots k_r i G$$

will yield the same metarational outcomes for player i. And so will any two metagames in which player i is followed last by every other player.

These two examples are important in connection with *symmetric* and *general* metarational outcomes—two types of metarational outcomes that we now examine.

General metarational outcomes for i have already been defined as those outcomes in the set

$$\Gamma_i = \bigcup_H \hat{R}_i(H).$$

Corollary 1.4

Alternative necessary and sufficient conditions for $\bar{s}$ to be general metarational for i are

i. $\bar{s}$ is metarational for i from some metagame;

ii. $\bar{s}$ is metarational for i from some complete metagame;

iii. $\bar{s}$ is metarational for i from some and every metagame in which all the other players follow i last;

iv. i does not possess a basic strategy that will guarantee that regardless of the others' strategy choices, he will obtain an outcome preferred by him to $\bar{s}$;

v. (applicable when G is a game with numerical payoff functions v_i such that the given "max min" expression exists) i's payoff $v_i(\bar{s})$ is greater than or equal to $\max_{s_i} \min_{s_{N-i}} v_i(s)$.

Proof: Condition i is a restatement of the definition of a general metarational outcome. Condition ii is equivalent to condition i because of Corollary 1.1 coupled with the fact that every metagame has a descendant that is complete. For the rest, condition iv is the statement

$$\sim \exists s_i \; \forall s_{N-i} : s \notin M_i \bar{s},$$

which is the same as

$$\forall s_i \; \exists s_{N-i} : s \in M_i \bar{s},$$

which by Theorem 1 is precisely the necessary and sufficient condition for the truth of condition iii. Moreover, it is equivalent to condition v in the special case noted under condition v. Hence conditions iii, iv, and v are equivalent. Next, condition iii clearly implies condition i. It remains to show that condition ii implies condition iii. Now if condition ii is true, $\bar{s}$ obeys

$$\exists s_P \; \forall s_i \; \exists s_F : s \in M_i \bar{s}$$

for some sets P and F. But this implies the above-quoted condition for the truth of condition iii.

Discussion. We have already described i's general metarational outcomes as including all those that can in any way be made to appear to him "best attainable" and hence can be stable for him. This is now seen to be quite weak, as indicated particularly by condition iv; which means, of course, that i's general metarational outcomes will often be very numerous.

But in a sense this should be so, for we recall that i's "possibly stable" outcomes must include all those that, *by any adjustments of i's beliefs about the others' preferences*, could possibly be made to seem to him "best attainable."

Figure 4.3a illustrates this. Here the (31) outcome is metarational for player 1 even though, since no outcome in the second column is metarational for 2, it is predictable that 2 will never choose the second column! This is more understandable if we recall that 1 may

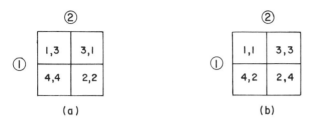

Figure 4.3. Actual and Believed Game. Misinformation about 2's preferences may lead 1 to regard as "best attainable" an outcome that is actually impossible.

believe, mistakenly, that 2's payoffs are as in Figure 4.3b.

We therefore have a weak theory, one that makes weak predictions. One reason for this is that we make no assumptions as to the players' knowledge of others' preferences. Strengthening the theory in this regard is discussed in Chapter 6. Meanwhile, note that a weak theory can be tested just as strongly as a strong one, provided the results of experiments are dealt with in a way that takes account of the theory's weakness (see Appendix B).

Mathematical Development

A subset of i's general metarational outcomes is the set of his *symmetric* metarational outcomes. These are the outcomes that are metarational for him from some descendant of any metagame. That is, they are the outcomes in the set

$$\bigcap_H \bigcup_{k_1 \ldots k_r} \hat{R}_i(k_1 \ldots k_r H),$$

where H is any metagame.

We shall denote this important set by "Σ_i." Alternative definitions are as follows (the proof of this corollary is left to the reader):

Corollary 1.5

The following are equivalent conditions for $\bar{s} \in \Sigma_i$:

i. $\bar{s}$ is metarational for i from some descendant of any metagame;

ii. $\bar{s}$ is metarational for i from every complete metagame;

iii. $\bar{s}$ is metarational for i from some metagame in which he follows every other player last;

iv. the other players possess a joint basic strategy by which they can guarantee that regardless of i's strategy choice, the outcome will be not preferred by i to $\bar{s}$;

v. (applicable when G is a game with numerical payoffs and the "min max" used here exists) i's payoff $v_i(\bar{s})$ is at least $\min_{s_{N-i}}\max_{s_i}v_i(s)$.

Discussion. Let us interpret this. First of all, i's symmetric metarational outcomes are those that can be made to appear "best attainable" for him whatever "path through the tree" (line of reasoning or bargaining process) he pursues, provided he pursues it until it yields no further metarational outcomes. This is an interpretation of conditions i and ii.

As for condition iii, let us recall our discussion of the free will paradox in Section 3.3. There we found that it seems easier to imagine a player believing that he can predict the others' free strategy choices than to imagine him believing that they can predict his.

On the other hand, we have also said, in effect, that it will often be easy for player i to imagine that the others can predict his policy; for (case 1) he will wish to communicate it to at least some of them, unless (case 2) it is "sure-thing."

But taken together, these two points lead to the conclusion that there will be a strong tendency for player i's subjective metagame to be one in which he follows all the others last. For such a metagame is precisely one in which he can predict the others' basic strategies, they cannot predict his, and they are possibly able to predict his policy. Indeed, if we add the condition that i believes there is complete mutual prediction (implying that i's subjective metagame is complete), then this precisely describes the complete metagames in which he follows all the others last.

We conclude that symmetric metarational outcomes are more likely to be stable for him than *asymmetric* (general but not symmetric) ones.

The point is brought out in the example of the merchant-warship game (Figure 2.2). Here every outcome is general metarational for both players, but only those that represent a "win" (escape for the merchant ship, encounter for the warship) are *symmetric* metarational. The psychology in this case is clear; each player is likely to try to predict the other and then to choose on the assumption that his own prediction is correct. To assume that the other's prediction will be correct, though logically just as defensible, would be to admit defeat.

Next, condition iv shows just how symmetric metarationality is stronger than general metarationality: it is not sufficient that i be unable to guarantee himself reaching an outcome preferred to $\bar{s}$, rather it is necessary that the others be able to guarantee that he not reach such an outcome. Condition v, as before, is simply the same as condition iv in the special case of numerical payoffs.

Summing up, we have defined two types of metarational outcomes: *general* (those that are metarational from some metagame) and *symmetric* (those that are metarational from some descendant of every metagame). What about those that are metarational from every metagame? Are not these interesting?

They are interesting but not new. By the descendance property (Corollary 1.1) they are simply the *rational* outcomes. Nevertheless let us list them as a third type, on a level with the other two. Clearly, they represent the strongest possible type of stability.

4.5 Discussion of Chapter 4

In this chapter we have presented the false theory of rational outcomes, pointing out that it is best interpreted as a theory about the individual player that knows his own preferences but need not know the others' preferences. Applied to the metagame tree, this theory becomes the theory of metarational outcomes. We have solved the chief mathematical problem of this theory—the basic characterization of metarational outcomes. Solving this problem was necessary before the empirical theory could be tested experimentally. We have discussed the empirical theory and noted that the experiments reported in Appendix B have confirmed it. Finally, we have deduced various properties of the sets of metarational outcomes found in the metagame tree.

In the next chapter we shall go further into metarationality theory. First we shall take up the problem of the role of coalitions in three-or-more-person games. Then we shall define various types of equilibrium found in the metagame tree.

Here an equilibrium will be regarded as an outcome that can

be stable (for all players) simply because it can be metarational for each player. Different types of metarationality thus give rise to different types of equilibrium, but there is nothing essentially new in this; it is simply a way of developing certain further implications of the theory of metarationality.

In the final section of the next chapter, we shall describe a technique for applying the theory to realistic conflict situations. This technique has been developed particularly for use in problems of international politics, but its scope is wider than this, and we shall end up applying it to the analysis of the plot of a contemporary play.

5
Further Developments in Metarationality Theory

5.1 Coalition Metarationality

When a game has more than two players, we must expect that coalitions of more than one player may form to achieve ends they have in common. Indeed, even in a two-person game, the coalition of both players may form to achieve joint ends. How is this possibility to be analyzed?

Previous approaches, beginning with the classical treatment of von Neumann and Morgenstern (1953), have laid down additional axioms supposed to govern the behavior of coalitions. The link between individual optimization and coalition optimization has not been made. It has not been explained how it may be to the individual advantage of player i to work for the collective ends of a coalition.

Our approach will concentrate on this aspect. In fact, we shall regard coalition metarationality as simply a special kind of individual metarationality.

Just as a player may be symmetric or general metarational, depending on the kind of prediction he makes of the others' strategies, so we shall see how the kind of prediction made by an individual player may cause him to be coalition metarational. In other words, because of the kind of prediction he makes, he may strive for the ends of the coalition in the very process of striving for his own individual ends.

The reason why he will make this kind of prediction will be tied up with trust in the cooperative intentions of the other members of the coalition. But the first and most important task is to specify what kind of predictions (by the individual player) will achieve this reconciliation between individual and group objectives.

Thus from our viewpoint the theory of coalition metarationality is still a theory predicting the "anticipated outcome" of the individual player, in this case an individual i belonging to a coalition.

No further experimental predictions beyond those already described can therefore be deduced from it. Thus our theory is really only another way of analyzing individual metarationality—albeit perhaps a particularly interesting way. We may say that it investigates the conditions under which individual interests may work together for joint ends.

To begin with, we define what we mean by the "joint ends" of a coalition. Our definition may seem somewhat narrow. The following discussion shows, however, that by appropriately defining players' strategy sets and preferences, it can be made wider than it appears. Moreover, to widen it in just this way is the most practical approach to modeling real situations.

Mathematical Development

A *coalition* is defined simply as a nonempty subset of players. This includes the *coalition of all players*, $C = N$; but the empty set is not a coalition.

Preferences are defined for coalitions as follows. If $\varnothing \subset C \subseteq N$, we write

$$M_C s = \bigcup_{i \in C} M_i s.$$

That is, an outcome is "not preferred" by a coalition if any member of the coalition does not prefer it. It follows that an outcome is "preferred" by C only if every member of C prefers it. That is, if we write

$$\tilde{M}_C s = S - M_C s,$$

as in the case of individual preferences M_i, we immediately obtain

$$\tilde{M}_C s = \bigcap_{i \in C} \tilde{M}_i s.$$

In particular, if $s \in \tilde{M}_N t$, s is preferred to t by every player. In this particular case we say that s *dominates* t.

Note that since individual preferences are reflexive ($s \in M_i s$ for all s), coalition preferences are also. (The reason why we do not allow the empty set as a coalition is that this would not be true for the "empty" coalition.)

But if individual preferences are ordinal, the reader may show that coalition preferences are partly ordinal but not necessarily ordinal. **Discussion.** Why do we define coalition preferences in this way? We can argue that if not every member of a coalition prefers an outcome, but only some members do, then that coalition does not prefer it. A subcoalition does.

This definition excludes certain possibilities. For instance, coalition members can have no feeling of loyalty to each other, such as would lead one member of C who was otherwise indifferent between s and t to prefer s because all the others do. If such feelings exist, they should already have been taken into account in forming the players' individual preference functions; for example, if i feels loyal toward j he will tend to prefer outcomes that j prefers. Hence no such feelings exist at this level.

This approach is the most practical when it comes to applications. It does not make much sense to ask a real-life player "what would your preferences be if you did not feel loyal toward so-and-so?" The only preferences he has are ones that have already absorbed the full influence of feelings such as loyalty.

We also exclude the possibility of so-called *side payments*, whereby members of a coalition induce each other to cooperate by "sharing their winnings" in some way with the others. Such possibilities should already have been taken into account in forming players' strategy sets; for example, if i can do something for j equivalent to "sharing his winnings," he should be assigned different strategies according to whether he does or does not do this thing. Again, this is the practical approach in applications.

The fact that if individual preferences are ordinal, coalition preferences need only be partly ordinal shows the real need to consider partly ordinal preferences. Even if we believed all players to have "consistent" (i.e., ordinal) preferences, we should still have to consider partly ordinal preferences when considering coalitions.

Mathematical Development

Rational outcomes for a coalition C may be defined as for individual players. Thus $\bar{s}$ is *rational for C* if

$$\forall s_C : (s_C, \bar{s}_{N-C}) \in M_C \bar{s},$$

and we write $R_C(G)$ for the set of rational outcomes for C.

Also, *metarational* outcomes for C may be defined. The set of metarational outcomes for C from a metagame H is the set

$$\hat{R}_C(H) = \beta^* R_C(H).$$

In particular, $R_N(G)$ is the set of *undominated* outcomes of G, that is, the set of outcomes s such that no outcome is preferred to s by all players. Hence

$$\hat{R}_N(H) = R_N(G) \qquad \text{for all } H.$$

Note that our definitions of coalition preferences and metarationality include individual preferences and metarationality as a special case—the case of a coalition $\{i\}$ containing only one member.

At this point we observe that our terminology is getting cumbersome. In the future, instead of saying "metarational for C from H" we shall say "(C, H)-metarational," and similarly we shall say "(i, H)-metarational" for the case of a single player. When it is clear which metagame H is being referred to we shall say "C-metarational" or "i-metarational."

We now state the theorem giving necessary and sufficient conditions for s to be (C, H)-metarational for any coalition C and metagame H. The theorem is a straightforward generalization of Theorem 1. The proof can be left to the reader: it follows the lines of the proof of Theorem 1 and, like that proof, is based wholly on the axiom of choice and the reflexive rule concerning preferences (which we have said applies also to coalition preferences).

Theorem 2

$\bar{s}$ is (C, H)-metarational if and only if

$$\forall s_{C-D} \, Q^1 s_{j_1} \ldots Q^m s_{j_m} : (\bar{s}_{N-C-D}, s_{C-D}, s_D) \in M_C \bar{s},$$

where D is the set of players named in H; $j_1 \ldots j_m G$ is the prime representative of H; and $Q^1, \ldots, Q^m$ are m quantifiers, one for each named player $j_1, \ldots, j_m$, such that

$$Q^i = \begin{cases} \forall, \text{ if } j_i \in C, \\ \exists, \text{ if } j_i \notin C. \end{cases}$$

EXAMPLE 1. Let $N = \{1, 2, \ldots, 9\}$, $C = \{2, 6, 7, 9\}$, and $H =$

$64649589686G$. Then $D = \{4, 5, 6, 8, 9\}$, $C - D = \{2, 7\}$, and the prime representative is $45986G$. Hence $\bar{s} \in \hat{R}_C(H)$ if and only if

$$\forall s_2, s_7 \; \exists s_4, \; s_5 \; \forall s_9 \; \exists s_8 \; \forall s_6 : (\bar{s}_1, s_2, \bar{s}_3, s_4, s_5, s_6, s_7, s_8, s_9) \in M_C \bar{s}.$$

Recalling the definition of M_C, we see that this is the same as

$$\forall s_2, s_7 \; \exists s_4, \; s_5 \; \forall s_9 \; \exists s_8 \; \forall s_6 \; \exists (i \in C) : (\bar{s}_1, s_2, \bar{s}_3, s_4, s_5, \ldots, s_9) \in M_i \bar{s}.$$

EXAMPLE 2. If G has numerical utilities v_i and the required minimum exists, we can see that "$s \in M_C \bar{s}$" means

$$\min_{i \in C} [v_i(s) - v_i(\bar{s})] \leqslant 0,$$

which we may write

$$v_C(s; \bar{s}) \leqslant 0,$$

where "$v_C(s; \bar{s})$" is defined to mean "$\min_{i \in C} [v_i(s) - v_i(\bar{s})]$."

Hence in this case the condition in Example 1 would become

$$\max_{s_2, s_7} \min_{s_4, s_5} \max_{s_9} \min_{s_8} \max_{s_6} v_C(\bar{s}_1, s_2, \bar{s}_3, s_4, \ldots, s_9; \bar{s}) \leqslant 0$$

provided this "min max . . . min" expression also exists.

EXAMPLE 3. The reader may check that if $C = \{i\}$, Theorem 2 reduces to Theorem 1.

All the corollaries of Theorem 1 discussed in Chapter 4 generalize to the case of coalition metarationality. We can show from Theorem 2 that

a. A (C, H)-metarational outcome is (C, H')-metarational, where H' is any descendant of H.

b. $\hat{R}_C(H) = \hat{R}_C(H^*)$ if H^* is the prime representative of H, so that the prime metagames yield all the distinct sets $\hat{R}_C(H)$.

c. The descendants of a complete metagame yield no further C-metarational outcomes.

d. $\hat{R}_C(iH) = \hat{R}_C(H)$ if $i \in C$.

Hence the situation, as with individual metarationality, is that as we proceed on a path through the metagame tree the set $\hat{R}_C(H)$ cannot lose elements; it may gain elements when a player not in C is added to its title; and after all players not in C have been added to its title, it remains the same.

Discussion. As before, following a path through the metagame tree means pursuing a certain thought process or bargaining process relative to the game G. This whole development parallels the case of individual metarationality.

Now we turn to the question of reconciling individual and coalition metarationality. To investigate C-metarationality is to investigate the thought processes of an individual player $i \in C$ that makes a certain assumption about the metastrategies that will be chosen by the other players in C. He assumes that they will not so choose as to make metarational for him an outcome that is not C-metarational.

If he makes this assumption, no conflict arises for him between i-metarationality and C-metarationality. His "best attainable" outcome, as he sees it, is also C-metarational. Consequently, his anticipated outcome (the outcome that is stable for him) will also be C-metarational. Obviously a further consequence is that the actual outcome will not be stable (anticipated by all players) unless it is C-metarational.

But just what is this assumption? A player $i \in C$ that makes the assumption we have described will always anticipate (predict) a joint metastrategy $\bar{x}_{N-i}$ such that

$$\forall x_i : (x_i, \bar{x}_{N-i}) \in R_i(H) \Rightarrow (x_i, \bar{x}_{N-i}) \in R_C(H),$$

which we define as a *C-cooperative* anticipation by player i. If his anticipations $\bar{x}_{N-i}$ always obey this condition, player i may be said to *trust* the coalition C.

But why should i make this assumption? Simply because if it were not fulfilled, the others in the coalition would be inducing him to accept a "best attainable" outcome that is worse for him and all the others in C than some other outcome they together could obtain. This is shown very simply as follows:

Let i have an anticipation $\bar{x}_{N-i}$ that is not C-cooperative. Then we have, on negating the preceding condition,

$$\exists \bar{x}_i : \bar{x} \in R_i(H), \bar{x} \notin R_C(H).$$

Here $\bar{x}_i$ is i's "best reply" to his anticipation, and $\bar{x}$ is his "best attainable" outcome. But on substituting the definition of $R_C(H)$ into the statement "$\bar{x} \notin R_C(H)$" we find that

$$\exists \hat{x}_C \; \forall (j \in C) : (\hat{x}_C, \bar{x}_{N-C}) \in \tilde{M}_j \bar{x},$$

so that, as we said, $\bar{x}$ is worse for i and all the members of C than another outcome $(\hat{x}_C, \bar{x}_{N-C})$ that they jointly could obtain.

Player i trusts them not to "cut their own throats" in this way. But note that this description assumes that player i

a. knows or guesses the preferences M_C of the coalition (otherwise he would not know when an i-metarational outcome is also C-metarational);[1]

b. believes that the others in C know or guess his (i's) preferences (otherwise they would not know when they are or are not making an outcome metarational for him);

c. believes that the others in C make the same prediction as he himself does of the metastrategies of the players not in C (for i- and C-metarationality will in general depend on these).

The above empirical conditions are necessary, but of course not sufficient, for i to be C-metarational. The sufficient condition is that i should make the "trusting" assumption we have described, in which case it follows from our general theory of metarationality that i will be C-metarational.

Empirically, we expect that if i makes this assumption he will often get together and confer with the other members of C. This he will do in order to change an anticipation that is not C-cooperative into one that is. For if player i's anticipation is C-cooperative, then his "best-attainable" outcome is such that there is no outcome better for him that is also better for the others in C and that he could obtain with their cooperation. Thus he has no reason to "get together" further with C. But the reverse is true if his anticipation is not C-cooperative. In this case, he has reason to "get together" with C in order to change his anticipation. He may change it by becoming convinced that they do not after all intend to do as he thought, or by persuading them to change their intentions. But certainly he has

1. But he still is not assumed to know the preferences of the players not in C—though neither is he assumed not to know this. We still make no assumptions either way.

reason to change his anticipation, for as he sees it his best attainable outcome is worse for him and all the others in C than some outcome they could jointly reach.

Of course, in our approach player i may trust the coalition C even if he is unable to communicate or "get together" with them. A coalition that works in this way would have an implicit, unspoken understanding between its members. However, such a coalition is vulnerable, since if player i does, for some reason, find himself anticipating an x_{N-i} that is not C-cooperative, he cannot reassure himself by communicating with and if necessary persuading the others in C.

EXAMPLE 4. Trivially, every x_{N-i} is $\{i\}$-cooperative toward i. (We may say that i cannot help "trusting" himself.)

EXAMPLE 5. Consider the game of prisoner's dilemma (Figure 2.20). In the basic game G, the strategy C is $\{1,2\}$-cooperative whereas D is not. However C "induces" the reply D—that is, D is the rational response. Thus if both players "trust" the coalition of both players, the actual outcome will be (D, D)—mutual defection. But (D, D) will not be stable; it will have come about through 1 anticipating (D, C) and 2 anticipating (C, D), both of which are in R_C. Each player "trusts" the coalition but betrays this trust.

This of course happens because (C, C) is not an equilibrium, so that even though both players trust the coalition, they are bound to betray it. (In a sense, it is "no use" their trusting each other.) If any player trusts the coalition of all players any stable outcome must be in R_N—that is, must be undominated. But if there is no undominated equilibrium, as in basic prisoner's dilemma, this simply means that no outcome can be stable.

The same holds for the two first-level metagames of prisoner's dilemma, but in the 1-2-metagame (Figure 3.3) it is of course possible for an outcome (the $(3, 3)$ outcome) to be stable with a player trusting the coalition. Note that in this game, all metastrategies are $\{1,2\}$-cooperative except D/D and $D/D/D/D$.

Altogether, prisoner's dilemma illustrates that if i trusts C, this merely means that his anticipated outcome will be C-metarational as well as i-metarational. It does not mean that his anticipated outcome will be individually metarational for the others in C; for example, in prisoner's dilemma the $(4,1)$ outcome is $\{1,2\}$-metarational but certainly not 2-metarational. (On the other hand of course the $(2,2)$ outcome is 1- and 2-metarational but not $\{1,2\}$-metarational.)

The question remains, therefore, How can i persuade the others in C to opt for an outcome that, though it may be advantageous for them all, cannot be stable for them because it is not individually metarational for them? This question will be answered in Section 6.2.

EXAMPLE 6. Consider the "test ban" game (Figure 2.16). Denote "either T or O" by a *blank* "–". Thus for example, $(-T-)$ stands for a set of outcomes—the set $\{(OTO),(OTT),(TTO),(TTT)\}$. Then we have

$$R_{\text{U.S.}} = (T--); \; R_{\text{SOV}} = (-T-); \; R_{\text{CHI}} = (--T);$$

so that (TTT) is the only equilibrium. Next,

$$R_{\{\text{U.S.,SOV}\}} = (OO-) \cup (TO-) \cup (OT-);$$

so that $(.OO)$ and $(.OT)$ are the $\{\text{U.S.,SOV}\}$-cooperative strategies toward the United States in the basic game. Similarly, $(O.O)$ and $(O.T)$ are the $\{\text{U.S.,SOV}\}$-cooperative strategies toward the Soviets in the basic game. Next,

$$R_{\{\text{U.S.,CHI}\}} = (T--) \cup (--T);$$

so that

$$R_{\text{U.S.}} \subseteq R_{\{\text{U.S.,CHI}\}} \supseteq R_{\text{CHI}},$$

and therefore all Chinese–Soviet strategies are $\{\text{U.S.,CHI}\}$-cooperative toward the United States and all U.S.–Soviet strategies are $\{\text{U.S.,CHI}\}$-cooperative toward the Chinese. This of course means that there is no point in the United States and the Chinese "getting together." They have nothing to gain from the $\{\text{U.S.,CHI}\}$ coalition. It may be called *inessential* for them. We define this next.

Mathematical Development

A coalition C containing i is *inessential* for i in a metagame H if every joint metastrategy x_{N-i} is C-cooperative toward i. Thus C is inessential for i in H (or, we may say, is "(i,H)-inessential") if

$$\forall x_{N-i} \, \forall x_i : x \in R_i(H) \Rightarrow x \in R_C(H),$$

or equivalently,

$R_i(H) \subseteq R_C(H)$,

or equivalently,

$\hat{R}_i(H) \subseteq \hat{R}_C(H)$.

In particular, the unit coalition containing just player i is always inessential for i.

Discussion. For example, we have seen above that in the "test ban" game, the coalition {U.S., CHI} is inessential for both the United States and the Chinese in the basic game G, since every outcome rational for either player is also rational for the coalition. In the basic game G, there is in a sense no way in which these two can cooperate, since merely by being selfishly rational they already exhaust all possibilities of cooperation. Note, however, that it is possible for a coalition to be essential for i in some metagames but not others. The reader may check that this does not happen in the "test ban" game: the {U.S., CHI} coalition is inessential for both its members in every metagame.

In all, then, the above gives an interpretation of how an outcome comes to be (C, H)-metarational. We can predict that if a member of a coalition C "trusts" C in the metagame H, an outcome stable for him will be (C, H)-metarational. But this prediction is nothing new; it is deduced from the theory of individual metarationality together with our definition of "trust."

We now discuss different types of coalition metarationality, generalizing the concepts of "general" and "symmetric" metarationality as defined for the individual player.

Mathematical Development

An outcome is *general* metarational for C if it is C-metarational from some metagame. Thus Γ_C, the set of general metarational outcomes for C, is the set

$$\Gamma_C = \bigcup_H \hat{R}_C(H).$$

The reader may prove from Theorem 2 the following:

Corollary 2.1

These conditions are equivalent:

i. $\bar{s} \in \Gamma_C$;

ii. $\bar{s}$ is C-metarational from some complete metagame;

iii. $\tilde{s}$ is C-metarational from some and every metagame in which the players not in C follow every player in C last;

iv. the players in C do not possess a basic strategy s_C that guarantees, for every s_{N-C}, an outcome preferred by C to $\tilde{s}$.

v. (applicable when G has numerical utilities v_i and the required "max min" exists):

$$\max_{s_C} \min_{s_{N-C}} v_C(s;\tilde{s}) \leqslant 0.$$

Next, a *symmetric* metarational outcome for C is an $\tilde{s}$ that is C-metarational from some descendant of any metagame. Thus Σ_C, the set of symmetric metarational outcomes for C, is given by

$$\Sigma_C = \bigcap_H \bigcup_{k_1 \ldots k_r} \hat{R}_C(k_1 \ldots k_r H).$$

And the reader may prove the following:

Corollary 2.2

These conditions are equivalent:

i. $\tilde{s} \in \Sigma_C$;

ii. $\tilde{s}$ is C-metarational from every complete metagame;

iii. $\tilde{s}$ is C-metarational from some metagame in which the players in C all follow every other player last;

iv. the players not in C possess a basic strategy s_{N-C} that guarantees, for every s_C, an outcome not preferred by C to $\tilde{s}$.

v. (applicable when G has numerical utilities v_i and the required "min max" exists):

$$\min_{s_{N-C}} \max_{s_C} v_C(s;\tilde{s}) \leqslant 0.$$

Discussion. What we have said about Γ_i and Σ_i applies, *mutatis mutandis*, to Γ_C and Σ_C. Once again we have weaker and stronger types of possibly stable outcomes. Again, too, if we define a third type of outcomes C-metarational from every metagame, this turns out to be R_C, the set of C-*rational* outcomes.

This then concludes our discussion of coalitions for the time being. We do think the subject needs more research. All we have done really is to set up some definitions based on individual metarationality.

We now turn to types of metagame *equilibria*—meaning outcomes simultaneously metarational for all players.

5.2 Types of Equilibria

INTERPRETATION. We have stressed that the theory of metarational outcomes is essentially a theory about the individual player and his reactions to (a) his own preferences, and (b) his beliefs about the others' strategies. It is tested experimentally by checking whether each individual player's anticipated outcome is (as the theory predicts it should be) metarational for him. Each player's behavior provides a separate test of the theory; the other players' behavior and the actual outcome are irrelevant to this test.

Nevertheless by forming the intersections of various sets of possible stable outcomes for each player, we do arrive at various sets of possible stable outcomes for the game, and this is what we shall do in this section.

Mathematical Development

An outcome which is general metarational for every player may be called a *general equilibrium*. That is, the set of general equilibria is defined by

$$\Gamma = \bigcap_i \bigcup_{k_1 \ldots k_r} \hat{R}_i(k_1 \ldots k_r G) = \bigcap_i \Gamma_i.$$

A general equilibrium is by definition metarational for every player. But for each player it may be metarational from a different metagame. An outcome that is metarational for every player from some one single metagame may be called a *metagame equilibrium*.

Thus the set T of metagame equilibria is defined by

$$T = \bigcup_{k_1 \ldots k_r} \bigcap_i \hat{R}_i(k_1 \ldots k_r G).$$

Clearly we have

$$T \subseteq \Gamma,$$

but the two sets are not the same. The set $\Gamma - T$ is called the set of *quasi equilibria*. A quasi equilibrium is metarational for every player, but there is no single metagame from which it is metarational for them all.

Figure 5.1 illustrates this.

Here the (22) outcome is not below the "max min" level of Corollary 1.4 for either player. Hence it is general metarational for

Figure 5.1. Game with a Quasi Equilibrium.

both players, and is therefore a general equilibrium. But it is not a metagame equilibrium, or it would be metarational for both players from one of the complete metagames $12G$, $21G$, requiring that it be not below the "min max" level of Corollary 1.5 for at least one player. But it is below this level for both.

Discussion. Now clearly the general equilibria include all outcomes that can possibly be stable in any way whatever. The metagame equilibria, on the other hand, are the outcomes that can be stable when all players have the same subjective metagame. The quasi equilibria, then, remain as those outcomes that cannot be stable via bargaining and negotiation except as a result of some kind of misunderstanding. The question is, When will players have the same subjective metagame?

In a sense we seem to have discounted the likelihood that they ever will: for in our discussion of "free will" and symmetric metarationality, we leaned to the view that each player will see himself as following the others last. This would mean that players will never have the same metagame.

If that is what we seem to have said, we should restate it as follows: each player will tend to think he is able (if he desires) to follow the others last. Clearly, if a player sees no disadvantage in doing so, he *can* let the others follow him last; often he can simply *tell* them his basic strategy. For example, in our discussion of prisoner's dilemma (Section 3.2) we imagined the players bargaining by 2 saying "I'll cooperate if you will" and 1 replying "In that case I'll cooperate too." Here 1 allowed 2 to follow him last—that is, he allowed 2 to carry out his (2's) stated first-level policy—by simply telling 2 his (1's) basic strategy choice.

We suggest then that it is precisely when players bargain and negotiate over the game that they are likely to have the same subjective metagame—provided, we should add, that they believe each other's statements of intention. "Bargaining in good faith" is perhaps the right phrase. If, on the other hand, the game is like the merchant-warship game, in which each player has obvious reasons to wish to follow the other last, then they will not be able to agree on a common subjective metagame, and no honest bargaining will be possible.

Mathematical Development

Next, just as general equilibria are defined as outcomes that are general metarational for all players, we can define *symmetric* equilibria as the outcomes that are symmetric metarational for every player. Thus we define

$$\Sigma = \bigcap_i \bigcap_{j_1 \ldots j_q} \bigcup_{k_1 \ldots k_r} \hat{R}_i(k_1 \ldots k_r j_1 \ldots j_q G)$$
$$= \bigcap_i \Sigma_i.$$

A symmetric equilibrium is a metagame equilibrium. Also, of course, the basic equilibria (outcomes rational for all players) are symmetric equilibria. Thus we have

$$E \subseteq \Sigma \subseteq T \subseteq \Gamma.$$

Discussion. Let us now discuss the existence of the above types of equilibria. Metagame equilibria, and even more, general equilibria, represent a type of stability "weak" enough to be almost always achievable. That is, metagame equilibria (and hence also general equilibria) do exist in all finite partly ordinal games. In fact, every complete metagame H yields at least one metagame equilibrium (one outcome metarational for all players from H), as the reader may care to prove. But symmetric equilibria and hence basic equilibria do not necessarily exist even in finite ordinal games. The merchant-warship game, for example, has no symmetric equilibrium. Thus our two smallest classes of equilibria may be empty.

A class of equilibria that has received attention from previous game theorists is the set of outcomes that are general metarational for every coalition. This set is called the α-*core*. Thus $\bar{s}$ is in the α-core if for every coalition C

$$\forall s_C \, \exists s_{N-C} : s \in M_C \bar{s}.$$

Also, the set of outcomes that are symmetric metarational for every coalition is called the β-*core*. Thus $\bar{s}$ is in the β-core if for every coalition C

$$\exists s_{N-C} \; \forall s_C : s \in M_C \bar{s}.$$

The α-core is a subset of Γ, and the β-core is a subset of Σ. Also, the β-core is a subset of the α-core.

Both may be empty, even in a finite ordinal game. This is illustrated by the game of "split the dollar."

There are three players. Any two who choose to "become partners" can split a dollar between them in any way they choose. A strategy for each player is a choice of another player as partner and of a number of cents (between 0 and 100) representing his share of the dollar if the partnership forms. If two players choose each other as partners and the numbers they have chosen add to 100, each receives the share he has chosen. Otherwise a player receives nothing.

In this game every outcome is symmetric and general metarational for any single player and for the coalition of all players. However, for any pair of players (coalition of 2), an outcome is not general metarational in which one of them receives 0 and the other less than 99: for these two have a joint strategy (forming a partnership and splitting the dollar) that guarantees an improvement to both of them.

Such a pair must always exist, however. Hence the α-core, and therefore the β-core, is empty. Whatever partnership forms, and however the dollar is split between the partners, the one who is left outside can suggest to at least one of the partners a more profitable arrangement.

In general, the α-core is the set of outcomes that can be stable regardless of what coalitions form. If, however, an outcome $\bar{s}$ is not in the α-core, there exists a coalition that can guarantee all its members an outcome preferred to $\bar{s}$, so that were $\bar{s}$ the current stable outcome, there would be an incentive for this coalition to form and overthrow $\bar{s}$ to the advantage of all its members.

However, we must not suppose that any coalition with an incentive to form will certainly do so! Prisoner's dilemma provides a counter example. Here the $(3,3)$ outcome is the only element of the α-core *and* β-core, since it is the only undominated general equilibrium. But the $(2, 2)$ outcome can certainly be stable, which means there is no certainty that the coalition of both players will form.

By contrast, if an outcome is not general metarational for an individual player, we can certainly predict that it will not be stable.

The β-core is naturally the set of outcomes that can be stable, regardless not only of what coalitions form, but regardless also of what processes of reasoning or bargaining (paths through the metagame tree) are pursued by the players. Also, if an outcome $\bar{s}$ is in the β-core, then for every coalition C, the other players $N - C$ have a strategy s_{N-C}^* that guarantees an outcome not preferred to $\bar{s}$ by some member of C. Hence if the coalition C were to attempt to move away from the outcome $\bar{s}$, the threat of the "sanction" s_{N-C}^* would suffice to deter them if this threat were made credible.

We now have to make an important but rather subtle distinction. We have defined and discussed the set

$$\bigcap_i \beta^* R_i(H),$$

which is the set of *metagame equilibria* yielded by H—that is, the set of outcomes metarational for all players from a metagame H. This is to be carefully distinguished from the set

$$\beta^* \bigcap_i R_i(H),$$

which is the set of *metaequilibria* from H.

We have actually encountered the metaequilibria before (in Section 3.2). They are the set $\beta^* E(H)$ of basic outcomes yielded by equilibria of H. What we are pointing out now is (we repeat) that they are not in general merely the outcomes metarational for all players from H.

In the case of $H = G$, the two sets are of course the same by definition. And the metaequilibria from H are naturally metarational for all players from H. The difference is that an outcome can be metarational for all players from H without being a metaequilibrium from H.

For suppose the game has three players. In the game $1G$ player 1 may have a policy f that makes $\bar{s}$ metarational for 2, and a policy f' that makes $\bar{s}$ metarational for 3. Then if $\bar{s}$ is rational for 1, $\bar{s}$ will be metarational from $1G$ for all three players. Yet $\bar{s}$ may fail to be a metaequilibrium from $1G$ because 1 may not have a single policy that makes $\bar{s}$ metarational for both 2 and 3 simultaneously.

This kind of situation creates a "policy dilemma" for a player, in that whatever he does to encourage one opponent to accept a certain proposed solution discourages another from accepting it. This appears to have been the dilemma of the United States in trying to withdraw from Vietnam on terms acceptable to the United States. To encourage the Communists (the North Vietnamese and National Liberation Front) to accept such terms, U.S. policy had to be that if its terms were not met, the United States would not withdraw from Vietnam. But to encourage the South Vietnamese government to accept the same terms, U.S. policy must be that if they are not met, the United States will withdraw from Vietnam. What then, in the current situation when the terms are not being met, can the United States do? Whatever she does will undermine the credibility of one or another of these policies. This example will be examined in more detail later.

However, this policy dilemma depends on the game having three or more players. We have, in fact

Theorem 3

If G is a two-person game, the metaequilibria from a metagame H are just the outcomes metarational for all players from H.

Hence, in the case of two-person games (but only in this case) the theory of metaequilibria may be regarded as part of the theory of metarational outcomes. In the three-or-more-person case, however, the theory of metaequilibria raises distinct problems of mathematical analysis and interpretation. The main mathematical problem is the basic characterization of metaequilibria. We need to be able to identify the metaequilibria from any metagame by examining the basic game G, just as Theorem 1 enables us to do for metarational outcomes.

Proof of Theorem 3: Let $H = k_1 \ldots k_r G$. The set of metaequilibria

$$\beta^r \bigcap_i R_i(H)$$

is a subset of the set of metarational outcomes

$$\bigcap_i \beta^r R_i(H)$$

by virtue of the easily proved fact that for any function f, $f(A \cap B) \subseteq f(A) \cap f(B)$.[2] Hence it suffices to show that an outcome metarational for all players is a metaequilibrium. Furthermore, from the definition of an equilibrium of G, it suffices to show this for $r \geqslant 1$. Now assume $k_1 = 1$. Write $x = (x_1, x_2)$ for an outcome of $k_2 \ldots k_r G$ and f for a function from X_2 to X_1, so that (f, x_2) is an outcome of $H = k_1 \ldots k_r G$. Since $\bar{s}$ is metarational for 1, we have, using Corollary 1.3,

$$\exists \bar{x} : \begin{cases} \forall x_1 : \beta^{r-1}(x_1, \bar{x}_2) \in M_1 \bar{s}, \\ \beta^{r-1} \bar{x} = \bar{s}. \end{cases}$$

Since $\bar{s}$ is metarational for 2 also, we have

$$\exists \bar{f} \, \forall x_2 : \beta^{r-1}(\bar{f}x_2, x_2) \in M_2 \bar{s}.$$

Hence, if we construct f such that

$$fx_2 = \begin{cases} \bar{x}_1 \text{ if } x_2 = \bar{x}_2, \\ \bar{f}x_2 \text{ if not,} \end{cases}$$

then $(f, \bar{x}_2)$ is an outcome that yields $\bar{s}$ and is in equilibrium. This proves the theorem.

What then is the status of an outcome metarational for all players from H but not a metaequilibrium from H?

If the players all see the situation in terms of H, then clearly this outcome can only be stable if some of them are mistaken as to each other's metastrategies in H. By the definition of stability, this says that the metagame outcome (the outcome of H) is not stable, since at least one player did not anticipate it; nevertheless the corresponding basic outcome may be stable—all players having correctly anticipated it, though some did so for the wrong reasons. This of course is possible because of the fact that two different metagame outcomes may yield the same basic outcome.

Despite these considerations, however, it *can* be shown that an outcome metarational for all players from H *is* a metaequilibrium— if not from H, then from some descendant of H. Thus we see that.

2. The function f meant in this case is of course the operator β^*.

in the end, the set of all metagame equilibria is the same as the set of all metaequilibria; that is, we have

$$\bigcup_H \beta^* \bigcap_i R_i(H) = \bigcup_H \bigcap_i \beta^* R_i(H),$$

and both sets are the set of all outcomes that can be stable when all players see the situation in terms of the same metagame.

This last is shown in Howard (1968c), where it is proved that if $\bar{s}$ is a metagame equilibrium from a game H with prime representative $j_1 \ldots j_m G$, then $\bar{s}$ is a metaequilibrium from the game $j_1 \ldots j_m H$ (which is, as required, a descendant of H). However, this theorem can (we believe) be strengthened considerably, and moreover its proof is laborious and cumbersome, so we shall not repeat it here. The whole subject of metaequilibria, in fact, requires a separate fundamental approach that has not yet been carried out. Mathematically and also in its interpretation, this subject is underdeveloped.

What we can say is this. The fact that a metagame equilibrium from H is always a metaequilibrium from some descendant of H allows us to add to our interpretation of metagame and symmetric equilibria. A metagame equilibrium is an outcome that is not merely metarational for all players from some metagame; it is also a metaequilibrium from some metagame. A symmetric equilibrium, too, is a metaequilibrium from some descendant of any metagame. Thus if the players share the same subjective metagame and also share the same predictions of each other's metastrategies, so that they are fully at one with each other in their understanding of the situation, then the outcomes that can be stable are the metagame equilibria; and the outcomes that can be stable regardless of which path through the tree (bargaining process) is pursued are the symmetric equilibria.

5.3 The Analysis of Options: A Method of Analyzing Real Problems

At this point it may seem that many problems lie in the way of applying the theory we have described. In this section we describe how these problems may be overcome. We shall describe a general procedure for analyzing quite large "realistic" problems. The procedure has already been sketched in Section 2.3 (see Figures 2.17 and 2.18). Here we give other examples and a more careful description.

The procedure is thoroughly practical. It is for use as follows. The "analyst" stands before an "audience" of persons with expert knowledge of the conflict problem being considered. Ideally, they should be involved in the problem as actual decision-makers. The analyst obtains from them various assumptions about the problem. From these assumptions a game-theoretic model is constructed and conclusions are deduced.

A computer may be used to help in handling the assumptions. Assumptions are made, one by one, and "fed into" a time-sharing terminal, which then "comes back" with the conclusions that follow from the assumptions made so far. This enables the whole exercise to be carried out in the mode of a discussion.

The "experts" really build and analyze their own model, guided by the analyst. The procedure is designed to be simple to understand, so that persons with no knowledge of mathematics or game theory can participate. A computer program for the analysis of options has been written by Stanley Monks and George Wileman of the Computer Usage Company, Philadelphia.

To start with, the analyst asks for a verbal list of the "issues" involved in the problem. In the case of an experimental analysis of the Vietnam problem, carried out in May 1968 (just prior to the Paris peace talks) by the author and members of the United States Arms Control and Disarmament Agency, this list of issues came out to be as follows:

1. U.S. bombing of North Vietnam (NVN).
2. U.S. military activity in South Vietnam.
3. U.S. withdrawal of most troops from Vietnam.
4. South Vietnamese Government (SVN) military activity in the South.
5. SVN willingness to accept a negotiated "settlement" of the conflict (implying some sharing of power with the NLF—i.e., the South Vietnamese Communists).
6. NVN military activity in the South.
7. NVN withdrawal from the South (involving the withdrawal of regular units and ceasing to infiltrate *men*, though possibly not supplies. The conception was that of a possible *quid pro quo* for U.S. withdrawal).

8. Military activity by the NLF in the South.

9. NLF willingness to accept the negotiated "settlement."

Each item in this list of issues usually contains a subject and a verb form such that the subject may be taken as a *player* in the game and the verb form may be taken as an *option* (a "yes/no" choice) open to that player. Thus from the list of issues a list of players and options may be formed, as on the left-hand side of Figure 5.2 for the Vietnam analysis.

It is not, of course, always as straightforward as here, where each option corresponds to a single item of the list. But with the exercise of some "art" and common sense it is usually possible to draw up a realistic list of options adequate to cover the issues—that is, adequate to represent the experts' view of the possibilities inherent in the problem situation.

The "settle" option for SVN and the NLF is defined to mean that if *both* choose to settle, there is a settlement; otherwise not.

A *strategy* for a particular player now appears as a subcolumn

U.S.
1. Cease Bombing   1   1
2. Cease-Fire   1   1
3. Withdraw   0   1

SVN
4. Cease-Fire   1   1
5. Settle   0   1

NVN
6. Cease-Fire   1   1
7. Withdraw   0   1

NLF
8. Cease-Fire   1   1
9. Settle   0   1

Figure 5.2. "Cease-Fire" and "Negotiated Settlement" Outcomes of the Vietnam Game.

of 1's and 0's, indicating which options that player decides to take. "1" represents "yes" (the option is taken) and "0" represents "no" (the option is not taken). Thus in Figure 5.2 the U.S. strategy in the first column is to cease hostilities but not to withdraw.

Note that this kind of simplification is probably warranted as representing the actual player's view of the situation. For example, the final U.S. decision as to whether to bomb North Vietnam probably was based on a simple dichotomy between "bomb" and "bomb to a negligible extent," as here represented by a yes/no option. We are in fact taking seriously the game-theoretic requirement that players must understand the game and applying it to mean that we must model the players' *subjective game*—the one and only game they do understand.

Our model is subjective also in another sense: we are modeling the view of the situation taken by the experts that are helping to build the model—in this case U.S. experts. This merely means that the analysis of options is a method for analyzing the assumptions of those whose knowledge is drawn upon—a necessary limitation.

Since a strategy for each player is a subcolumn of 1's and 0's, an *outcome* is a whole column, as in Figure 5.2, where the "cease-fire" and "negotiated settlement" outcomes are shown.

Essentially we have now built a model of the game in that we have defined *players, strategies,* and *outcomes.* Later we shall classify certain outcomes as "infeasible" when a player combines certain options that he cannot feasibly combine; for example, the United States cannot both withdraw and continue fighting. But apart from this, the problem now is to make assumptions about preferences.

To define a complete preference relation for each player over all feasible outcomes would be a tremendous task. How shall we proceed?

Observe that if we wish to answer one particular question about the game—for example, whether some particular outcome can be stable for some particular player—then we do not need to know all about the preferences of each player. Indeed, let us ask what are the minimum assumptions necessary in order to answer some particular question.

If we can discover beforehand what these minimum necessary assumptions are, then we can proceed by making only those assumptions. This will (a) save us the trouble of making many unnecessary assumptions and (b) give us valuable extra information in that it will tell us exactly which assumptions are responsible for our conclusions.

In general, then, we proceed to analyze the game sequentially. We first choose a particular outcome $\bar{s}$ for which we are interested in whether or not it can be stable. This means we should ask whether it can be reached as a result of some implicit or explicit agreement between the players or, more generally, whether it can be the final outcome after players have realized the truth about each other's strategy choice.

A particular outcome that concerned us in the case of Vietnam was the "negotiated settlement" in Figure 5.2. After analyzing the potential stability of this outcome, we can go on to analyze others.

Next, we choose a particular player i in order to ask whether $\bar{s}$ can be stable for i. Afterwards, we can ask the same question about other players. We recall that an outcome can be stable only if it can be stable for each player separately.

To decide whether $\bar{s}$ can be stable for i, we ask first whether it is rational for him. If it is, there is no need to go further: if the others continue to choose as they are choosing at $\bar{s}$, and if $\bar{s} \in R_i$, then certainly $\bar{s}$ will be stable for i.

Now $\bar{s} \in R_i$ if and only if

$$\forall s_i : (s_i, \bar{s}_{N-i}) \in M_i \bar{s},$$

or equivalently,

$$\sim \exists s_i : (s_i, \bar{s}_{N-i}) \in \tilde{M}_i \bar{s}.$$

The s_i here required not to exist may be called a *unilateral improvement* for player i: it is a strategy by which (if $\bar{s}_{N-i}$ remains fixed) i can improve his position. So first we make assumptions necessary to find all unilateral improvements (if any) for player i.

For this we need to take each s_i (each combination of i's options) and assign each outcome $(s_i, \bar{s}_{N-i})$ to one of three sets: the set I of outcomes judged to be infeasible (on the grounds that such an option

	Preferred by NVN	Particular Outcome $\bar{s}$	Not Preferred by NVN	Infeasible
U.S.				
1. Cease Bombing	1	1		1
2. Cease-Fire	1	1		1
3. Withdraw	1	1		1
SVN				
4. Cease-Fire	1	1		1
5. Settle	1	1		1
NVN				
6. Cease-Fire	–	1		0 ⎫
7. Withdraw	0	1		1 ⎭ Ω-set
NLF				
8. Cease-Fire	1	1		1
9. Withdraw	1	1		1

Unilateral
Improvements

Figure 5.3. NVN Unilateral Improvements. The symbol "–" stands for "either/ or," meaning the option may or may not be taken.

combination is impossible or not worth considering); the set $M_i\bar{s}$ of outcomes not preferred to $\bar{s}$; or the set $\tilde{M}_i\bar{s}$ of outcomes preferred to $\bar{s}$.

This is done in Figure 5.3, where we investigate unilateral improvements for NVN starting from a negotiated settlement. Here a *blank* (the symbol "–") stands for "either/or"—the option may or may not be taken. Thus the first column stands for a set of two outcomes, either of which is preferred by NVN to the particular outcome.

The analysis (here very simple) tells us that $\bar{s} \notin R_{NVN}$; but more than this, it gives a full explanation of this fact by listing all the unilateral improvements for NVN.

Note that this stage of the analysis is complete when every combination of the options in a certain set, labeled the "Ω-set" in Figure 5.3, has been included in some column of the tableau.

The content of the assumptions in Figure 5.3 is quite straightforward: by not withdrawing as required under the settlement, NVN
could reach a preferred position assuming the others did not react.
Also it is impossible for them to withdraw and at the same time
continue fighting; this is shown in the column assigned to "infeasible."
These two assumptions complete the Ω-set.

Having discovered that $\bar{s} \notin R_{\text{NVN}}$, we still do not know that $\bar{s}$ cannot
be stable for NVN. We have seen theoretically and experimentally
that $\bar{s}$ can still be stable for i provided that $\bar{s} \in \hat{R}_{\text{NVN}}(H)$ for some metagame H. We investigate this next.

First we investigate whether $\bar{s}$ is symmetric metarational for i
(NVN). If it is, then we need go no further; for certainly then it is
general metarational for i.

Now $\bar{s}$ is symmetric metarational for i if and only if

$$\exists s^{*}_{N-i} \, \forall s_i : (s^{*}_{N-i}, s_i) \in M_i \bar{s}.$$

The s^{*}_{N-i} here required to exist may be called a *sanction* against i.
It is a joint strategy of the other players such that, should they
carry it out, i cannot in any way reach a position preferred to $\bar{s}$.
Thus if i believes that a sanction would be applied if he moved away
from $\bar{s}$, he will not move away.

Our task is then to make assumptions necessary to determine all
the sanctions (if any) that exist against i.

To do this we need to take each s^{*}_{N-i} (each combination of the
other players' options) and write it in a column assigned again to
one of three sets: I (the set of infeasibles); $M_i \bar{s}$; or $\tilde{M}_i \bar{s}$. Figure 5.4
shows how this is done for an analysis of the sanctions against NVN
for a settlement.

In Figure 5.4, the "Ω-set" is now the set of options open to the
players other than the NVN, since this is now the set of options of
which all combinations have to be listed to complete this stage of the
analysis; for we must consider each joint strategy s_{N-i} of these
players. Now concerning each combination of Ω-options one of
three things is true. The combination may be infeasible and can be
listed in the infeasible set with all blanks against player i's options.
This is done in Figure 5.4 with all combinations in which the United

	Preferred by NVN	Particular Outcome $\bar{s}$	Not Preferred by NVN	Infeasible
U.S.				
1. Cease Bombing	1	1	–	0
2. Cease-Fire	1	1	0	1
3. Withdraw	1	1	0	–
SVN				
4. Cease-Fire	1	1	0	–
5. Settle	–	1	0	–
NVN				
6. Cease-Fire	0	1	–	– Ω-set
7. Withdraw	0	1	–	
NLF				
8. Cease-Fire	–	1	–	–
9. Settle	–	1	–	–

Sanctions

Figure 5.4. Assumptions for Sanctions against NVN.

States adopts a cease-fire in the South but does not cease bombing the North (though physically possible, this was thought not worth considering). Second, the combination may represent a feasible s^{*}_{N-i} that is a sanction, when it can be listed in the not-preferred set $M_i\bar{s}$ again with all blanks against i's options. For writing it thus with blanks is merely saying that

$$\forall s_i : (s^{*}_{N-i}, s_i) \in M_i\bar{s}.$$

This is done in Figure 5.4 with all Ω-combinations in which the United States fires and does not withdraw and SVN fires and refuses to settle, it being assumed that all feasible outcomes containing this combination will be not preferred by NVN to the settlement.[3] Or

3. Actually, a "settlement" was *defined* to be such that it would be preferred by NVN to continued fighting, it having been found in a pilot study that no other kind of settlement had a chance of stability.

finally, the only third possibility is that the combination represents a feasible s_{N-i}^* that cannot be written as a sanction, in which case it can be written in the "preferred" set $\tilde{M}_i\tilde{s}$ with some fixed combination of i's options. This is done in Figure 5.4 with all Ω-combinations in which the United States withdraws and ceases fighting and SVN does not fight, the assumption being that in this case NVN can guarantee itself a preferred outcome by fighting and not withdrawing.

We note that when blanks are written in a "preferred" or "not preferred" assumption, it is not implied that every way of filling in these blanks is feasible but merely that there is some feasible way of filling them in.

Another comment: it might seem that we are making rather bold, general assumptions in writing "preferred" or "not preferred" columns containing large numbers of blanks, as in Figure 5.4. In practice, the best way of making assumptions is to "try out" bold assumptions, containing many blanks, which are subjected to critical discussion before being finally entered. The discussion, in the case of a "preferred" assumption, aims at trying to fill in the blanks so as to make the column "not preferred," if possible; in the case of a "not preferred" assumption, the aim is to fill in the blanks so as to make the column "preferred." If an assumption survives these critical efforts, it is accepted.

We have said that the current stage of analysis is complete when all "Ω-combinations" (combinations of Ω-options) have been listed. (The word "Ω-set" is merely an arbitrary term for a set of options, found at each stage of the analysis, which has the property that all combinations in the set must be examined.) The reader may see therefore that the stage illustrated in Figure 5.4 is not complete, since not all Ω-combinations have been listed. Figure 5.5 shows those that remain.

These Ω-combinations that currently remain to be considered constitute what we call the current *residual*. The computer will recalculate the current residual after each assumption is put in. When there is no residual left, the computer will state that the analysis is complete.

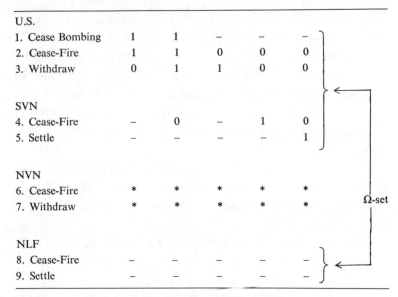

U.S.					
1. Cease Bombing	1	1	–	–	–
2. Cease-Fire	1	1	0	0	0
3. Withdraw	0	1	1	0	0
SVN					
4. Cease-Fire	–	0	–	1	0
5. Settle	–	–	–	–	1
NVN					
6. Cease-Fire	*	*	*	*	*
7. Withdraw	*	*	*	*	*
NLF					
8. Cease-Fire	–	–	–	–	–
9. Settle	–	–	–	–	–

Ω-set

Figure 5.5. Residual for Sanctions against NVN after Three Assumptions Have Been Entered.

	P	N	P	N	I	P	N	I
U.S.								
1. Cease Bombing	1	1	1	1	–	–	–	–
2. Cease-Fire	1	1	1	1	0	0	0	0
3. Withdraw	0	0	1	1	1	0	0	0
SVN								
4. Cease-Fire	–	–	0	0	–	1	1	0
5. Settle	–	–	–	–	–	–	–	1
NVN								
6. Cease-Fire	0	–	0	–	–	0	–	–
7. Withdraw	0	–	0	–	–	0	–	–
NLF								
8. Cease-Fire	0	1	0	1	–	0	1	–
9. Settle	–	–	–	–	–	–	–	–

Figure 5.6. Further Assumptions for Sanctions against NVN. The letters "P", "N", and "I" stand for "preferred," "not preferred," and "infeasible."

To complete this stage of the analysis, therefore, the Ω-combinations in the residual must be assigned in one of the three ways: to "infeasible," with blanks against player i's options; to "not preferred," with blanks against i's options; or to "preferred," with some combination against i's options. A set of assumptions sufficient to achieve this is shown in Figure 5.6. Here the assumptions are the following:

a. If the United States ceased military activity but did not withdraw (first column of the residual), it was assumed that this would constitute a sanction if at the same time the NLF ceased military activity. If the NLF continued to fight, however, then the North Vietnamese could reach a preferred outcome by fighting and not withdrawing. These assumptions are shown in the first two columns of Figure 5.6.

b. If the United States ceased military activity and withdrew while SVN continued to fight (second column of residual), the assumption again was that this would be a sanction if and only if the NLF gave up fighting (third and fourth columns of Figure 5.6). The third column of the residual was obviously "infeasible" (fifth column of Figure 5.6).

c. The fourth column of the residual, in which the United States continued fighting while SVN gave up, was perhaps "far fetched" from the U.S. point of view, but might well seem a possibility to the North Vietnamese. It too was seen as a sanction if and only if the NLF "gave up." The last column of the residual was regarded as "infeasible" on the grounds that SVN should not be considered as "willing to settle" unless it had agreed to a cease-fire.

Clearly at this point the residual has been exhausted, and so this stage of the analysis is complete. Logical manipulations performed on the vectors of 1's and 0's now enable the preference assumptions that have been made to be reexpressed as in Figure 5.7. Here the preference assumptions have been written with as many blanks as possible—a representation that seems to be the most informative of the many equivalent ways of writing a set of assumptions.

From Figures 5.3 and 5.7, the conclusions from the analysis so far may be summed up as follows: (a) From Figure 5.3, in the absence of credible sanctions, NVN will not keep to the settlement. (b) From

	Preferred by NVN			Particular Outcome $\tilde{z}$	Not Preferred			
U.S.								
1. Cease-Bombing	–	–	–	1	–	–	–	
2. Cease-Fire	–	1	–	1	0	–	–	
3. Withdraw	1	–	–	1	–	0	–	
SVN								
4. Cease-Fire	1	–	1	1	0	–	0	
5. Settle	–	–	–	1	–	–	–	
NVN								
6. Cease-Fire	0	0	0	1	–	–	–	
7. Withdraw	0	0	0	1	–	–	–	Ω-set
NLF								
8. Cease-Fire	1	0	0	1	–	1	1	
9. Settle	–	–	–	1	–	–	–	

Sanctions

Figure 5.7. Sanctions against North Vietnam for a Settlement.

Figure 5.7, possible sanctions are that if NVN departed from the settlement

i. the United States *and* SVN would resume fighting;

ii. the United States would not withdraw and the NLF would cease fighting;

iii. SVN would continue fighting while the NLF would cease.

Note that it is because the sanctions have been expressed as in Figure 5.7, using maximal numbers of blanks, that this simple description of them is found to be possible.

Now clearly the method we are using only tells us all the sanctions that exist against NVN. It does not tell us whether these sanctions might be *credible*—that is, whether NVN is likely to believe that the others' metagame policies are such that these sanctions would be carried out. It cannot tell us this because (this being the theory of metarational outcomes) no assumptions about the other players' preferences are relevant; yet clearly these are highly relevant to the question of credibility.

Credibility must therefore be estimated on extratheoretic grounds. In our example, the first sanction might be credible provided the United States had not already withdrawn from South Vietnam. If U.S. troops had actually been withdrawn, however, it might not seem credible to NVN that they would return. In this case, only the third sanction would remain. This too is not very credible, but it does tell us that if the NLF wishes to keep to the settlement, it would have a means of exerting pressure on NVN.

At this point we have completed two stages of the analysis. We have found that a negotiated settlement is not rational for NVN but is symmetric metarational. This means that it can be stable for them provided they find certain sanctions credible—a matter that has to be judged on extratheoretic grounds.

Since the particular outcome $\tilde{s}$ is symmetric metarational for NVN, it is also general metarational, and therefore a third stage in which we would investigate this is unnecessary (as the second stage would have been had we found in the first stage that $\tilde{s}$ was rational). The analysis of the stability of the settlement outcome from the NVN viewpoint is therefore complete.

Next, the same outcome can be analyzed from the viewpoints of other players—or from the viewpoints of coalitions of players, which may be treated exactly like individual players. Their preferences, we recall, are defined by saying that a coalition prefers an outcome only if every member of the coalition prefers it.

Having finished analyzing the stability of this particular outcome, one can go on to analyze other outcomes. The total procedure is like exploring a large, dark warehouse with a small flashlight. We have to select, one after the other, various small parts of the game to examine, since the whole game is too large to examine at once. Also, many parts of the game are quite uninteresting, so that the area to be explored has to be chosen with some skill if the analysis is to be at all useful. Exploration of one part of the game may give clues as to which other parts would be interesting to explore.

In the case of the Vietnam analysis, it was found that the negotiated settlement could be stable, but from the viewpoint of credibility it seemed unlikely that it would be. For stability, the Communist players had to believe that if the settlement were not accepted, the United States would stay in Vietnam. Probably, on the contrary, the Communists believed that, even if there were no settlement, the United States would withdraw sooner or later.

In addition, we also found the difficulty we have discussed above in connection with metaequilibria—the "policy dilemma" for the United States that for the settlement to be accepted, the South Vietnamese would have to believe that otherwise the United States would withdraw whereas the Communists had to believe that otherwise the United States would not withdraw.[4]

The Vietnam analysis is given in more detail in Howard (1968b). Here we conclude this section by using another example to illustrate the analysis of (a) coalition metarationality and (b) general metarationality.

Can game theory be used to analyze a work of art? Let us see what can be done along these lines. We take as our example Harold Pinter's play *The Caretaker*. Let us review the plot.

Aston is a solitary man in his early thirties, who apparently has suffered brain damage from electric-shock treatment authorized by his family. Mick, his younger brother, apparently feeling guilty about this, has bought a London house in which he has installed Aston; Aston will fix up the house but he does this work very slowly.

One night Aston brings back Davies, an old, embittered tramp, whom he invites to stay until he (Davies) can sort out his life. The tramp agrees, suspiciously. This is the first act.

In the second act Mick appears; he torments and bullies the old man, but, discovering that Aston has suggested that Davies stay on as "caretaker," he suddenly changes his tune. He pretends to respect Davies, asks his advice concerning Aston's slowness, and as owner of the house says he will himself hire Davies as caretaker. Davies is taken in by this.

4. This analysis was conducted in May 1968; since then the Vietnam problem has no doubt changed a great deal. The analysis may be regarded as illuminating the difficulties faced in 1968 by Averell Harriman; it is now (in 1971) of historical interest.

In the third act Davies turns against Aston, whom he now despises as "queer in the head"; but when Aston is thereby driven to turn Davies out, and Davies appeals to Mick, Mick withdraws support, torments him again, and pays him off with half-a-dollar. Bereaved of support, Davies goes back and appeals to Aston, but in vain. He will have to leave.

The issues are the relationships between the actors. Will Aston and/or Mick give Davies psychological as well as material support and respect? Or will Mick, who can be a bully, torment and bully the old man? Will Davies, in return, be loyal to Aston or to Mick?

The actors' preferences are fairly clear. Aston wants to support Davies, in return for a relationship in which he, Aston, will be treated as "normal"—not mentally defective. Davies wants support and respect from either brother, but preferably from Mick. Mick would like neither brother to support Davies or have his loyalty, but if necessary would rather he alone had this relationship with Davies than that Aston should have it.

The play may be regarded as a "reaction game" in which the players move from one outcome to another, jockeying for position. The players and options may be listed as in Figure 5.8. Davies's

	Preferred by Davies and Aston	Particular Outcome $\bar{s}$	Not Preferred by Davies or Aston	
Davies				
Nor.A	1	0	0	–
Loy.A	–	0	–	–
Loy.M	–	0	–	–
Aston				
Sup.D.	1	0	–	0
Mick				
Sup.D.	–	0	0	0
Per.D	–	0	0	1

Figure 5.8. Inescapable Improvements for Coalition of Aston and Davies in *The Caretaker*, Act 1.

options are: to treat Aston as normal; to be loyal to Aston; to be loyal to Mick. Aston has the single option of supporting Davies. Mick can support Davies or persecute him.

In the first act, Davies and Aston move from the particular outcome "no relationships" (central column in Figure 5.8) to one of the improvements shown in Figure 5.8. The analysis here is one that asks whether the particular outcome is general metarational for this coalition.

Now $\bar{s}$ is general metarational for C if and only if

$$\sim \exists s_C^* \ \forall s_{N-C} : (s_C^*, s_{N-C}) \in \tilde{M}_C \bar{s}$$

and the s_C^* here required not to exist may be called an *inescapable improvement* for the coalition. It is an improvement that remains better than $\bar{s}$ for all players in C, regardless of what reaction is forthcoming from those not in C. Hence in order to test for general metarationality, we look for all inescapable improvements (if any) as in Figure 5.8. We do this by choosing as our Ω-set the set of options open to C, just as we did when looking for unilateral improvements (Figure 5.3); but now each feasible Ω-combination must be assigned either to "preferred" with all blanks against the options of $N-C$ or to "not preferred" with some entry against the options of $N-C$.[5] In the first case the Ω-combination is an inescapable improvement, in the second case it is not. The analysis is thus similar to the analysis when looking for sanctions, the difference being that "preferred" becomes "not preferred" and "C" becomes "$N-C$."

In Figure 5.8, an improvement is assumed to exist even if Mick persecutes Davies. Mick's persecution of Davies at the beginning of act 2 may in fact be interpreted as an attempt to overthrow this improvement. However, when Aston intervenes to protect Davies, Mick realizes that persecution will not suffice to make the outcome "not preferred" by the Aston-Davies coalition. Mick then changes his tactic. (In Figure 5.8 the first "not preferred" column is, of course, not preferred by Aston, while the second is not preferred by Davies.)

Figure 5.8 thus shows that $\bar{s}$ is not general metarational for the coalition, and it is clear from the technique that therefore it cannot

5. There might also be infeasibilities, but here none are relevant.

be rational for the coalition (i.e., a unilateral improvement must exist) and cannot be symmetric metarational either (no sanction can exist). This is what we have already seen to follow from Theorem 1. As for interpreting the result, recall that whereas an inescapable improvement for an individual player must be taken, if one exists, this is not so for a coalition: an outcome is definitely unstable if it is not general metarational for an individual, but it may be stable even though it fails to be general metarational for a coalition.

In the second act Mick sets up a coalition with the tramp, Davies. They start from the particular outcome in Figure 5.9, where Mick is persecuting the tramp, who, while not loyal toward Aston, treats him as "normal" and is supported by him. From this position the coalition of Mick and Davies has a number of inescapable improvements as shown. We suppose that an improvement is guaranteed for Mick provided Davies does not treat Aston as normal (for Mick is probably jealous of his brother's need for the tramp); and for Davies an improvement is guaranteed provided Mick gives him support. It is assumed to be infeasible for Davies to be loyal to Aston without treating him as "normal," or for Mick to support Davies and persecute him also.

	Preferred by Davies and Mick	Particular Outcome $\tilde{s}$	Not Preferred by Davies or Mick		Infeasible		
Davies							
Nor.A	0	1	1	–	0	– ⎫	
Loy.A	–	0	–	–	1	– ⎬ ←	
Loy.M	–	0	–	–	–	– ⎭	
Aston							
Sup.D.	–	1	1	0	–	–	Ω-set
Mick							
Sup.D.	1	0	–	0	–	1 ⎫	
Per.D	–	1	–	–	–	1 ⎬ ←	

Figure 5.9. Inescapable Improvements for Mick and Davies in The Caretaker, Act 2.

	Preferred by Aston and Mick	Particular Outcome $\check{s}$	Not Preferred by Aston or Mick	
Davies				
Nor.A	–	0	1	0
Loy.A	–	0	1	0
Loy.M	–	1	0	1
Aston				
Sup.D	0	1	1	–
Mick				
Sup.D	0	1	–	1
Per.D	–	0	–	–

(The Aston Sup.D, Mick Sup.D, and Per.D rows are grouped by a brace labelled Ω-set.)

Figure 5.10. Inescapable Improvements for Aston and Mick in *The Caretaker*, Act 3.

Mick and Davies take their inescapable improvement, leading at the beginning of act 3 to the particular outcome shown in Figure 5.10. This is probably the best possible outcome for Davies, but it is short-lived. There is now an inescapable improvement for the coalition of the two brothers if both cease to give support to Davies, as shown in Figure 5.10. (In Figure 5.10 the first column on the "not preferred" side is not preferred by Mick; the second is not preferred by Aston.)

In the end, the outcome "no relationships" with which the play began, is apparently stable, though in act 1, it was not stable against the coalition of Aston and Davies. This coalition will not now form, however, as Aston will no longer trust Davies, despite Davies's offer to go further than before and be loyal to Aston. Davies says, after proposing a rearrangement of beds to suit Aston: "... and then we could get down to what we was saying, I'd look after the place for you, for you, like, not for the other ... not for ... for your brother, you see, not for him, for you, I'll be your man, you say the word, just say the word ...."

Pause.
DAVIES. What do you think of this I'm saying?

Pause.
ASTON. No. I like sleeping in this bed.
DAVIES. But you don't understand my meaning![6]

This meaning is that the two of them have an inescapable improvement. But Aston cannot now believe that Davies would treat him as normal, let alone be loyal, if he were to give Davies support once more. He does not believe, that is to say, that Davies can be trusted to be {Aston, Davies}-cooperative.

The Caretaker is almost classically austere and simple from a game-theoretic point of view. It has three characters and three acts, in each of which one of the three possible two-person coalitions negotiates, forms, and achieves its ends. The circularity of the whole process, whereby the final outcome is the same as the first, may be seen to arise from the fact that the α-core is empty, as in the game of "split the dollar" discussed in Section 5.2: starting from any outcome, a coalition of two of the players can achieve an inescapable improvement at the expense of the third player. It is therefore appropriate that when the curtain falls Davies has not actually left; we cannot be sure that Aston will not accept his offered renewal of their coalition causing the three acts to be repeated in sequence again and again.

To sum up, the analysis of options technique starts with a list of issues and from this defines the players and their options. Then outcomes are taken one at a time and their stability examined from the viewpoint of one player (or coalition) at a time. In doing this, separate investigations are made of rationality (looking for unilateral improvements), symmetric metarationality (looking for sanctions), and general metarationality (looking for inescapable improvements).

Computationally, the only problems are calculating the residual of the Ω-set so as systematically to exhaust all Ω-combinations and calculating the "generalized form" of the assumptions made so as to reexpress these in the strongest and most informative way. A real-time computer system may be used for these computations, not because the calculations cannot be done by hand, but because leaving them to the machine helps to maintain continuity of discussion during the process of building the model.

6. Harold Pinter, *The Caretaker* (London: Methuen and Co., 1960), p. 80.

If we accept that real-life players actually see themselves confronted with a rather small and simple set of options, models large enough to be realistic can be analyzed in this way. However, this is only possible because small, selected areas of the game are examined; to examine the whole of a realistic game is still usually impractical. Hence skill and intuition must be used in preselecting those parts of the game it is useful to analyze—even in addition to the intuitive skill and constant exercise of common sense needed in all successful model building.

We have not discussed the special requirements of analyzing the plot of a work of fiction. Clearly it is necessary that the actions analyzed be actions that would, or might, actually be taken by real people in the given situation; if the actions are symbolic, or otherwise nonrealistic, the approach makes no sense. Even then, the analysis is interesting only from this realistic point of view. Game theory is about real people, not about certain authors' representations of real people; so that unless these are within limits the same, game theory is inapplicable. Another difficulty is that skillful authors often conceal certain essential motivations of their characters in order to reproduce the mystery we often feel in real life as to why people behave in the way they do.

6
Knowledge
of Others'
Preferences

6.1 Special Types of Games

In this chapter we shall deal our final blow to the concept of rationality—even (what we have failed to do so far) to the concept of metarationality. Our positive theory of metarationality is not overthrown, but we shall find that even metarationality will not bear the constructions we are intuitively inclined to place upon it.

We begin quietly enough, however. We intend to look at the question, What difference does it make if we assume players that know each other's preferences? We should say that we do not think this question has yet really been answered, so that what follows is in the mode of notes for future research.

The question turns out to be connected with the question, What can we say if we assume a game that has a more special structure than the general (reflexive) game? That is, it turns out that the additional things that can be said if we assume (let us say) an ordinal game are things that concern players that know each other's preferences.

Hence in this section we begin by describing certain special types of games.

We have already defined and discussed partly ordinal and ordinal games. These are interesting because they model decision-makers that are either coalitions of "reasonable," "consistent" actors or are themselves "reasonable" and "consistent" in their preferences.

We shall also discuss a type of ordinal game we call *mutually ordinal*. In these games, a player is never indifferent between two outcomes unless all players are indifferent.

This is interesting because it is realistic: a player is likely to obey this rule, since the mere fact of other players having preferences between two outcomes is likely to induce preferences in him—either in line with or against the preferences of the others.

To see this, it is sufficient to point out that it would be next to impossible to set up an experimental ordinal game that was not mutually ordinal. In experiments, subjects are usually paid different amounts of money according to the outcome in order to give them the desired preferences. To make sure that this does give them the right preferences is hard enough, as altruism, competitiveness, and so on, may cause their preferences to be at variance with monetary considerations. Hence it would be foolhardy to try to make a subject indifferent between two outcomes unless all the others were also;[1] for the tiniest amount of altruism or competitiveness would suffice to overthrow such indifference.

This suggests the research question, Are there strategic reasons for a player to prefer or not to prefer a certain outcome preferred or not preferred by others? If so, can we build a theory to predict these preference changes? Indeed, suppose that by altering his preferences, a player can change the game so as to better his own chances. Will there not be a tendency for him to do so?

In the case when initially he is indifferent, the existence of this tendency would mean that a change takes place with certainty; in other cases, it would sometimes take place, sometimes not. This might be called a theory of "preference deterioration."

We shall discuss the possibility of such a theory in our last section. In the meantime, this consideration gives us an added reason to think that in the end most real-life ordinal games will be mutually ordinal.

Formally, a game is *mutually ordinal* if it is ordinal and also satisfies the condition

$$(\exists i : M_i s \supset M_i t) \Rightarrow (\forall i : M_i s \neq M_i t).$$

NOTE. We recall that in an ordinal game, "$s \in M_i t$" is equivalent to "$M_i s \subseteq M_i t$," and "$s \in \tilde{M}_i t$" is equivalent to "$M_i s \supset M_i t$"; that is, in these games the subset relation "$\subseteq$" between not-preferred sets behaves just like the less-than-or-equal-to relation "$\leqslant$" between

1. The only exception would be under these experimental conditions: a one-shot game is played; subjects are given wrong information about each other's payoffs and are not allowed to communicate or interact before making their choices. (To give them no information and forbid them to interact would be useless, as they would then have no basis on which to predict the others' choices, and no way of measuring stability would exist.)

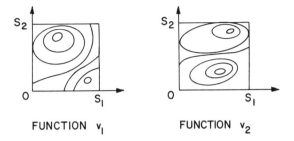

FUNCTION v_1 FUNCTION v_2

Figure 6.1. Contour Lines Representing Numerical Payoffs of Two Players for a Game on the Unit Square.

numerical preferences. "$M_i s = M_i t$" simply means that i is *indifferent* between s and t.

An interesting fact about mutually ordinal games is that infinite games with numerical payoffs will normally fail to be mutually ordinal. For example, a two-person numerical game on the unit square with continuous payoff functions v_1, v_2 will usually be representable as in Figure 6.1, where the "contour lines" of the functions v_1 and v_2 are shown. These contour lines, like the contour lines on a map, show sets of points at which the function v_i is of uniform height—that is, each contour line represents a set of points between which player i is indifferent. This means that in a mutually ordinal game the contour lines of the two players must coincide. Normally this will imply that player 1 prefers the outcomes either in the same order as player 2 or else in the inverse order. But these are two very special and rather uninteresting cases. (The second, we shall see in a moment, is the case of a two-person zero-sum game.)

In fact, without going into this rigorously, it soon becomes clear that *analytic* games with numerical payoffs (games, usually infinite, that have mathematically tractable payoff functions) will scarcely ever be mutually ordinal.

Yet we have argued that in practice realistic games are almost all mutually ordinal; so much so that it seems impossible to set up experimentally any game that is not.

We seem to face a desperate gap between mathematical convenience and realism. The gap, however, is easily bridged if we introduce so-called lexicographic payoff functions.

A *lexicographic payoff function* v_i is a sequence $v_i = (v_i^1, \ldots, v_i^m)$ of payoff functions, the interpretation of which is that s is preferred to t

if $v_i^1(s) > v_i^1(t)$;
or $v_i^1(s) = v_i^1(t), v_i^2(s) > v_i^2(t)$;

$\ldots$;

or $v_i^1(s) = v_i^1(t), \ldots, v_i^{k-1}(s) = v_i^{k-1}(t), v_i^k(s) > v_i^k(t)$;

$\ldots$;

or $v_i^1(s) = v_i^1(t), \ldots, v_i^{m-1}(s) = v^{m-1}(t), v_i^m(s) > v_i^m(t)$;

so that in effect the v_i^k's are taken in a priority ordering, v_i^k having no effect unless each $v_i^j (j<k)$ is unable to discriminate between the outcomes s and t.

The word "lexicographic" is used because the process of determining preferences is similar to the process of looking up words in a dictionary.

Our suggestion is to use lexicographic functions to model the fact that, though player i's "own" payoffs $v_i(s)$ may have greatest priority for him, nevertheless he will be influenced, lexicographically, by the others' payoffs whenever his "own" payoffs v_i would reveal indifference. Thus if we find ourselves using nice analytic functions $v_1, \ldots, v_n$ with which to model an n-person game, the suggestion is to improve the model by introducing lexicographic functions $\bar{v}_i$ of the form

$$\bar{v}_i = (v_i, \pm v_{j_1}, \ldots, \pm v_{j_{n-1}}),$$

where $j_1, \ldots, j_{n-1}$ is some ordering of the players $N - \{i\}$, an ordering that represents the importance to player i of the payoffs accruing to the other players, and each v_{j_k} is preceded by a plus or minus sign according to whether player i feels friendly or antagonistic to player j_k. This will change the game to a mutually ordinal game that will, we feel, be somewhat more realistic than the original game.

To illustrate, suppose that in modeling an arms race between the United States and the Soviets, the United States is given the numerical payoff function

$$v_{\text{U.S.}}(a_{\text{U.S.}}, a_{\text{SOV}}) = f\left(\frac{a_{\text{U.S.}}}{a_{\text{SOV}}}\right) - g(a_{\text{U.S.}}),$$

where $a_{\text{U.S.}}$, a_{SOV} are the armament levels of the two sides, f is a function representing U.S. security as a function of the arms ratio, and g represents cost to the United States as a function of U.S. armaments. Then the suggestion is that this payoff function is likely to be unrealistic precisely at the point where it may state that two situations are indifferent to the United States, even though the Soviets suffer more at one than at the other. The suggestion would be to amend it by writing the lexicographic function.

$$\bar{v}_{\text{U.S.}} = (v_{\text{U.S.}}, -v_{\text{SOV}}),$$

indicating that under such circumstances the United States would prefer the outcome not preferred by the Soviets. The result, if this were done for both sides, would be to create a mutually ordinal game.

The other special type of game we shall discuss will be the *two-person zero-sum game.*

This is necessarily mutually ordinal. It describes a completely competitive situation in which there is no possibility of cooperation, because whatever is gained by one player is necessarily lost by the other.

We can set up our formal definition as follows. Any preference function M_i will have a unique *inverse* M_i^{-1}, defined as the preference function M_i^{-1} such that

$$s \in M_i^{-1}t \Leftrightarrow t \in M_i s$$

or, equivalently,

$$s \in \tilde{M}_i^{-1}t \Leftrightarrow t \in \tilde{M}_i s,$$

where, of course, $\tilde{M}_i^{-1}$ is the *complement* of M_i^{-1}, that is, the function defined by $\tilde{M}_i^{-1}s \equiv S - M_i^{-1}s$.

These inverse preferences M_i^{-1} and $\tilde{M}_i^{-1}$ are the exact opposite of player i's preferences M_i and $\tilde{M}_i$: s is preferred to t if and only if i prefers t to s. If M_i is ordinal, M_i^{-1} is ordinal also, but the ordering is the reverse ordering to that given by M_i. One who has the preferences M_i^{-1} is the worst enemy (as far as motivation goes) that i could possibly have.

Now a *two-person zero-sum* game is defined as a two-person ordinal game $G = (S_1, S_2; M_1, M_2)$ in which we have

$$M_1 = M_2^{-1}$$

(and hence also $M_2 = M_1^{-1}$). That is, it is a game in which each player's motivation is solely to "harm" the other player. (The reader may show that such a game must be *mutually* ordinal.)

The results obtainable here are extremely strong. But the condition is not at all realistic. It is hard to think of any real-life situation satisfying this condition apart from artificial conflicts such as parlor games and sporting events.

It is sometimes thought that military conflicts should qualify; but even in a battle, both sides normally prefer exactly the same final strategic balance to be achieved with fewer casualties on both sides rather than more, so that not even war is zero-sum.

Why then should we be interested in such a hypothetical condition? Because there is an influential body of misleading, intuitive, common-sense folklore about conflict situations that can be called "the zero-sum mentality." It consists of general statements about conflict that are not generally true except in two-person zero-sum games.

This folklore is influential because—unlike, for example, the New Testament attitude toward conflict—it is regarded as hard-headed, tough-minded, and realistic. But it is false and misleading, and the direction in which it misleads is peculiarly unfortunate, since it causes people to behave as if their interests were more opposed (i.e., more zero-sum) than they actually are. Our interest in two-person zero-sum games, then, is in investigating a number of generally accepted bromides, which, it is important to realize, are usually untrue.

It is indeed hard to exaggerate the threat posed by an approach based on the two-person zero-sum game, particularly when it is armed by modern weapons. Whence does it arise? One source may be parlor games and sports, which (we repeat) are virtually the only area in which the zero-sum approach is appropriate, yet which are used from the earliest age to train people in conflict behavior.

Also used for training are so-called war games and business games. These are used to train generals and businessmen for their respective non-zero-sum pursuits. They are generally set up so that each participant's motive is to do better than the other participants; that is, in the two-person case they are set up as two-person zero-sum games, so that, again, the wrong approach toward the real world is instilled.

But a deeper cause than these may be the concept of rationality we have discussed before—the idea that "obviously," given one's preferences, one should choose the course of action that will optimize those preferences in the given situation; for as we shall see, in two-person zero-sum games this concept does not suffer from many of the defects we have found it to possess in the general case. In two-person zero-sum games rationality is, to a large extent, "saved"; and this is probably the basic reason why the zero-sum mentality appears to so many to be the hardheaded, "practical" approach and why decision-makers resort to distortions of the reality they are faced with rather than abandon this approach.

It is indeed, a rational approach in the limited sense we have specified: it is "irrational" only in that it is erroneous, illogical, and mutually destructive.

6.2 Ordinal Games: Saddle Points

Having now defined the various special types of games in which we are interested, we proceed to develop their special characteristics. In this section we discuss ordinal and partly ordinal games.

The problem posed by the prisoner's dilemma game is essentially that there exists an outcome that is not a (basic) equilibrium and that nevertheless *dominates* such an equilibrium (that is, all players prefer it to a basic equilibrium). This is the essence of the second breakdown of rationality.

We now point out that in a partly ordinal game this cannot happen with general equilibria, metaequilibria, or symmetric equilibria. Indeed, it is easy to see from Theorem 1 that the following is true:

Theorem 4

In a partly ordinal game, if s is metarational for i from a complete metagame H and if i prefers s^* to s, then s^* is also metarational for i from H. Hence if s is a metagame equilibrium from a complete metagame H, and s^* dominates s, then s^* is also a metagame equilibrium from H. Hence also if s is a general (respectively symmetric) equilibrium, and s^* dominates s, s^* is also a general (respectively symmetric) equilibrium; and if s is a metagame equilibrium from any H (not necessarily complete), and s^* dominates s, then s^* is a metagame equilibrium from some descendant of H.

Also from Theorem 1 we see that this can be strengthened in the ordinal case as follows:

Theorem 5

In an ordinal game, if s is metarational for i from a complete metagame H and if s^* is preferred-or-indifferent to s, then s^* is also metarational for i from H. Hence if s is a metagame equilibrium from H and s^* either weakly dominates[2] s or is indifferent to s for all players, then s^* is also a metagame equilibrium from H. Hence also the general (respectively symmetric) equilibria include all outcomes that either weakly dominate or are indifferent for all players to a general (respectively symmetric) equilibrium; and the descendants of any H (not necessarily complete) yield as metagame equilibria all outcomes that either weakly dominate or are indifferent for all players to some metagame equilibrium from H.

Because of the above we can say that in the metagame tree, the second breakdown of rationality is "solved"; it cannot occur in a complete metagame based on a partly ordinal game.

But we have also seen that the first breakdown of rationality (the fact that an equilibrium may not exist) is likewise "solved" by going to the metagame tree. Every complete metagame based on a (finite) partly ordinal game, possesses an equilibrium. (Recall that we regard the finite case as being "typical" when we consider questions of existence.)

Thus far, therefore, we have in a sense "rescued" rationality. But this state of affairs will not last; we shall find that not even a complete metagame is exempt from our third breakdown.

Next, we may draw from Theorem 4 a corollary concerning the *modus operandi* of a coalition C.

Suppose $\bar{x}$ is an outcome of H that makes an outcome $\bar{s}$ i-metarational for some player $i \in C$, even though $\bar{s}$ is not C-metarational; that is,

---

2. An outcome s^* *weakly* dominates s if no player prefers s and at least one player prefers s^*.

$\beta^* \bar{x} = \bar{s}$; $\quad \bar{x} \in R_i(H)$; $\quad \bar{s} \notin \hat{R}_C(H)$;

so that in fact $\bar{x}_{N-i}$ is a non-C-cooperative anticipation for player i. We have suggested that under these circumstances player i, if he is to continue to operate as a member of the coalition, must attempt to persuade the other members of C to abandon $\bar{s}$ in favor of another outcome $s' = \beta^*(\bar{x}_{N-C}, x_C')$ that is better for all of them (and that does exist).

But how is he to persuade them? Well, first, we may assume that $\bar{s}$ is (j, H)-metarational for all $j \in C$. Otherwise he will not be able to persuade all $j \in C$ of the danger of ending up at $\bar{s}$. Second, we assume that all members of C can agree on the coalition anticipation $\bar{x}_{N-C}$; so that in fact $\bar{s}$ must be $(j, H(\bar{x}_{N-C}))$-metarational for all $j \in C$— where $H(\bar{x}_{N-C})$ stands for the *submetagame* formed by *fixing* the metastrategy x_{N-C} at the constant value $\bar{x}_{N-C}$.

But given the above, it follows from Theorem 4 that in the partly ordinal case, the players in C can, starting from $H(\bar{x}_{N-C})$, form among themselves a submetagame

$H' = j_1 \ldots j_m H(\bar{x}_{N-C})$; $\quad j_1, \ldots, j_m \in C$

such that s' is (j, H')-metarational for all $j \in C$. For from Theorem 4 such an H' always exists. Here s' is, as before, the outcome preferred by all $j \in C$ to $\bar{s}$.

Thus player i's method of persuasion is clear. He must first obtain agreement on the policy $\bar{x}_{N-C}$ of the players outside the coalition and the consequent danger of the outcome $\bar{s}$. If he can do this, then negotiations between the players in C will always, by building up the metagame H', be able to lead to agreement on the outcome s'.

We turn now to some consequences of the fact that, in an ordinal game, the relation "$\subseteq$" between sets $M_i s$, $M_i t$ behaves just like the relation "$\leqslant$" between numbers.

The nonquantitative approach adopted throughout this book forbids us to let anything depend upon assigning numerical values to outcomes to represent a player i's preferences. Nevertheless, we shall now in the case of an ordinal game, introduce the word "value" in describing player i's preferences for the outcome s relative to the other outcomes of a game.

We shall call the set $M_i s$—which is to say the set of outcomes not preferred by i to s—the *value* of s to player i. This usage allows us to say that i is *indifferent* between s and t when they have the same value for him—that is, when $M_i s = M_i t$; and that he prefers s to t when its value is "greater"—that is, when $M_i s \supset M_i t$.

This is a natural way of talking, and it does not involve us in the unnatural mode of thinking that requires a numerical value to be assigned to outcomes. The approach is to admit that often it does not make sense to ask what numerical utility we attach to an outcome such as, for example, nuclear war; but to insist that it is extremely sensible and practical to ask, Which (if any) of these other outcomes is not preferred to nuclear war? The practicality of such questions is seen in the analysis of options technique described previously.

A *value*, in an ordinal game, is thus a subset of outcomes. Player i's values are the sets $V \subseteq S$ such that $V = M_i s$ for some s. Because of the properties of ordinality, these sets (player i's values) are "nested": that is, given any two values V and V', either $V \subseteq V'$ or $V' \subseteq V$.

Next, recall that in a "well-behaved" numerical game[3] with numerical utility functions v_i, the condition for $\bar{s}$ to be (i, H)-metarational may be written

$$v_i(\bar{s}) \geqslant \min_{s_P} \max_{s_i} \min_{s_F} v_i(\bar{s}_U, s_P, s_i, s_F),$$

where P, F, and U are defined as in Theorem 1. This says that given any fixed $\bar{s}_U$, the (i, H)-metarational outcomes s in which $s_U = \bar{s}_U$ are just the outcomes s such that (a) $s_U = \bar{s}_U$ and (b) $v_i(s)$ is greater than or equal to a certain minimum value, the "min max min" value. In particular, if U is empty, which will be the case if H is complete, then the (i, H)-metarational outcomes are simply all outcomes that have at least a certain minimum value for i.

It would be nice if we could generalize this to "well-behaved" ordinal games, and in fact we can do so. For first, consider the set

3. The term "well behaved" is used in mathematics to mean, roughly speaking, "obeying certain general rules that are to be regarded as normal and typical." In the present context, a well-behaved game is one in which certain things exist that always do exist in the finite case.

$$V = \bigcap_{s_F} M_i(\bar{s}_U, s_P, s_i, s_F),$$

which, of course, is in general different for each given $(\bar{s}_U, s_P, s_i)$. Clearly this set V has the property that

$$\forall s_F : M_i(\bar{s}_U, s_P, s_i, s_F) \supseteq V,$$

and moreover we may describe a "well-behaved" game as one in which there does always exist an s_F^* such that

$$V = M_i(\bar{s}_U, s_P, s_i, s_F^*),$$

so that the set V is in fact a *value* and we may well use the notation

$$V = \min_{s_F} M_i(\bar{s}_U, s_P, s_i, s_F)$$

to denote this value. For first, it is a value of M_i obtainable by some choice of s_F; second, it is the "least" value so obtainable.

Next, consider the set

$$V = \bigcup_{s_i} \bigcap_{s_F} M_i(\bar{s}_U, s_P, s_i, s_F),$$

which we may also write

$$V = \bigcup_{s_i} \min_{s_F} M_i(\bar{s}_U, s_P, s_i, s_F),$$

and which depends upon $(\bar{s}_U, s_P)$. This set clearly has the property that

$$\forall s_i : V \supseteq \min_{s_F} M_i(\bar{s}_U, s_P, s_i, s_F);$$

and moreover we may say again that in a "well-behaved" game there will exist s_i^* such that

$$V = \min_{s_F} M_i(\bar{s}_U, s_P, s_i^*, s_F),$$

so that V is a value, and we may use the notation

$$V = \max_{s_i} \min_{s_F} M_i(\bar{s}_U, s_P, s_i, s_F)$$

to denote this value. Similarly we can write

$$V = \min_{s_P} \max_{s_i} \min_{s_F} M_i(\bar{s}_U, s_P, s_i, s_F)$$

to denote the value

$$V = \bigcap_{s_P} \bigcup_{s_i} \bigcap_{s_F} M_i(\check{s}_U, s_P, s_i, s_F).$$

But this last value, which we may write

$$V_i(\check{s}_U, F) = \min_{s_P} \max_{s_i} \min_{s_F} M_i(\check{s}_U, s_P, s_i, s_F),$$

is just the value we were looking for—the value that has the property
that

$$\hat{R}_i(H) = \{\check{s} \mid M_i\check{s} \supseteq V_i(\check{s}_U, F)\},$$

where U is the set of unnamed players in H excluding player i, and F
is the set of players who follow i last in H.

If H is complete, this becomes

$$\hat{R}_i(H) = \{s \mid M_i s \supseteq V_i(F)\},$$

following the convention that if K is empty, "s_K" and the notations
that depend upon it stand for blank spaces on the page. If H is
complete we thus have a single value $V_i(F)$ that alone suffices to
determine membership in $\hat{R}_i(H)$.

EXAMPLE. Figure 6.2 shows a preference ordering for player 1 in a
three-person game in which $S_1 = S_2 = S_3 = \{0, 1\}$. The outcomes
(s_1, s_2, s_3) are listed in order of preference for player 1; for example,
(011) is his most preferred outcome. The values $V_1(F)$, which are
minimal for 1's metarational outcomes from each complete metagame, are, as shown in the figure:

$$
\begin{aligned}
V_1(\varnothing) \quad &= \{100, 110, 101, 111, 000\} &&= M_1(100); \\
V_1(\{2\}) \quad &= \{110, 101, 111, 000\} &&= M_1(110); \\
V_1(\{3\}) \quad &= \{101, 111, 000\} &&= M_1(101); \\
V_1(\{2, 3\}) &= \{111, 000\} &&= M_1(111).
\end{aligned}
$$

Finally let us note that in a "well-behaved" ordinal game (including
any finite ordinal game) a certain minimum value for player i may
be associated with any metagame H (not just with the complete
metagames)—this being the minimum value for him of any metarational outcome from H or from any descendant of H. Let us write
this minimum value as $V_i(H)$. We see that $V_i(H) = \min_{\check{s}_U} V_i(\check{s}_U, F)$
$= V_i(F)$.

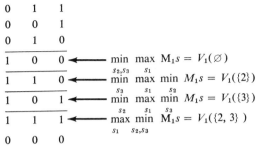

$$
\begin{array}{ccc}
0 & 1 & 1 \\
0 & 0 & 1 \\
0 & 1 & 0 \\
\hline
1 & 0 & 0 \\
1 & 1 & 0 \\
1 & 0 & 1 \\
1 & 1 & 1 \\
0 & 0 & 0
\end{array}
$$

$\leftarrow$ min max $M_1 s = V_1(\varnothing)$
      s_2, s_3 s_1

$\leftarrow$ min max min $M_1 s = V_1(\{2\})$
      s_3 s_1 s_2

$\leftarrow$ min max min $M_1 s = V_1(\{3\})$
      s_2 s_1 s_3

$\leftarrow$ max min $M_1 s = V_1(\{2, 3\})$
      s_1 s_2, s_3

Figure 6.2. Player 1's Preferences in a $2 \times 2 \times 2$ Game. The minimum values $V_1(F)$ are shown.

The value $V_i(H)$ has a certain importance for player i. It represents the worst he may expect if the bargaining process or thought process he is engaged in goes through the metagame H.

But $V_i(H)$ is at its minimum value when $H = G$ and at its maximum value for $H = iG$. That is, we have

$$V_i(G) = \max_{s_i} \min_{s_{N-i}} M_i s = \min_H V_i(H);$$

$$V_i(iG) = \min_{s_{N-i}} \max_{s_i} M_i s = \max_H V_i(H).$$

If therefore player i wishes to maximize the value $V_i(H)$, he may do so by endeavoring to directly predict the others' basic strategies, meanwhile not allowing them to predict directly his own basic strategy but only his policy. This places him in the game iG or one of its descendants.

Thus we can now state clearly our suggested reason why it should seem more natural for player i to assume he can predict the others' basic strategies than to assume that they can predict his. It puts him in a better position (at least as regards the worst that can happen). This is the fact that throws light on the "free will" paradox. To refuse to believe that one's free choice can be predicted (which is the instinct we all share that causes free will to seem a paradox) is, after all, a sound attitude to take from a strategic point of view. By taking this attitude one protects oneself.

Of course, we see from the foregoing that $\min_H V_i(H)$ is the minimum value of a general metarational outcome, while $\max_H V_i(H)$ is the minimum value of a symmetric metarational outcome.

But what if the two are equal? Then and only then every metarational outcome is symmetric metarational. In this case player i does not mind which path through the metagame tree is taken; all lead to the same metarational outcomes. He might as well permit the other to guess his basic strategy in exchange for him guessing the other's policy, for either way his minimum value is the same. Prisoner's dilemma illustrates this.

In this case we may call the game *determinate* (or *strictly determined*) for player i. We investigate this in the remainder of this section.

If all general metarational outcomes for player i are symmetric metarational for him, this means that relative to any outcome s there are two alternatives: either i can guarantee himself a preferred outcome, or the others can guarantee him a not-preferred outcome. Other alternatives are excluded. Such a game we have called *determinate for player i*, and the game as a whole can be called *determinate* if it is determinate for all players.

In a determinate game, the metagame equilibria from each complete metagame are the same and are just the symmetric equilibria; and of course if the game is finite, they exist.[4] There are no quasi equilibria.

Now consider an ordinal game G, and define a *saddle point* for player i as an outcome $\bar{s}$ such that

$$\forall s_{N-i}, s_i : M_i(s_{N-i}, \bar{s}_i) \supseteq M_i\bar{s} \supseteq M_i(\bar{s}_{N-i}, s_i).$$

This says that at a saddle point player i is doing the best thing for himself ($\bar{s}$ is rational for him), while the others are doing the worst they can for player i: given his strategy choice $\bar{s}_i$, any other joint strategy they could choose would be no worse for him.

To fix these ideas, imagine a (numerical) two-person game matrix as a board on which player i's payoffs are represented by vertical blocks of various heights. If $\bar{s}$ is a saddle point for player i, then as player i moves from $\bar{s}$ (along a column, say) the height of the blocks can only go down; as the other player moves (along a row), the height can only go up. Hence the name "saddle point" for the outcome $\bar{s}$.

---

4. Actually they exist in any "well-behaved" game, as earlier defined.

Looked at another way, a saddle point is an equilibrium of the two-person zero-sum game,

$$(S_i, S_{N-i}; M_i, M_i^{-1}),$$

in which the players $N - \{i\}$ are merged into a single player with preferences that are the inverse of i's preferences.

Theorem 6

If an ordinal game G has a saddle point for i, it is determinate for i. Moreover if G is well behaved, the converse is also true; G determinate for i implies G has a saddle point for i.

Proof of Theorem 6: Let $\bar{s}$ be a saddle point for i. We show that there cannot exist for player i a general metarational outcome s^* that is not symmetric metarational. For if s^* is general metarational we have

$$\forall s_i \, \exists s_{N-i} : M_i s \subseteq M_i s^*.$$

In particular, therefore,

$$\exists s_{N-i} : M_i(\bar{s}_i, s_{N-i}) \subseteq M_i s^*.$$

But since $\bar{s}$ is a saddle point, we have

$$\forall s_{N-i} : M_i(\bar{s}_i, s_{N-i}) \supseteq M_i \bar{s},$$

and therefore $M_i s^* \supseteq M_i \bar{s}$.

On the other hand, if s^* is not symmetric metarational we have

$$\sim \exists s_{N-i} \, \forall s_i : M_i s \subseteq M_i s^*,$$

or

$$\forall s_{N-i} \, \exists s_i : M_i s \supset M_i s^*.$$

In particular, we have

$$\exists s_i : M_i(s_i, \bar{s}_{N-i}) \supset M_i s^*.$$

But since $\bar{s}$ is a saddle point, we have

$$\forall s_i : M_i(s_i, \bar{s}_{N-i}) \subseteq M_i \bar{s},$$

implying that $M_i \bar{s} \supset M_i s^*$, contrary to the earlier result.

This shows that if a saddle point exists, G is determinate. Now we suppose that G is well behaved and determinate and show that i must have a saddle point.

Since G is well behaved, there exist two values

$$\max_{s_i} \min_{s_{N-i}} M_i s; \quad \min_{s_{N-i}} \max_{s_i} M_i s,$$

which are the minimum values in the sets Γ_i and Σ_i, respectively. But since G is determinate, $\Gamma_i = \Sigma_i$, and therefore the preceding two values are the same.

Therefore we have

$$\max_{s_i} \min_{s_{N-i}} M_i s \supseteq \min_{s_{N-i}} \max_{s_i} M_i s,$$

which is equivalent to

$$\exists \bar{s} : \min_{s_{N-i}} M_i(\bar{s}_i, s_{N-i}) \supseteq \max_{s_i} M_i(s_i, \bar{s}_{N-i}).$$

This says that there exists $\bar{s}$ such that

$$\forall s_i : \min_{s_{N-i}} M_i(\bar{s}_i, s_{N-i}) \supseteq M_i(s_i, \bar{s}_{N-i});$$

$$\forall s_{N-i} : M_i(\bar{s}_i, s_{N-i}) \supseteq \max_{s_i} M_i(s_i, \bar{s}_{N-i}).$$

Here the first line implies

$$\min_{s_{N-i}} M_i(\bar{s}_i, s_{N-i}) \supseteq M_i\bar{s}$$

and the second implies

$$M_i\bar{s} \supseteq \max_{s_i} M_i(s_i, \bar{s}_{N-i}).$$

Therefore, $\bar{s}$ is a saddle point.

EXAMPLES. Figure 6.3a shows a game which is determinate (has a saddle point) for both players. This game has no equilibrium.

The game in Figure 6.3b, on the other hand, is not determinate for either player. It has two equilibria. In this game, although for both players there exist metarational outcomes that are not symmetric, yet it so happens that all general equilibria are symmetric.

The two-person zero-sum game in Figure 6.3c is not determinate. It has no equilibria nor symmetric equilibria and is not determinate for either player. But the two-person zero-sum game in Figure 6.3d is determinate for player 1. It has an equilibrium that is also the only general equilibrium, and it is determinate for both players. We shall

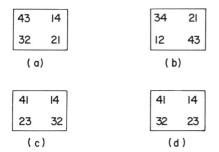

Figure 6.3. Determinate and Indeterminate Games with and without Equilibria.

in fact see that all these things go together in the case of a two-person zero-sum game—the special type of game that we turn to in the next section.

6.3 Two-Person Zero-Sum Games

We have pointed out already that game theory is full of simple, intuitive, convincing theories and arguments that, however, are false.

They are, that is, false in general. But many of these arguments, though they fail in general, are valid for determinate two-person zero-sum games.

A "rational" approach can, in this special case, be justified. That is why these games are misleading.

Let us enumerate the misleading characteristics we shall find in determinate two-person zero-sum games.

i. An equilibrium always exists.

ii. It has a unique value for each player.

iii. Though the equilibrium itself may not be unique, yet if $\bar{s}$ and s^* are two equilibria, $(\bar{s}_1, s_2^*)$ and $(s_1^*, \bar{s}_2)$ are also equilibria. Hence if both players choose equilibrium strategies (strategies, such as $\bar{s}_1$, which "lead to" an equilibrium) the result will be an equilibrium.

iv. A strategy is an equilibrium strategy if and only if it is a "safe" strategy (meaning a strategy s_i that maximizes the value $\min_{s_j} M_i(s)$).

v. Because of characteristics iii and iv, one may describe any equilibrium strategy as "optimal." Hence one may say that there exists an optimal way to play this game.

vi. The general equilibria are unique in value. Thus no conflicts arise between them, such as are found in prisoner's dilemma or the game of Figure 2.14c.

vii. Because of characteristics i and vi, all equilibria found from any metagame have the same value as an equilibrium of the basic game. Hence there is no point in exploring the metagame tree at all: any process of reasoning (path through the tree) that goes further than the basic game G will lead to no conclusions essentially different from those obtained already from G.

viii. Suppose player 1 asks, "What strategy should I choose assuming he (2) will be able to predict my choice and will then optimize for himself?" The answer is, an equilibrium strategy.

ix. Suppose 1 asks, "What strategy should I choose if I were able to predict and he (2) knew this and assumed I would optimize?" The answer again is, an equilibrium strategy.

x. The value to player i of an equilibrium may be called the *value of the game* to player i. By playing an equilibrium strategy, player i cannot obtain less than this value, and may obtain more if the other does not play optimally (choose an equilibrium strategy). If player i does not play an equilibrium strategy, the other player's "best reply" will give player i less, and the other player more, than their respective "values of the game."

This list of characteristics of course contains some repetitions.

It is clear that "rationality" does indeed seem justified in determinate two-person zero-sum games.

Rationality does not lead one astray, nor does it prove inadequate to the task of solving one's decision problem. The situation is almost as rational as in a "game against nature," where one chooses from a set of alternatives that which leads to a most-preferred result. With almost equal obviousness, in a two-person zero-sum game one chooses an equilibrium strategy.

Indeed this is so obvious that determinate two-person zero-sum games that are understood by the players (the only ones to which game-theoretic predictions apply) are quite uninteresting. An example is noughts-and-crosses (ticktacktoe in U.S. parlance). Once one understands how to play this game, one loses interest because it is quite predictable.

Most parlor games are two-person zero-sum. But most of them are so complicated that they cannot be understood. This is why they continue to be interesting. Chess is an example. Although a game-theoretic analysis of chess is a finite problem, this problem is too large ever to be solved.

The problems involved in "understanding" a determinate two-person zero-sum game are in fact analogous to the scientific and mathematical problems that may arise in finding the "results" that will follow from alternative choices made in a one-person "game against nature." Essentially, the game-theoretic problem is answered.

Rationality—the concept that seems so obvious initially—can, therefore, be carried a little way into the sphere of game theory. It performs satisfactorily for determinate two-person zero-sum games. Realizing this, von Neumann (1959) extended rationality a little further with his proof that any mixed strategy game based on a finite two-person zero-sum game is determinate. At the cost of allowing mixed strategies, rationality can thus be stretched a little further still.

But in the end, this path peters out. As we have seen many times not one of the above characteristics is true in general for non-zero-sum or many-person games—not even if these are determinate. And as we have said, zero-sum games are an artificial type scarcely ever found outside parlor games and sports. So rationality is abandoned.

We now investigate mathematically these special properties of the two-person zero-sum game.

Mathematical Development

Firstly we show that if $\bar{s}$, s^* are both equilibria of a two-person zero-sum game G, then

$$M_1(\bar{s}) = M_1(s^*),$$

from which $M_2(\bar{s}) = M_2(s^*)$ follows because G is mutually ordinal.

By the definition of a saddle point, a saddle point for one player is a saddle point for both in the two-person zero-sum case. And the saddle points are just the equilibria.

Both $\bar{s}$ and s^* are therefore saddle points for 1, so that we have

$$M_1(s_1^*, \bar{s}_2) \subseteq M_1(\bar{s}) \subseteq M_1(\bar{s}_1, s_2^*),$$

$M_1(\check{s}_1, s_2^*) \subseteq M_1(s^*) \subseteq M_1(s_1^*, \check{s}_2),$

from which we do obtain

$M_1(\check{s}) = M_1(s^*) = M_1(s_1^*, \check{s}_2) = M_1(\check{s}_1, s_2^*).$

Thus if $\check{s}$ and s^* are two equilibria they do have the same value (for each player). Moreover, this value is shared also by the points $(\check{s}_1, s_2^*)$, $(s_1^*, \check{s}_2)$. Hence $(\check{s}_1, s_2^*)$ is an equilibrium also, for we have

$\forall s_1 : M_1(s_1, s_2^*) \subseteq M_1 s^* = M_1(\check{s}_1, s_2^*);$

$\forall s_2 : M_1(\check{s}_1, s_2) \supseteq M_1 \check{s} = M_1(\check{s}_1, s_2^*).$

And similarly, $(s_1^*, \check{s}_2)$ is an equilibrium.

Thus we have that any two equilibria are *equivalent* (have the same value) and *interchangeable* (such that if one player aims at one equilibrium and the other at another, the result will be an equilibrium).

Now we prove the following theorem for a well-behaved two-person zero-sum game. It gives alternative necessary and sufficient conditions for G to have an equilibrium.

Theorem 7

The following are equivalent conditions for a well-behaved two-person zero-sum game G.

i. An equilibrium exists.

ii. G is determinate.

iii. All general equilibria are symmetric equilibria.

iv. All general equilibria have the same value for each player.

v. A symmetric equilibrium exists.

Proof: We shall prove that condition i ⇒ condition ii ⇒ condition iii ⇒ condition iv ⇒ condition v ⇒ condition i.

Condition i ⇒ condition ii. An equilibrium is a saddle point for both players. Therefore if an equilibrium exists, both players have a saddle point, and therefore from Theorem 6, G is determinate.

Condition ii ⇒ condition iii. If G is determinate, $\Gamma_1 \subseteq \Sigma_1$ and $\Gamma_2 \subseteq \Sigma_2$. Therefore, $\Gamma_1 \cap \Gamma_2 \subseteq \Sigma_1 \cap \Sigma_2$.

Condition iii ⇒ condition iv. From condition iii, any two general equilibria $\check{s}$, s^* are symmetric. Hence they are metarational for both players from $12G$ (or $21G$). Hence (using Theorem 3) they are metaequilibria from $12G$. But then they have the same value, for both are yielded by equilibria of the two-person zero-sum game $12G$. Condition iv $\Rightarrow$ condition v. If all general equilibria have the same value, all metagame equilibria have the same value. But this means that all metagame equilibria are symmetric equilibria; for each complete metagame yields some metagame equilibria; and from Theorem 1 the metagame equilibria yielded by one complete metagame could only differ from those yielded by another if the values of the equilibria differed. Next, metagame equilibria exist, since the game is well behaved. Therefore symmetric equilibria exist.

Condition v $\Rightarrow$ condition i. If a symmetric equilibrium exists, let it be $\bar{s}$. Then we have

$$\exists s_2 \, \forall s_1 : M_1 s \subseteq M_1 \bar{s},$$
$$\exists s_1^* \, \forall s_2^* : M_1 s^* \supseteq M_1 \bar{s};$$

or, equivalently,

$$\exists (s_1^*, s_2) \, \forall (s_1, s_2^*) : M_1 s \subseteq M_1 \bar{s} \subseteq M_1 s^*.$$

We may write this

$$\exists s^* \, \forall s : M_1(s_1, s_2^*) \subseteq M_1 \bar{s} \subseteq M_1(s_1^*, s_2),$$

and since on setting $s = s^*$ this yields $M_1 s^* = M_1 \bar{s}$, it tells us that there exists s^* obeying

$$\forall s : M_1(s_1, s_2^*) \subseteq M_1 s^* \subseteq M_1(s_1^*, s_2);$$

that is, it tells us that there exists a saddle point, which is to say an equilibrium.

Discussion. Hence in a well-behaved two-person zero-sum game, the "complete" sets of metaequilibria,

$$\beta^2 E(12G), \, \beta^2 E(21G),$$

are either disjoint or identical.[5] They are disjoint if G has no equilibrium, identical if G has an equilibrium. Thus either every path through the tree leads to the same metaequilibria (which are simply all outcomes having for each player the "value of the game"—i.e., the unique value of an equilibrium of G), or else the paths leading

5. Recall that in any two-person game, the metaequilibria from H are simply the outcomes metarational from H for both players.

through $2G$ lead to one set of equilibria while the paths through $1G$ lead to another, disjoint set.

Indeed, we can say in general that

$$\beta^2 E(12G) = \{\bar{s} | M_1 \bar{s} = \max_{s_1} \min_{s_2} M_1 s\}$$

$$= \{\bar{s} | M_2 \bar{s} = \min_{s_1} \max_{s_2} M_2 s\},$$

and

$$\beta^2 E(21G) = \{\bar{s} | M_1 \bar{s} = \min_{s_2} \max_{s_1} M_1 s\}$$

$$= \{\bar{s} | M_2 \bar{s} = \max_{s_2} \min_{s_1} M_2 s\},$$

from which we see that these sets are the same when G is determinate.

The situation therefore is that either G has an equilibrium, in which case G is determinate, there is no advantage in a player guessing the other's basic strategy, all general equilibria are symmetric, and all have the same value for each player; or else G has no equilibrium and everything depends on guessing the other's basic strategy, for on this depends which of the two values, one more advantageous and one less advantageous, one is able to obtain.

The second case is illustrated in the merchant ship–warship game, Figures 2.12 and 2.13, as well as in Figure 6.3c. Figure 6.3d illustrates the first case.

How does our theory compare, in the two-person zero-sum case, with the theory of rational outcomes? This predicts that only equilibria will be stable. Provided equilibria exist, our prediction differs from this only slightly; we predict that only outcomes with the same value as an equilibrium will be stable.

When equilibria do not exist there is, according to our theory, no strong (symmetric) stability: but there is a possible asymmetric stability if one player recognizes the other's superior ability to predict.

6.4 Inducement: The Third Breakdown of Rationality

In the remainder of this chapter we shall be discussing mutually ordinal games. In fact, we shall be discussing two-person mutually ordinal games in particular.

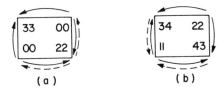

Figure 6.4. Games with Rational and Inducing Moves.

We have said that in this chapter we are assuming players that know each other's preferences. But so far we have merely developed various mathematical facts that will be important, interesting, or relevant to such players. We have not presented a predictive theory, testable by experiments, concerning the special behavior of such players. We have not in fact presented any predictive theory at all beyond the theory of metarationality, which is applicable whether or not players know each other's preferences.[6]

We shall not present in any final testable form a predictive theory concerning players that know each other's preferences. But we wish to indicate what we believe to be the main lines such a theory should follow.

We believe this theory must hinge on the idea of *inducement*. By inducement, we mean roughly the following. According to our previous theory, a player will be rational—if not in the original game, then in a metagame. This allows us to predict players' behavior to some extent. But then, if a player knows the other players' preferences, he too can predict, to some extent, their rational behavior. He may then deliberately take actions that, if the others react rationally, will lead to a preferred outcome for himself. Such actions we call *inducement*.

Two examples are given in Figure 6.4. Here each player's rational moves are shown by unbroken lines; his inducing moves are shown by broken lines. By a "rational" move we mean here simply a move to a rational outcome—rational, that is, for the player that moves.

6. To make this distinction clear, note the following. We could have presented metarationality theory, not as a predictive theory, but as a series of mathematical facts presumed to be of interest to players in a game. Then we would merely have said: metarational outcomes, defined in such-and-such a way, have such-and-such characteristics. Stability would not have entered the picture as a concept with any definite meaning, and no experimental tests would have been relevant.

Figure 6.5. The Basic Game of Prisoner's Dilemma. It has no inducing moves. The rational moves lead to (22).

By an "inducing" move we mean a move such that, if the other player responds with a rational move, the first player gains more than he could from any rational move.

(Row-player, of course, moves up and down columns, and column-player, along rows.)

In the first game, the result, if the players move according to the arrows (for example, at random) long enough, is that they must end up at the (33) outcome, and stay there. In the second game, they will continue to move about among the three outcomes (34), (43), and (11).

In the first game, there is no conflict between the players: each is trying to induce the same outcome. This is why they must end up at this outcome. In the second game, there is a conflict. Each is trying to induce a different outcome. Hence they end up in a set of outcomes containing the two outcomes they are trying to induce and what we may call a "conflict point," (11), at which each is trying to induce the other.

This then is the germ of a theory of inducement. We could build up a theory based on the possible "moves" from one outcome to another that a player might make. When we speak of a player "moving" in this way we mean that he "moves" either mentally, in the course of thinking about the game, or in the course of a bargaining process that precedes the playing of the game.

But this, as we have described it, would be a "basic" theory; that is, a theory about the original game G. In the same way, the theory of rational outcomes is a "basic" theory. To achieve truth, it has to be applied to the metagame tree, where it becomes the theory of metarationality.

Our proposed theory of inducement would also need to be applied to the metagame tree. Otherwise, like the theory of rational outcomes, it would be false. This is illustrated by prisoner's dilemma. Figure 6.5

shows that in the basic game G, the (33) outcome cannot be brought about by inducement. The players inevitably end up at (22). In order to obtain the (33) outcome at which, experimentally, players may end up, it is necessary to apply the concept of an inducing move to the metagame tree.

Our method of building the theory of inducement must, then, be the same as for the theory of metarational outcomes. We construct a neat, plausible, but false, theory of the basic game. We then deduce the consequences of applying it to the metagame tree, hoping that there it will "come true." Predictions are deduced by asserting that the theory must be true for some metagame; but we assert that the players may take any metagame as their subjective game.

These should, we believe, be the main lines of a theory of inducement (theory of players who know each other's preferences). But many problems remain.

The basic theory has to be stated precisely and in general; only then can its consequences when applied to the metagame tree be deduced. But to obtain these consequences is a considerable mathematical problem; it is a problem of "basic characterization," like the characterization of metarational outcomes; and till it is solved, how are we to know that we have stated the basic theory correctly—that is, in the form (if any!) that will "come true" in the metagame tree?

There thus lies ahead a process of iteration: to state a basic theory, deduce its metagame consequences, then if these are unsatisfactory, to amend the basic theory, and so on. We hope this process may end in the truth.

In the meantime, we can give, and try to interpret, some mathematical results that appear relevant to this problem.

The results we shall discuss have not, for the most part, been generalized beyond two-person mutually ordinal games. Now we have already said that all realistic ordinal games may be expected to be mutually ordinal. Hence the reader may, for the time being, accept this as not a drastic limitation. The limitation to two-person games is drastic, but leaves much that is of interest.

We shall also confine ourselves to finite games. The problem of generalizing the theory to infinite games is one that can certainly be postponed until the theory is in a more final form.

Mathematical Development

In any mutually ordinal game, a given value of the function M_i determines uniquely the values of all the functions $M_1, \ldots, M_n$. Write "Ms" for the n-tuple of values, one for each player, obtained from the outcome s, so that we have

$$Ms = (M_1 s, \ldots, M_n s);$$

and call such an n-tuple of values, obtained from an outcome, a *value-outcome*. Then we may say that in a mutually ordinal game, all outcomes that yield the same value for player i, yield the same *value-outcome*.

Because of this fact, each joint strategy $\bar{s}_{N-i}$ of the players other than player i "induces" from player i a unique value-outcome. That is to say, if player i responds "rationally" to $\bar{s}_{N-i}$, the result will be an outcome in the set

$$\{s \mid s \in R_i; \, s_{N-i} = \bar{s}_{N-i}\};$$

and each outcome in this set has the same n-tuple of values. We call this n-tuple of values the value-outcome *induced by* $\bar{s}_{N-i}$.

EXAMPLE 1. Figure 6.6 illustrates how this may fail in the non-mutually ordinal case. If column-player chooses column a, this certainly induces a unique value (2) for row-player; but it does not induce a unique value for column-player; it may induce either 1 or 4. (Note: Of course strictly we should say that column a induces for row-player the set $M_{\text{ROW}}(a, a) = M_{\text{ROW}}(b, a) = \{(a, a), (b, a), (b, b)\}$—that is, the set of outcomes not preferred by row player to (a, a) or (b, a); for this is our definition of a *value*. But we are identifying these set-theoretic values with payoff numbers. This is legitimate because

	a	b
a	21	42
b	24	13

Figure 6.6. A Possible Ambiguity of "Inducement" in a Non–Mutually Ordinal Game.

each payoff number determines a unique value, and vice versa, and it makes life easier when discussing simple examples.)

EXAMPLE 2. Consider the game with numerical payoffs defined by

$$v_1(s_1, s_2) = 4s_1s_2 - s_1;$$
$$v_2(s_1, s_2) = s_2^2 - \tfrac{1}{2}s_1s_2;$$
$$0 \leqslant s_1, s_2 \leqslant 1.$$

This game is not mutually ordinal; and if player 2 chooses $s_2 = \tfrac{1}{4}$, this does not induce a unique value for player 2. For player 1 it induces the value 0, but for player 2 it induces any value equal to

$$\tfrac{1}{16} - \tfrac{1}{8}x,$$

where $0 \leqslant x \leqslant 1$.

EXAMPLE 3. We may convert Example 2 into a mutually ordinal game by assigning the players lexicographic payoff functions

$$\bar{v}_1 = (v_1, -v_2),$$
$$\bar{v}_2 = (v_2, v_1);$$

and now $s_2 = \tfrac{1}{4}$ does induce a unique value-outcome, since if player 2 chooses $s_2 = \tfrac{1}{4}$, player 1 will choose s_1 so as to minimize v_2 (maximize $-v_2$). He does this because his choice of s_1 does not affect v_1, so he moves on to the second item in his list of priorities, which is to minimize v_2. Setting $s_1 = 1$ minimizes v_2, and the induced value-outcome is

$$(0, \tfrac{1}{16}; -\tfrac{1}{16}, 0),$$

where $(0, \tfrac{1}{16})$ is the induced value of v_1 and $(-\tfrac{1}{16}, 0)$ is the induced value of v_2. (Note that a (numerical) value of a lexicographic function is a list of numbers, in this case a pair of numbers, ordered in their order of priority.)

Now let us consider, in particular, two-person games.

As the previous example illustrates, in a two-person mutually ordinal game each strategy $\bar{s}_i$ of player i induces a unique value for player i. This is the unique value of M_i in the set

$$\{M_i s | s_i = \bar{s}_i; s \in R_j\}, \qquad j \neq i,$$

and we may call it the *inducement value* for player i of $\bar{s}_i$. We may write it "$D_i(\bar{s}_i)$."

Thus we attach an inducement value $D_i(\bar{s}_i)$ to each *strategy* $\bar{s}_i$ of player i. But this same inducement value may also be attached to any *outcome* s such that $s_i = \bar{s}_i$. That is, the inducement value, for player i, of an outcome $\bar{s}$ is again the unique value of M_i in the set

$$\{M_i s | s_i = \bar{s}_i; s \in R_j\}, \qquad j \neq i,$$

and the inducement value of s for i will be written "$D_i(s)$."

Discussion. A player in a two-person game that knows the other player's preferences may be expected to be concerned with the inducement values of his strategies and outcomes. Figure 6.7 shows a game in which both (a, c) and (a, d) are rational for player 2; yet if player 1 seemed likely to choose strategy a, player 2 would surely choose strategy c rather than strategy d; for $D_2(c) = D_2(a, c) = 3$, whereas $D_2(d) = D_2(a, d) = 1$. Strategy c, and hence outcome (a, c), has a higher inducement value for 2. (As before we imagine player 1 "offering" to choose a in the course of a bargaining process of some kind, possibly one that takes place only in the mind of a player.)

Hence we may regard the inducement value of an outcome as conferring a kind of preference on it—what we might call a "strategic" preference. We shall not express this by altering the actual preferences $M_i s$ of the players. In Figure 6.7, $M_2(a, c) = M_2(a, d) = 3$, so that player 2 is certainly indifferent as to whether (a, c) or (a, d) is the final outcome. Nevertheless he has strategic reasons for "moving" from (a, d) to (a, c); that is, he has reasons for behaving "as if" he preferred (a, c).

This may seem unimportant. It may seem that the situation illustrated in Figure 6.7 will occur infrequently. On the contrary, it is extremely important. Such situations occur "all the time" in the metagame tree. For this reason we make the following definitions.

	c	d
a	33	33
b	22	41

Figure 6.7. A Rational Outcome That Is Not Inducement Rational.

Mathematical Development

Let us write "M_i^d" for the *lexicographic* preference function $M_i^d = (M_i, D_i)$.[7] That is, we write "$M_i^d s \subseteq M_i^d t$" to mean

$$\begin{cases} M_i s \subset M_i t \\ \text{or} \\ M_i s = M_i t, D_i s \subseteq D_i t. \end{cases}$$

Alternatively, M_i^d might be defined as $\tilde{M}_i^{-1} \cup (M_i \cap D_i)$.

Discussion. The function M_i^d would thus represent the preferences of a player i whose first priority is to achieve preferred outcomes but who, as between outcomes otherwise indifferent, prefers one with a greater inducement value.

Mathematical Development

We now define an outcome $\bar{s}$ of a finite two-person mutually ordinal game as *inducement rational for player i* if

$$\forall s_i : M_i^d(s_i, \bar{s}_j) \subseteq M_i^d \bar{s},$$

which, by the definition of M_i^d, is equivalent to

$$\forall s_i : \begin{cases} M_i(s_i, \bar{s}_j) \subset M_i \bar{s} \\ \text{or} \\ M_i(s_i, \bar{s}_j) = M_i \bar{s}, D_i(s_i, \bar{s}_j) \subseteq D_i \bar{s}. \end{cases}$$

Next, writing $R_i^d(G)$ for the set of all outcomes that are inducement rational for player i, we may define an *inducement equilibrium* as an outcome in the set

$$E^d(G) = R_1^d(G) \cap R_2^d(G).$$

That is, an inducement equilibrium is an outcome which is inducement rational for both players.

Just as with rational outcomes and equilibria, we can go on to define *inducement metarational* outcomes and *inducement meta-equilibria*. An outcome is *inducement metarational for player i from H* if it is in the set

$$\hat{R}_i^d(H) = \beta^* R_i^d(H),$$

and it is an *inducement metaequilibrium from H* if it is in the set

---

7. Lexicographic preferences are here being used in a quite different way from the way discussed previously, and the reader should not confuse the two uses.

$$\hat{E}^d(H) = \beta^*(R_1^d(H) \cap R_2^d(H))$$
$$= \beta^* E^d(H).$$

Inducement equilibria are, by definition, equilibria. Hence they need not exist, as equilibria need not exist. In fact, a game that possesses an equilibrium may nevertheless not possess an inducement equilibrium. Figure 6.8 illustrates this.

Another illustration is provided by a first-level metagame of prisoner's dilemma (Figure 2.20b). Here $(D, D/D)$, though an equilibrium, is not an inducement equilibrium. For player 2 will move from there to $(D, C/D)$, which yields the same value and has a higher inducement value.

Figure 2.20 also illustrates some further facts. It is not true that an outcome that is d-metarational (short for inducement metarational) for both players from a metagame H is necessarily a d-metaequilibrium from H—though we have seen (Theorem 3) that this is true in the two-person case for ordinary metarational outcomes and ordinary metaequilibria. From Figure 2.20 we see that (D, D) is d-metarational for both players from $2G$, yet it is not a d-metaequilibrium from $2G$. Again, the hereditary property $\hat{E}(H) \subseteq \hat{E}(H^*)$, if H^* is a descendant of H, though true for ordinary metaequilibria, is false for d-metaequilibria. In Figure 2.20, for example, we find that $(D, D) \in \hat{E}^d(G)$, $(D, D) \notin \hat{E}^d(2G)$.

On the other hand, the hereditary property $\hat{R}_i^d(H) \subseteq \hat{R}_i^d(H^*)$, if H^* is a descendant of H, does hold for d-metarational outcomes as for ordinary metarational outcomes, as the reader may easily prove.

Discussion. To interpret the above, we can follow our interpretation of the distinction, in three-or-more-person games, between metaequilibria from H and metagame equilibria (outcomes metarational for all players) from H. If player i believes player j to perceive the same metagame as himself and believes that each correctly predicts

33	33
25	44

Figure 6.8. Game with an Equilibrium but No Inducement Equilibrium.

the other's metastrategy, he must anticipate a d-metaequilibrium. But if he believes that the other is mistaken in his metastrategic prediction, he may anticipate merely an outcome d-metarational for both players. For example, in Figure 2.20b player 2 may anticipate (D, D), though he perceives the metagame $2G$, because he believes that 1 will choose D even though he himself will choose C/D. He is willing to cooperate if 1 will, but he does not believe that 1 believes this. (He cannot, in fact, believe that 1 believes this in the game $2G$; for if he did, he would believe that 1 would choose C and not D.)

Mathematical Development

The (i, H)-d-metarational outcomes (outcomes d-metarational for i from H) have a very simple basic characterization in the case when i is named in H. They are, in fact, simply the (i, H)-metarational outcomes! That is to say $\hat{R}_i^d(H) = \hat{R}_i(H)$, if i is named in H. We leave the proof of this theorem to the reader.

Discussion. Thus a named player that knows the other's payoffs, and hence behaves inducement rationally, may nevertheless be led to accept as "best attainable" any outcome he might ordinarily have been led to accept. This happens because, even though such a player will "induce" whenever he does not lose by so doing, he may not believe that he will succeed: he may believe that the other player will fail to predict his "inducements." We have already illustrated this in the 2-metagame of prisoner's dilemma, where we saw that (D, D) remains d-metarational for 2.

This fact about d-metarationality must, however, be contrasted with the following surprising fact about d-metaequilibria.

Mathematical Development

Theorem 8

If H is complete, the d-equilibria of H are the equilibria of H that are *undominated*. That is, $E^d(H) = E(H) \cap R_N(H)$. Hence also $\hat{E}^d(H) = \hat{E}(H) \cap R_N(G)$: the d-metaequilibria from H are the undominated metaequilibria from H.

Proof: Suppose, without loss of generality, that player 1 is named first in H. Then an outcome of H has the form (f, x_2), where $(x_1, x_2) \in X_1 \times X_2$ is a typical outcome of the immediate ancestor of H, and f, a function $f: X_2 \to X_1$, is a metastrategy of player 1 in H.

First we prove that if (f^*, x_2^*) is a d-equilibrium, it is an undominated equilibrium.

If it is a d-equilibrium, it must be an equilibrium, by definition. Hence it induces the value of (f^*, x_2^*).

Next, suppose it is a dominated equilibrium. Then by Theorem 4, it is dominated by another equilibrium outcome, say $(\bar{f}, \bar{x}_2)$. Write

$$f^*x_2^* = x_1^*, \quad \bar{f}\bar{x}_2 = \bar{x}_1.$$

Then player 1 can change to a strategy f' such that $f'x_2^* = x_1^*$, $f'\bar{x}_2 = \bar{x}_1$. (That is, he can say "if you change to $\bar{x}_2$, the result will be $\bar{x}$, but if you play x_2^*, the result will be x^*, which is worse for us both.") This f' yields the same value against x_2^* as f^* does, yet it induces more, since it induces at least the value of $(\bar{f}, \bar{x}_2)$. Hence (f^*, x_2^*) is not, after all, a d-equilibrium, since it is not d-rational for 1.

Next we prove that if (f^*, x_2^*) is an undominated equilibrium, it is a d-equilibrium.

For it not to be a d-equilibrium, one of the players must be able to move to a strategy that allows the other to obtain the value of (f^*, x_2^*), yet induces more for the first player. This is impossible, for since (f^*, x_2^*) is undominated any outcome preferred by the first player is worse for the second.

NOTE. The second part of the proof actually shows that in any game, an undominated equilibruim is a d-equilibrium. That is,

$$E \cap R_N \subseteq E^d.$$

Discussion. The fact is that while d-metarational outcomes add nothing essentially new, d-metaequilibria show us a simple, "costless" way for two players in a complete metagame to avoid dominated equilibria—that is, to act as a coalition. There is always a path in the complete matrix (shown in Figure 3.3 for prisoner's dilemma) by which they can move from a dominated equilibrium to one that is better for both players without passing through any outcome worse for either. The interpretation of this given by d-rationality is simply, "Why not induce more, if it costs nothing?" It is surprising that such a weak axiom of inducement should lead to such a strong result.

Why then would players that know each other's preferences ever end up at a dominated outcome? The two reasons are that each may not believe that he or the other can predict. These are the two sources of "mistrust" that may lead two players to act other than as a coalition.

In Appendix B we report on some experiments that confirm this. These are the so-called experiments with certainty, described previously, in which two players played in a manner equivalent to playing in the complete metagame matrix. One stated a "policy": "If you choose ———, I choose ———, and so forth"; the other then chose in knowledge of the first player's policy. As we should predict, the players invariably reached an undominated metaequilibrium; for here they were forced to play in the complete metagame, and each was able with "certainty" to predict the other's choice.

We now go on to develop some further facts about inducement in two-person mutually ordinal games. These lead to the third breakdown of rationality.

So far we have defined the *value* $D_i(\bar{s}_i)$ *induced* by a strategy $\bar{s}_i$ of player i. We have not defined an *outcome induced* by $\bar{s}_i$.

Clearly the *induced outcome* should be in the set $\{s \mid s_i = \bar{s}_i;$ $s \in R_j\}, j \neq i$. Since player j is assumed to know i's payoffs, however, we place it in the smaller set $\{s \mid s_i = \bar{s}_i; s \in R_j^d\}$. Any outcome in this set is said to be *induced* by $\bar{s}_i$.

We can now ask what outcomes are induced by particular types of strategies. One interesting type, mentioned already, is the *sure-thing* strategy. What does this induce?

We recall that a *sure-thing* strategy for player i is an $\bar{s}_i$ such that

$$\forall s : M_i s \subseteq M_i(\bar{s}_i, s_j),$$

or equivalently,

$$\forall s_j : (\bar{s}_i, s_j) \in R_i,$$

so that a sure-thing strategy guarantees a rational outcome.

A sure-thing strategy may or may not exist. But a sure-thing strategy exists, for some player, in every proper metagame; for player i has a sure-thing strategy in any metagame iH, where H is a metagame (assumed to be finite).

Sure-thing strategies were discussed in connection with both previous breakdowns of rationality. The "defect" strategy in prisoner's dilemma is sure-thing. A game in which a player has a sure-thing strategy is the one kind of game in which he can be sure of being objectively, not merely subjectively, rational. There is a strategy choice that is best for him, whatever the others do.

It might be thought, therefore (and it has been claimed), that in this kind of game a player certainly "should" choose his sure-thing strategy, that in this one case a game-theoretic recommendation can certainly be made. Of course, we have contested this view. But the strongest thing that can be said against it is contained in the following theorem—according to which in a two-person game, choosing one's sure-thing strategy is "usually" the most foolish thing one can do.

Theorem 9

In a (finite) two-person mutually ordinal game, a sure-thing strategy induces the best possible equilibrium for the other player. (In a complete metagame, this is necessarily a d-equilibrium.)

Proof: First, the sure-thing strategy induces an equilibrium. For what it induces must be rational for the player that chooses it, since a sure-thing strategy guarantees a rational outcome; and it must be rational for the other player, since an induced outcome is by definition rational for the player that is being induced. Second, it is the best possible equilibrium for the other player since, if $\tilde{s}_1$ is sure-thing for player 1, we have, in a mutually ordinal game,

$$\{Ms|s_1 = \tilde{s}_1\} = \{Ms|s \in R_1\};$$

that is, $\tilde{s}_1$ "offers" to player 2 just those value-outcomes that are rational for 1. Hence the induced value-outcome is best for player 2 of all those in R_1. Therefore it is also best for him of those in E, since if it is preferred or indifferent to any in R_1, it must be preferred or indifferent to any in a subset of R_1, and $E = R_1 \cap R_2 \subseteq R_1$.

The essential message of this theorem is that the rule that one should choose a sure-thing strategy if one exists is very foolish unless it so happens that the best equilibrium for the other player is also the best for oneself. We shall examine this possibility when we discuss "rational" games in the next section. If, however, there is any possibility of conflict between possible stable outcomes; that is, if there are two or more possible compromises, of which the one most favored by player 1 is not the one most favored by player 2; then to choose a sure-thing strategy is to be a "sucker" that capitulates entirely to the other side.

This is our third breakdown of rationality.

For example, if a buyer and seller are haggling over a price, the buyer who is "sure-thing" rational will accept any price, no matter how high, provided only that it is better for him than the "no sale" alternative. If two countries are seriously negotiating peace terms, a "sure-thing" rational player will accept the best feasible settlement for the other side, though it is most unlikely to be also the best for himself. Suppose a candidate for democratic office proposes the seemingly quite sensible approach: "We shall, in all circumstances we face in foreign affairs, choose that strategy which leads to the best result for ourselves." He is really proposing a policy of complete appeasement, which would make his country a doormat for others in any international conflict.

Of course, such a completely "selfish" approach is never proposed for a country's foreign policy. Theorem 9 suggests that it would be surprising if it were. At most, a country's foreign policy declarations become slightly more "selfish" when, as with the United States in Southeast Asia, it is in retreat.

Theorem 9 in fact provides a reason why "idealism," "unselfishness," "honor," "loyalty," and so forth, should appear as elements in a country's foreign policy: by appealing to such unselfish motives, a country can more effectively bluff and bully others into capitulation—or, to put it another way, can more effectively resist the temptation to capitulate in the face of others' bluffs.

These remarks apply to other kinds of players, not just to nation states. They refer of course to sure-thing strategies in proper metagames (where sure-thing strategies always exist) as well as to sure-thing strategies in the basic game.

To illustrate this final weakness of rationality, we analyze a highly simplified model of the 1962 Cuba missile crisis using the game known as "chicken."[8]

We suppose that there are just two players—the United States and the Soviet Union. Thus Cuba, the other South American countries, and so on, are not regarded as having any influence on the simple issues we analyze. These are

1. Shall the Soviets maintain their missiles in Cuba?
2. Shall the United States invade Cuba?

To cover these issues we give each player two strategies, leading to the 2×2 game shown in Figure 6.9. We suppose that if both sides "give in"—the United States by abandoning its invasion plans and the Soviets by withdrawing their missiles—the result will be the "compromise" settlement that was actually reached. If one side but not the other gives in, then clearly this is a "victory," of some sort, for the side that does not give in. If neither side gives in, we suppose that this leads to nuclear war, or a high probability thereof.[9]

These assumptions lead, we should say, quite inevitably to the (ordinal) preferences shown in Figure 6.9. We obtain a game with two equilibria; victory for one side or the other. Each player can try to induce victory for himself by refusing to give in; but if both do this, the result is nuclear war.

In this basic game, neither side has a sure-thing strategy. But Figure 6.10 shows, as it must, that the Soviets have a sure-thing strategy in the Soviet-metagame. It induces victory for the United States. Next, in Figure 6.11 we see that the United States has a sure-thing strategy in the U.S.–Soviet-metagame. It induces victory for the Soviets. And so it continues throughout the metagame tree: a sure-thing strategy always induces victory for the other side.

Next consider the "compromise" outcome, which appears in Figure 6.11 as a metaequilibrium from the U.S.–Soviet metagame. In order to induce this outcome, the United States must pursue what we have called a *retaliatory* policy. Its essential characteristic is

8. Based on the California sport in which two teenagers drive toward a head-on collision, the loser being the one who swerves first.
9. Robert F. Kennedy's *Thirteen Days: A Memoir of the Cuban Missile Crisis* provides some backing for these assumptions; though our simple model was presented, in Management Science Center (1968), before Kennedy's memoir was published. At the time the Soviets denied that they had any missiles and the United States that it had any invasion plans.

		'W'	'M'
U. S. INVASION PLANS:	ABANDON 'A'	33 COMPROMISE	(24) SOV. VICTORY
	CONTINUE 'C'	(42) U. S. VICTORY	11 NUCLEAR WAR

Figure 6.9. Cuban Missile Crisis. Equilibria are circled.

SOVIET POLICIES:

		W/W	M/M	W/M	M/W
U.S. STRATEGIES	A	33	(24)	33	24
	C	(42)	11	11	(42)
					↑ SOVIET SURE-THING POLICY

Figure 6.10. The Soviet-Metagame. The symbol "X/Y" stands for the Soviet policy "X against A, Y against C." Equilibria are circled.

SOVIET POLICIES:

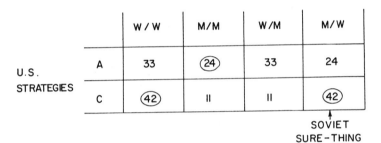

		W/W	M/M	W/M	M/W
U.S. COUNTER-POLICIES:	A/A/A/A	33	(24)	33	24
	C/C/C/C	(42)	11	11	(42)
SURE-THING POLICY →	C/A/A/C	42	(24)	33	42
'RETALIATORY' POLICY →	C/C/A/C	42	11	(33)	42

Figure 6.11. Excerpt from the U.S.–Soviet-Metagame. The symbol "$V/X/Y/Z$" stands for "V against W/W, X against M/M, Y against W/M, Z against M/W."

that if the Soviets refuse ever to give in (i.e. the policy M/M), the United States will incur nuclear war rather than give in. This induces the (equally retaliatory) Soviet response W/M, which may be called "tit for tat": we won't give in unless you do.

It can in fact be shown quite easily that

1. For the compromise outcome to be stable, both sides must be ready to risk nuclear war.

2. If one side but not the other is willing to risk nuclear war, that side wins.

3. If neither side is willing to risk nuclear war, no stable outcome is possible.

These conclusions are surprising in that from the original game (Figure 6.9) it appears that the "safe" outcome, obtained by neither side being willing to risk nuclear war, is compromise.

We stress the essential rationality of the idea that in a situation such as this one should, before deciding to "hold out" for one's best outcome, try to estimate whether the other will respond by giving in. If one thinks he will do so, then by all means hold out. But if one is convinced he will *not* yield, one should not deliberately bring disaster on one's own head.

This, we repeat, is rational. It describes the "sure-thing" Soviet policy in Figure 6.10, and it induces the best equilibrium for the United States. It is weak and foolish.

Of course, one may pretend to be irrational while in fact pursuing a sure-thing policy; that is, one may proclaim that one will not give in if the other will not, while secretly being ready to do the opposite. This is "bluff." By bluffing, one may hope to obtain the advantages of both inducement and rationality in a case where these conflict.

The other player then has to decide the question, which we have seen that he always must decide, whether one's policy is what one says it is or whether it is sure-thing. If the metagame outcome is to be stable, then by definition he will come to the correct conclusion about this.

6.5 Optimal Inducement: Perfect Games and Conflict Points
Our first breakdown of rationality was that a game might have no equilibrium; the second was that it might have no undominated

equilibrium. These problems are, we have seen, solved in the meta-game tree, in that a complete metagame always has an undominated equilibrium.[10]

What is the essential characteristic of the third breakdown, exemplified by the game of chicken (the Cuban missile crisis game)? It is a problem that we know is not necessarily solved in the metagame tree.

It is that a sure-thing first-level policy may not be *maximally inducing*; that is, there may exist another first-level policy that induces more.

This is the case in chicken, where we see from Figure 6.10 that the sure-thing policy M/W induces less than M/M. Indeed, Theorem 9 tells us that it must always be the case for player i unless the best equilibrium of iG for the other player is also the best outcome i can induce for himself.

Clearly this also is a crisis for rationality, introducing as it does a reason why player i should not be "sure-thing" rational. It throws doubt on the rational prescription—choose a sure-thing strategy if there is one, otherwise choose a sure-thing policy by trying to predict the other's choice and responding rationally.

In this section we shall show, however, that if a game has none of these problems—that is, it has an undominated equilibrium and for each player his sure-thing policy is maximally inducing—then essentially it has no problems at all. We shall call it *perfect*.

A special class of perfect games that we have already encountered is the determinate two-person zero-sum games. We have seen that these games really do present no problems; and now we shall see that all perfect games share most of the desirable characteristics of this special case.

Furthermore we shall see that any complete metagame is either perfect or else has what we shall call a *conflict point*. This is a point, like the (1, 1) outcome in Figure 6.9, at which each player is holding out for an undominated equilibrium that suits him better. It is a point at which there is a conflict between two undominated equilibria, one of which is preferred by player 1 and the other by player 2.

10. At least this is so in the finite case, which we take as typical.

We now develop this theory. Though here it is confined to finite games, the extension to infinite games will probably add nothing essential. Some care will be required. As before, however, the limitation to two-person games is serious, and an intensive effort should be made to extend the theory to the n-person case. The limitation to mutually ordinal games is, we have argued, less serious.

Mathematical Development

We consider a (finite) two-person mutually ordinal game G. Let f_1, f_2 be typical metastrategies for players 1 and 2 in the games $1G$ and $2G$ respectively. Let f_1^r, f_2^r be the players' sure-thing metastrategies in these games. We have seen that such sure-thing metastrategies always exist, and their inducement values $D_1 f_1^r$, $D_2 f_2^r$ are unique.

Then G is called *rational* if these inducement values are maximal: that is, G is rational if

$$\forall f_1 : D_1 f_1^r \supseteq D_1 f_1;$$

$$\forall f_2 : D_2 f_2^r \supseteq D_2 f_2.$$

Discussion. We are, then, saying that a game that suffers from the third breakdown is "irrational." The term is justified in that, in such a game, irrationality "pays."

The merchant ship–warship game is rational. But prisoner's dilemma is irrational, for Figure 2.20b shows that the sure-thing policy D/D is not maximally inducing in the 2-metagame. Chicken is also irrational, of course.

We now introduce some further notation.

Mathematical Development

In a mutually ordinal game, by definition, a unique value for player j is attached to each one of player i's values. Hence we may define a function "M_j^i" that takes any one of player i's values into the corresponding value for player j.

For example, in Figure 6.9,

$$M_2^1(4) = M_1^2(4) = 2;$$

$$M_2^1(3) = M_1^2(3) = 3.$$

In this game, $M_2^1 = M_1^2$ because the game is symmetric. In the game of Figure 6.3a, however,

$$M_2^1(4) = 3;$$

$$M_1^2(4) = 1.$$

Of course we always have

$M_j^i M_i^j = M_j^j =$ the identity function.

Using this notation, we can give a necessary and sufficient condition for G to be rational.

Theorem 10

G is rational if and only if

$$\max M_1(\Gamma_2) = M_1^2 \max M_2(R_1)$$

and

$$\max M_2(\Gamma_1) = M_2^1 \max M_1(R_2).$$

It follows also that any descendant of a rational game is rational.

Proof: Player 1's maximal inducement value[11] from a metagame H is obviously max $M_1(\hat{R}_2(H))$,[12] since he can induce just those values in the game H that are rational for player 2. But $\hat{R}_2(1G) = \Gamma_2$, so that max $M_1(\Gamma_2)$ is 1's maximal inducement value from $1G$. On the other hand, 1's sure-thing policy f_1^r induces 2 to obtain the basic value max $M_2(R_1)$. Hence the first condition of the theorem is necessary and sufficient for f_1^r to be maximally inducing. Similarly, the second condition is necessary and sufficient for f_2^r to be maximally inducing.

Discussion. Interpreting this proof, we can say that 1's sure-thing policy in $1G$ induces 2 to induce the most he can in G. Hence it is that a game is rational for 1 only if allowing 2 to induce the most he can in G yields 1 his maximal inducement value in $1G$.

---

11. By "player 1's maximal inducement value [from H]" we naturally mean the basic value corresponding to his maximal inducement value in the metagame H. Basic values are not the same as metagame values; for values are sets of outcomes, and basic outcomes are not the same as metagame ones. But there is a one–one correspondence between the two.

12. If T is a set of outcomes, we may as here write "$M_i(T)$" for the set $\{M_i s \mid s \in T\}$ and "max $M_i(T)$" for the maximum value in $M_i(T)$.

Mathematical Development

Now, as we have said, a game is called *perfect* if (a) it is rational and (b) it has an undominated equilibrium.

By definition, such a game suffers from none of our breakdowns of rationality. We have to show, however, that a perfect game justifies its name in that it presents no real problems of any kind.

We show first that a determinate two-person zero-sum game is perfect. For first it possesses an undominated equilibrium. Second, any two-person zero-sum game is rational, since in such a game the operators

$$M_1^2 \max M_2, \; M_1^2 \min M_2$$

are the same respectively as

$$\min M_1, \; \max M_1,$$

and hence

$$
\begin{aligned}
M_1^2 \max M_2(R_1) &= \min M_1(R_1) \\
&= \min_{s_2} \max_{s_1} M_1 s \\
&= M_1^2 \max_{s_2} \min_{s_1} M_2 s \\
&= M_1^2 \min M_2(\Gamma_2) \\
&= \max M_1(\Gamma_2).
\end{aligned}
$$

And similarly, of course, we have

$$M_2^1 \max M_1(R_2) = \max M_2(\Gamma_1).$$

Thus we have proved

Theorem 11

Any two-person zero-sum game is rational; and a determinate two-person zero-sum game is perfect.

Determinate two-person zero-sum games are thus a special case of perfect games. Now we show that all perfect games share most of the desirable characteristics of the determinate two-person zero-sum case.

First note that an equilibrium of a two-person zero-sum game has a characteristic not shared by equilibria in general. It is not just an equilibrium: it is an *optimum*, defined as a point $\bar{s}$ that is not only rational for each player i,

$\forall s_i : M_i(s_i, \bar{s}j) \subseteq M_i\bar{s},$

but is also such that each player i cannot induce more than he is getting,

$\forall s_i : D_i(s_i, \bar{s}_j) \subseteq M_i\bar{s}.$

An outcome having these two characteristics for player i may be called *optimal for i*. Another way of writing the conditions is

$\bar{s} \in R_i;$
$M_i\bar{s} \supseteq \max M_i(R_j), j \neq i,$

for we have said that $\max M_i(R_j)$ is the maximum value that player i can induce in the basic game.

In the zero-sum case, player i can never induce more than he obtains at any rational outcome. For the most he can induce is

$$\max_{s_i} \min_{s_j} M_i s = \max M_i(R_j),$$

and this is a subset of $\min_{s_j} \max_{s_i} M_i s$, which is his smallest value from a rational outcome. Hence we have

Theorem 12

In a two-person zero-sum game, an outcome is optimal for i if and only if it is rational for him; hence the equilibria are the optima.

We write "O_i" for the set of outcomes optimal for i. If $s = \beta^* x$, where x is an outcome optimal for i in a metagame H, s may be called *metaoptimal for i* from H; and we write $\hat{O}_i(H) = \beta^* O_i(H)$ for the set of such outcomes. Clearly $\hat{O}_i(H) = \hat{R}_i(H)$ in the zero-sum case.

An optimal outcome always exists in finite games; for player i's best outcome over the whole game is obviously optimal for him. But there is not, as there is with rational outcomes, always an optimal response to every strategy of the other player.

At an optimal outcome $\bar{s}$ player i has no motive of either kind—"rational" or "inducing"—for moving away. He can neither get nor induce more than he is getting. Does this mean that player i can be expected to "accept" an optimal outcome if it is proposed to him by the other player? Not necessarily; for player i may be able to induce more by going to the metagame. For example, in prisoner's dilemma the $(2, 2)$ outcome is optimal for both players in the basic

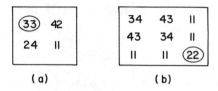

(a) (b)

Figure 6.12. Two Rational Games, One with and One without an Optimum. Equilibria are circled.

game, but is not metaoptimal for i from any metagame in which i is named. We might say that if he could be confined to the basic game, i could be got to accept this outcome, but "for metagame reasons" he might refuse.

In Figure 6.12a, the (3, 3) and (4, 2) outcomes are optimal for player 1. In Figure 6.12b, the two (4, 3) outcomes are optimal for 1; the (2, 2) outcome is rational but not optimal.

If we consider the (infinite) game of Example 3, page 173, we find that

$$R_1 = \{s|(s_1 = 1, s_2 \geqslant \tfrac{1}{4}) \text{ or } (s_1 = 0, s_2 < \tfrac{1}{4})\};$$

$$R_2 = \{s|s_2 = 1\}.$$

Hence max $M_1(R_2) = (3, -\tfrac{1}{2})$, max $M_2(R_1) = (\tfrac{1}{4}, 3)$. Only (1, 1) is optimal for player 1, whereas for player 2, $O_2 = R_2$.

Now, as we have said, an outcome optimal for both players is called an *optimum*. We write $O = O_1 \cap O_2$ for the set of optima.

We may write

$$\hat{O}(H) = \beta^* O(H)$$

for the set of *metaoptima from H*, that is, the set of basic outcomes yielded by optima from H. We have then the following theorem.

Theorem 13

$$\beta^*(O_1(H) \cap O_2(H)) = \beta^* O_1(H) \cap \beta^* O_2(H) = \hat{O}(H).$$

This is just as for metarational outcomes and metaequilibria in the two-person case (Theorem 3). That is, the metaoptima from H are just the outcomes metaoptimal for both players from H.

Proof: If s is metaoptimal for both players from H, it is a metaequilibrium from H, hence H has an equilibrium x that yields s; but then x is an optimum of H, because it is an equilibrium at which both players are getting at least their maximal inducement values in H.

This is in contrast with d-metarational outcomes and d-metaequilibria. We have seen that an outcome d-metarational for both players from H is not necessarily a d-metaequilibrium.

On the other hand, d-metaequilibria exist from every complete metagame, whereas metaoptima certainly may not. In chicken, for example (the Cuban missile crisis game) no optima exist in any metagame, since each player can always induce a value of 4, and no outcome exists at which both players obtain this much.

The difference between the two concepts is that whereas a rational outcome is d-rational for a player provided only that to induce more would mean moving to a worse outcome, for a rational outcome to be optimal for him, he must be obtaining the most he can induce. If to insist on inducement rationality is the weakest response a player can make to knowing the others' preferences, then to insist on optimality is the strongest.

It is clear that optima, though not necessarily unique, are unique in value. Indeed, the value-pair (value-outcome) from an optimum is

$$(\max M_1(R_2), \max M_2(R_1));$$

for i receives at least his maximum inducement value $\max M_i(R_j)$, and cannot receive more since the optimum is rational for j, hence belongs to R_j.

The value-pair of an optimum is thus better for both players than that of any nonoptimal equilibrium. For $\max M_i(R_j) \supseteq \max M_i(E)$ since $R_j \supseteq E$. Hence the optimum is the best equilibrium for both players. These remarks are summed up in

Theorem 14

$\tilde{s}$ is an optimum if and only if

$\tilde{s} \in E$

and

$M\tilde{s} = (\max M_1(R_2), \max M_2(R_1)).$

Theorem 15

If $\bar{s}$ is an optimum,

$$M\bar{s} = (\max M_1(E), \max M_2(E)).$$

However, an equilibrium best for both players is not necessarily an optimum. Figure 6.12b provides an example of such an equilibrium that is not an optimum.

The $(2, 2)$ outcome of prisoner's dilemma is an optimum, though it is not a metaoptimum from any proper metagame. The $(3, 3)$ outcome of Figure 6.12a is an optimum; but Figure 6.12b has no optimum, despite the fact that it has an equilibrium. The outcome $s = (1, 1)$ is the optimum of the game in Example 3 on page 173.

The characteristics of optima would make them the "obvious solution" to a game (and hence would confer on games with optima a unique value) were it not for the worrisome fact that metaoptimal outcomes lack the *descendance property* (i.e., $\hat{R}_i(H^*) \supseteq \hat{R}_i(H)$, if H^* is a descendant of H) enjoyed by metarational outcomes. This is disturbing because, as we have seen in prisoner's dilemma, it means that a player may find an optimal outcome unacceptable because by going to a metagame he can induce more.

If, however, an outcome is a metaoptimum from every metagame, this will not be so. Then it will be both rational for each player and also the best that either player can in any way induce, even by going to a metagame.

We call such an outcome a *perfect optimum*. Thus the set Π of perfect optima is defined by

$$\Pi = \bigcap_H \hat{O}(H) = \bigcap_H \bigcap_i \hat{O}_i(H).$$

This is of course the same as

$$\bigcap_H \hat{O}_1(H) \cap \bigcap_H \hat{O}_2(H),$$

so we may say that a perfect optimum is an outcome that is *perfectly optimal* for both players, or

$$\Pi = \Pi_1 \cap \Pi_2,$$

where

$$\Pi_i = \bigcap_H \hat{O}_i(H)$$

is defined to be the set of *perfectly optimal outcomes for player i.*

Now we have a number of theorems. First we have from Theorem 12 and from the descendance property of metarational outcomes:

Theorem 16

In a two-person zero-sum game, an outcome is perfectly optimal for i if and only if it is rational for him; hence the equilibria are the perfect optima.

Thus in the zero-sum case, $R_i = O_i = \Pi_i$. But the general basic characterizations of optimal outcomes, perfectly optimal outcomes, and perfect optima are obtained as follows:

Theorem 17

For any metagame H, $s \in \hat{O}_i(H)$ if and only if

$$s \in \hat{R}_i(H)$$

and

$$M_i s \supseteq \max M_i(\hat{R}_j(H)), \quad j \neq i.$$

Hence $s \in \Pi_i$ if and only if

$$s \in R_i$$

and

$$M_i s \supseteq \max M_i(\Gamma_j), \quad j \neq i,$$

and $s \in \Pi$ if and only if

$$s \in E$$

and

$$Ms = (\max M_1(\Gamma_2), \max M_2(\Gamma_1)).$$

The reader may prove this himself, noting that since

$$\Gamma_i \supseteq \hat{R}_i(H), \quad \text{for all } H,$$

it is the case that $\max M_i(\Gamma_j)$, which is the best value that player i can induce from iG, is also the best value he can induce from any metagame.

The best outcome for player i over the whole game is in Π_i. Hence perfectly optimal outcomes always exist. Perfect optima may not, of course. In Figure 6.12a the $(3, 3)$ optimum is perfect. Figure 6.12b has no optimum, therefore no perfect optimum.

In the game of Example 3, page 173, $(1, 1)$ is an optimum. Is it perfect? To decide, we have to find Γ_1 and Γ_2. We find

$$\Gamma_1 = \{s \,|\, \bar{v}_1(s) \geqslant (0, -1)\};$$
$$\Gamma_2 = \{s \,|\, \bar{v}_2(s) \geqslant (\tfrac{1}{2}, 3)\}.$$

For example, Γ_1 is formed by calculating

$$\max_{s_1} \min_{s_2}(4s_1 s_2 - s_1, \, -s_2^2 + \tfrac{1}{2}s_1 s_2)$$
$$= \max_{s_1} \begin{cases} (-s_1, 0) & \text{if } s_1 \neq 0 \\ (0, -1) & \text{if } s_1 = 0 \end{cases}$$
$$= (0, -1).$$

Therefore $\max M_2(\Gamma_1)$ is found by maximizing $\bar{v}_2(s) = (s_2^2 - \tfrac{1}{2}s_1 s_2, \, 4s_1 s_2 - s_1)$, subject to the side condition requiring that

$$(4s_1 s_2 - s_1, \, -s_2^2 + \tfrac{1}{2}s_1 s_2) \geqslant (0, -1).$$

But this side condition is redundant, since the maximum $(1, 0)$, obtained by setting $s_1 = 0$, $s_2 = 1$, is in any case obtained without violating the side condition. Thus $\max M_2(\Gamma_1) = M_2(0, 1) = (1, 0)$.

This is not the same as $M_2(1, 1)$, therefore the optimum $(1, 1)$ is not perfect. Indeed, in the game $2G$ player 2 can induce more than he can in G. In G, we have seen that he can induce at most $(\tfrac{1}{2}, 3)$; but in $2G$, he may adopt the policy

"If you choose $s_1 \neq 0$, I will set $s_2 = 0$.

If you choose $s_1 = 0$, I will set $s_2 = 1$."

This policy induces player 1 to set $s_1 = 0$, since if he does not, he obtains a negative payoff $4s_1 s_2 - s_1$. By setting $s_1 = 0$, he at least ensures that his payoff is zero.

Of the games in Figure 2.14, (a) and (b) have perfect optima, (c) and (d) do not, in fact they have no optima at all. Figure 2.14b of course has two perfect optima; and this brings out the one difficulty with perfect optima—if they are not unique, there may be a problem of coordination in order for the players to obtain a perfect optimum.

We have seen that this cannot be a problem in the zero-sum case, but it may be in the general case.

Apart from this difficulty, it seems that a game with a perfect optimum presents no real problems. The solution is obvious: players that understand the game and know each other's preferences must anticipate an optimum. The game therefore has a unique value for each player.

This has to be tested experimentally, of course. Meanwhile, let us show that a game with a perfect optimum is precisely one that suffers from none of our three breakdowns of rationality; that is, it is what we have defined as a "perfect" game.

Theorem 18

A game has a perfect optimum if and only if it is perfect.

Proof: We prove first that a perfect game has a perfect optimum. Suppose that G is perfect. Then G has an undominated equilibrium $\bar{s}$; but since $\bar{s} \in E$, it suffices to prove that

$$M\bar{s} = (\max M_1(\Gamma_2), \max M_2(\Gamma_1)).$$

Now G is also rational, so that a sure-thing policy f_1^r induces for player 1 precisely the value $\max M_1(\Gamma_2)$. Moreover, it induces 2 to obtain the value $\max M_2(R_1)$. Hence f_1^r induces the value-outcome

$(\max M_1(\Gamma_2), \max M_2(R_1))$.

But

$\max M_1(\Gamma_2) \supseteq \max M_1(R_2) \supseteq M_1\bar{s}$,

since $\bar{s} \in R_2$. Also $\bar{s} \in R_1$, so that

$\max M_2(R_1) \supseteq M_2\bar{s}$.

Hence f_1^r induces a value-outcome as good for both players as $M\bar{s}$. But $\bar{s}$ is undominated, therefore f_1^r induces $M\bar{s}$, and therefore

$M_1\bar{s} = \max M_1(\Gamma_2)$.

Similarly we can prove that $M_2\bar{s} = \max M_2(\Gamma_1)$, and this concludes the first part of the proof.

It remains to prove that a game with a perfect optimum is perfect. Such a game G has an undominated equilibrium, since a perfect optimum is undominated and an equilibrium. It remains to prove that G is rational.

Now a perfect optimum $\bar{s}$ belongs to R_1 and obeys

$$M_2\bar{s} = \max M_2(\Gamma_1) \supseteq \max M_2(R_1).$$

Hence $M_2\bar{s} = \max M_2(R_1)$. But $M_1\bar{s} = \max M_1(\Gamma_2)$, so that

$$\max M_1(\Gamma_2) = M_1^2 \max M_2(R_1),$$

and similarly

$$\max M_2(\Gamma_1) = M_2^1 \max M_1(R_2),$$

which from Theorem 10 is all we need.

Before leaving the subject of perfect games, let us note that though they are certainly more common than determinate two-person zero-sum games, they are still not likely to occur very often in real-life situations. They are mainly interesting in that they define for us the "problem area" of *imperfect* games.

We have said that a perfect game presents no problems. An *imperfect* game, on the other hand, certainly presents problems, since it embodies some kind of breakdown of rationality. Yet we have seen that the first two breakdowns of rationality are "solved" in the metagame tree; that is, they cannot occur in a complete metagame.

What else can we say about a complete metagame? Are there other problems that cannot occur in a complete metagame, even an imperfect one? Indeed there are. The situation in a complete meta-game is comparatively simple. The first point to note is that if player i attempts to induce $\max M_i(R_j)$, the best value he can induce, then he can always find an equilibrium that has this value. This is an advantage, as player j may be unwilling to be induced to accept an outcome having this value that, though it is rational for him, j (it must be, since player i is inducing it), is not rational for player i: player j may fear that if he accepts such an outcome, i will then move away.

This difficulty, which can occur in general, is illustrated in Figure 6.13. In Figure 6.13a, player 1 can try to induce $(3,3)$, but since this is not an equilibrium, player 2 may refuse to believe that if he (2) accepts, 1 will not move away to $(4, 1)$. Figure 6.13b provides an even

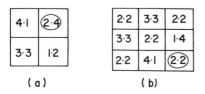

Figure 6.13. Games in Which max $M_i(R_j)$ Is Not an Equilibrium Value.

worse case. Here there are two outcomes with the value-pair

$$(\max M_1(R_2), \max M_2(R_1)) = (\max M_1(\Gamma_2), \max M_2(\Gamma_1)),$$

that is, the value-pair of a perfect optimum. Yet neither of these is an equilibrium.

That this difficulty cannot occur in a complete metagame is the content of

Theorem 19

A complete metagame H yields metaequilibria s^1, s^2 such that

$$M_1 s^1 = \max M_1(\hat{R}_2(H)),$$

$$M_2 s^2 = \max M_2(\hat{R}_1(H)).$$

NOTE. This is equivalent of course, to the statement that H has equilibria x^1, x^2 such that

$$M_1 x^1 = \max M_1(R_2(H)), \; M_2 x^2 = \max M_2(R_1(H)).$$

Proof: Player 2's sure-thing policy in $2H$ induces an equilibrium $(\bar{x}_1, \bar{f})$ such that

$$M_1 \beta^*(\bar{x}_1, \bar{f}) = \max M_1(\hat{R}_2(2H))$$

(see Theorem 9 and its proof). But since H is complete, $\hat{E}(2H) = \hat{E}(H)$. Therefore $\beta^*(\bar{x}_1, \bar{f})$ is a metaequilibrium from H. Also, $\hat{R}_2(2H) = \hat{R}_2(H)$. Therefore $s^1 = \beta^*(\bar{x}_1, \bar{f})$ satisfies the theorem. The proof for s^2 is similar.

We now have

Theorem 20

If H is complete, the following are alternative necessary and sufficient conditions for H to be perfect:

i. H is rational;

ii. H has an equilibrium that is the best equilibrium for both players;

iii. $Ms^1 = Ms^2$ (where s^1, s^2 are as in Theorem 19);

iv. max $M_i(\hat{R}_j(H)) = M_i^j$ max $M_j(\hat{R}_i(H))$ (where $j \neq i$).

Proof: Condition i is necessary and sufficient by the definition of a perfect game, since we know that a complete metagame possesses an undominated equilibrium. Hence condition i $\Rightarrow$ condition ii, since a perfect game possesses an optimum (Theorem 18) and an optimum is an equilibrium best for both players (Theorem 15). Next, condition ii $\Rightarrow$ condition iii, since s^i is certainly the best equilibrium for player i. Also condition iii $\Rightarrow$ condition iv by the definition of s^1, s^2. Finally condition iv $\Rightarrow$ condition i; using Theorem 8 and the fact that if H is complete, $\hat{R}_j(H) = \hat{R}_j(H')$ for every descendant H' of H, so that

$$M_i(\beta^*\Gamma_j(H)) = M_i(\hat{R}_j(H)).$$

To sum up, difficulties of various kinds may occur in incomplete metagames. But when we reach a complete metagame, it is either perfect or else it contains a simple conflict between various equilibria, there being no equilibrium that is the best for both players.

When we have such a conflict between equilibria s^1, s^2, where s^i is better for player i, then the point (s_1^1, s_2^2) will be a *conflict point*. The $(1, 1)$ outcome in Figure 6.4b is an example. This conflict point will be dominated by both s^1 and s^2. But it is nevertheless likely to have a kind of stability. It is not truly stable, since neither player is willing to accept it, but each may be unwilling to move, hoping that the other will move instead.

In the next section we shall suggest that, though not stable, it may become so through a process of preference change.

6.6 Possible Directions for Further Research

Vast numbers of problems remain in the development of an empirical theory of inducement. In other areas also, for example, in coalition theory and in the theory of metaequilibria in many-person games, the theory of metagames is underdeveloped. As we have said, the best methodological approach seems to be to find simple, intuitive theories for the basic game and then to apply them to the metagame tree in the hope that there they will be, not merely simple and intuitively obvious, but also true. The main difficulty is to choose among an embarrassingly large number of simple, obvious theories that cannot all be used, as they contradict each other.

Here we shall offer a number of research ideas that seem promising. First, there is the idea of *preference deterioration*.

This arises in connection with conflict points. We have seen that these are important in that a complete metagame (in the two-person mutually ordinal case) is either perfect—has no real problems—or else involves a conflict between conflicting equilibria; and this conflict is carried on by each player refusing to budge from a conflict point, hoping that the other will move instead. Figure 6.4b contains a clear, simple example of a conflict point.

Now experimentally it has been observed that this conflict (staying at a conflict point) has the effect of making players cross with each other. They feel that their opponent "should" give way, and begin to adopt the attitude conveyed by such clichés as "I'll see you in hell first," "better dead than red," and "over my dead body." This may go so far that a player may change his preferences. He may come to prefer the conflict point to the equilibrium preferred by his opponent. For example, starting from the game in Figure 6.4b or Figure 6.14a, player 1's preferences may change so that the game becomes that shown in Figure 6.14b. We call this kind of change *preference deterioration*.

Is this a matter of player 1 developing such dislike for his opponent that he prefers the conflict point simply because it is worse for 2? This is unlikely, as this motivation would also lead player 1 to prefer the conflict point to s^1, the equilibrium preferred by 1 himself, a phenomenon that does not occur. A psychological explanation might be provided by Festinger's theory of "cognitive dissonance"

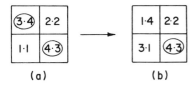

(a)   (b)

Figure 6.14. Preference Deterioration Acting on Player 1's Preferences.

(Festinger 1957), according to which inner conflict between preferences and policy choice, as when a player's policy is not sure-thing, might lead, as here, to a change in preferences designed to make the player's actual policy a sure-thing policy. This is a most interesting idea. However, here we feel that the deepest explanation is to point out that the preference change is in a way strategically motivated. It causes the equilibrium preferred by the other player to cease to be an equilibrium; all that is left is the equilibrium preferred by player 1. The game in fact becomes a perfect game, the perfect optimum being s^1. Player 1, by allowing his preferences to deteriorate, will therefore get what he wants—provided, that is, that 2's preferences do not deteriorate and 2 can be persuaded that 1's preferences *have* in fact deteriorated.

If player 2's preferences also deteriorate, however, we again obtain a perfect game, shown in Figure 6.15. But now the perfect optimum is the point that was previously the conflict point itself. This is now the only stable outcome, although initially it was the worst outcome for both players. The players have in a sense worked themselves into a corner so that no further compromise is possible.

We remind the reader that this has been achieved by way of emotions such as anger and frustration; these emotions appear to be a concomitant of preference deterioration. A player who "cold-bloodedly" changes his preferences has not, we would say, really changed them at all: he has merely pretended to change them, which may of course be justified as a sensible thing to do if one thinks the opponent's preferences have not really changed. An example of all this might be the conflict between the United States and North Vietnam, in which the conflict consisted of the United States bombing North Vietnam while the North Vietnamese killed U.S. troops. North Vietnam wanted

1·4	2·2
③·③	4·1

Figure 6.15. A Fully Deteriorated Game.

the United States to withdraw, while the United States wanted North Vietnam to cease aiding the NLF. Perhaps North Vietnamese preferences actually deteriorated, while U.S. preferences did not really deteriorate. This is merely a suggestion that we throw in to give a concrete example.

These ideas might lead to an important role for perfect games as being "fully deteriorated" games, that is, games in which no further preference deterioration is possible.

It is of course urgently necessary to generalize our ideas about inducement to the many-person case. This might also provide a more far-reaching analysis of coalitions than we have at present. A suggested approach is to complete an adequate theory of the two-person case first. Then player 3 might be brought in by regarding his various strategies as creating various two-person games between players 1 and 2. What player 3's choice of a strategy "induces" is this two-person game between 1 and 2. If this two-person game is perfect, then player 3's strategy has an inducement value that, in the mutually ordinal case, is unique. Otherwise, it has a range of possible inducement values. Clearly, player 3 will try to persuade the other players to go to the solution of the two-person game that player 3 likes best. An intriguing possibility is that 3 may wish to exacerbate the conflict between 1 and 2, leading their preferences to deteriorate until they reach a fully deteriorated game with a perfect optimum that player 3 happens to like!

Baffling problems arise for inducement theory if we start with a game that is not mutually ordinal. It is necessary to tackle these problems, as we ought to provide further reasons for supposing that a realistic game will be mutually ordinal. These reasons may form part of the theory of preference deterioration, in that we may be able to show that if initially a game is not mutually ordinal, there are strategic reasons for players to change their preferences so as to make it so.

The application of game theory to realistic problems has only been touched on in this book. A detailed account of the technique of analysis of options (described generally in Section 5.3) is given in Management Science Center (1969b). Elaborate and sophisticated computer-aided methods for storing and analyzing assumptions about current political problems may soon be developed and used by governments to analyze foreign policy problems. Theoretically this is not so interesting as the mathematical and conceptual problems that we have discussed, but feedback from the field of applications is invigorating for theoretical research. We believe that game theory is becoming a unifying force in the social sciences, encompassing economics, psychology, politics, and history within a single mathematical theory capable of being applied to the understanding of all interactions between conscious beings.

Appendix A
Elementary
Set Theory
and Logic

Mathematics may be regarded as a language for making statements and deducing one statement from another. Let us see how quite ordinary statements appear when written in the language of mathematics.

The statement

John is a coward

may be written "John $\in C = \{x \mid x$ is a coward$\}$." Let us explain this.

Here C is a *set*. Without attempting to define a set, we shall simply describe it. A set is a collection of objects of any kind. A particular set may be specified in one of two ways.

We may list the objects contained in the set, using the notation

$A = \{$the king of Spain, 1, my head$\}$,
$B = \{1, 2, 3, \ldots\}$.

Here two sets are defined. The set A contains three objects—the king of Spain, the number one, and my head. The set B contains the positive integers $1, 2, 3, \ldots$. Thus A is *finite* (contains a finite number of objects) and B is *infinite*. When we list the objects in a set, no object can appear in the list more than once.

Alternatively, we may define a set by giving a *property* that characterizes the objects in the set; that is, any object belongs to the set if and only if it possesses this stated property. In this case we use the notation

$X = \{x \mid x$ has the property ——— $\}$

to define a set. This is read "X is the set of all x such that x has the property ——— ." For example, using this notation, we defined C as being the set of all cowards.

The objects belonging to a set are called *elements* of the set; and we write "$\in$" to mean "is an element of." For example, we have according to our previous definition (my head) $\in A$,

and our translation of the statement "John is a coward" reads

John is an element of C, where C is the set of all x such that x is a coward.

It is not clear whether C is finite or infinite.

EQUALITY. Two sets are said to be *equal* ("the same") when they contain the same elements. This is so even if they are defined quite differently. For example, at a party it might happen that the only married couple were Australian; then if they were the only Australians present, the two sets

$Y = \{y \mid y$ is an Australian at the party$\}$,
$Z = \{\alpha \mid \alpha$ is accompanied to the party by a spouse$\}$

would be the same set, despite the difference in their definitions. We would write

$Y = Z.$

Equivalently, two sets are different when one of them contains an element not contained in the other. For example, if A and B are defined as above we have

$A \neq B,$

since

(my head) $\in A$, (my head) $\notin B$.

DUMMY VARIABLES. Note that the symbol used in defining a set—for example, the symbol "α" used to define Z—is immaterial: any other symbol substituted throughout would have precisely the same effect. Had we written

$Z = \{\cdot \mid \cdot$ is accompanied to the party by a spouse$\}$,

the meaning attached to Z would have been the same. A symbol such as this, for which any other symbol can be substituted, is said to represent a *dummy variable*. Thus in our previous definition of Z, α is a dummy variable. If a mathematical statement is hard to understand, it is often useful to sort out the dummy variables in it.

THE EMPTY SET. There are of course many sets, indeed an infinite number. Among them we include the *empty set*—the set containing no elements. There is only one empty set; for if there were two, one would have to contain an element not in the other, which is impossible, since neither contains any elements. This leads to conclusions, at first sight puzzling, such as that the set of good French restaurants in Waterloo, Ontario, is the same as the set of perfect social systems—both being empty. The symbol $\emptyset$ denotes the empty set.

UNION OF SETS. Given two sets P and Q we may form another set, called the *union* of P and Q, and written

$P \cup Q$.

This is defined as the set

$\{x | x \in P \quad or \quad x \in Q\}$;

that is, it contains the elements of P *and* those of Q. For example,

$\{a, x, y\} \cup \{a, b\} = \{a, b, x, y\}$.

We can go on to form unions of more than two sets. We write

$P \cup Q \cup R = (P \cup Q) \cup R = P \cup (Q \cup R)$.

INTERSECTION OF SETS. Given P and Q we may also form a set called their *intersection*, and written

$P \cap Q$.

This is the set

$\{v | v \in P \text{ and } v \in Q\}$

containing the elements belonging to *both* P and Q. For example,

$\{a, x, y\} \cap \{a, b\} = \{a\}$.

(*Note:* The set $\{a\}$ is called a *singleton* set, or *unit* set, since it contains just one element. The singleton set containing a is not to be confused with a itself. For example, (my head) $\in A$, but $\{(\text{my head})\}$ $\notin A$. However, of course,

$\{(\text{my head})\} \in A \cup \{ \{(\text{my head})\} \}$,

where $\{ \{(\text{my head})\} \}$ is the singleton set containing the singleton set containing my head.)

We can form the intersection of more than two sets, writing

$$P \cap Q \cap R = P \cap (Q \cap R) = (P \cap Q) \cap R.$$

SUBSETS. If every element contained in P is contained also in Q, then P is said to be a *subset* of Q, and we write

$$P \subseteq Q.$$

Thus according to our previous definition, $P = Q$ if and only if $P \subseteq Q$ and $Q \subseteq P$.

If P is a subset of Q, we also say that Q is a *superset* of P, and write

$$Q \supseteq P.$$

If P is a subset of Q that is not equal to Q (so that Q contains an element not in P), then P is said to be a *proper subset* of Q, and Q to be a *proper superset* of P, and we write

$$P \subset Q, Q \supset P.$$

The empty set is a subset of every set, and a proper subset of every nonempty set. Also we have

$$P \cap Q \subseteq P,$$

$$P \cup Q \supseteq P$$

for any sets P and Q.

COMPLEMENTARY SETS. Given P and Q, we may form a set called the *complement of P in Q*, written

$$Q - P.$$

This is the set

$$\{x | x \in Q, x \notin P\},$$

containing the elements of Q that are not in P. Clearly, $Q - P \subseteq Q$. Forming $Q - P$ may also be called "subtracting P from Q."

If $P \cap Q = \varnothing$, P and Q are called *disjoint*. In this case $Q - P = Q$. The empty set is disjoint from every set.

The foregoing operations with sets may be illustrated by a *Venn diagram* as in Figure A.1. Here a set is represented by an area on the page.

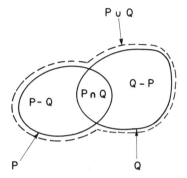

Figure A.1. Venn Diagram Illustrating Set Operations.

Various operational rules are obeyed by sets. For example, we have for any sets P, Q, and R

$$P \cap (Q \cup R) = (P \cap Q) \cup (P \cap R),$$

$$P \cup (Q \cap R) = (P \cup Q) \cap (P \cup R).$$

FUNCTIONS. A *function* is a rule that assigns to each element of one set (called the *domain* of the function) a unique element of another set (called the *codomain* of the function). For example, if a person follows a daily routine, there is a function connecting the time of day (the domain is the set of distinct moments in a day) with the action he customarily performs at that time (the codomain is the set of mutually exclusive actions he may perform). At any given time, he customarily is performing one and only one action.

Another example is the function "multiply by 2" with domain and codomain equal to the set $\{1, 2, 3, \ldots\}$. This function takes any number $x \in \{1, 2, 3, \ldots\}$ to the number $2x \in \{1, 2, 3, \ldots\}$.

Functions are also called "transformations" or "mappings." To specify a function, we have to specify the domain and codomain (which may be the same) and the rule that takes (or "transforms" or "maps") any element of the domain into a unique element of the codomain. We write

$$f : P \to Q$$

to signify that f is a function from P (the domain) to Q (the codomain). This of course does not define the function f. It merely gives it a name "f" and specifies the domain and codomain—P and Q.

Elements of the domain P are called *arguments* of the function. The element of the codomain that corresponds to a given element x of the domain is written

$f(x)$,

or simply

fx,

and is called *the value of f at x.*

This enables us to specify the function. Thus, to specify the function "multiply by 2" mentioned earlier, we could write

$g : \{1, 2, 3, \ldots\} \rightarrow \{1, 2, 3, \ldots\};$

$g(x) = 2x.$

This gives the function the name "g" and specifies exactly what the function is. Here x is a *dummy variable. (Note:* To emphasize that a certain equality is true for every argument of a function, we sometimes write "$\equiv$" instead of "$=$". Thus above we might have written "$g(x) \equiv 2x$." The symbol "$\equiv$" is read "identically equal to.")

If $f: P \rightarrow Q$ is a function, an element of Q must correspond to each element of P, but there may well be elements of Q that correspond to no element of P. In the foregoing example, where domain and codomain were equal, there was a value $g(x) = 2x$ for every $x \in \{1, 2, 3, \ldots\}$. But it was not the case that for every $y \in \{1, 2, 3, \ldots\}$ there was an x such that $g(x) = y$. This was true only for the numbers $2, 4, 6, \ldots$.

The set[1]

$\{\alpha \,|\, fx = \alpha, x \in P\}$

is the subset of Q for which it is true that each element is a value of the function $f: P \rightarrow Q$. It is in fact just the set of values of f and is called the *image* of f.

A clear distinction must be made between a *function f*, and a *value* of that function, written $f(x)$. These are obviously two quite different things. Yet at times mathematicians do not bother to make this distinction. For instance, in this book we talk of the set of outcomes

1. Here both α and x are dummy variables.

of a game that are "equilibria" of that game. We write "E" to denote this set of equilibria; but when we wish to specify what particular game E is the set of equilibria of—for instance, when we wish to denote the equilibria of a certain game H—we write "$E(H)$." This is not really correct. Strictly we ought to define a function e from the set of games to the set of subsets of outcomes of games and write "$e(H)$" for the set of equilibria of H. But we do not do this because it requires more notation, making the development harder to follow though more nearly correct. At other times, however, particularly when discussing functions f that are metagame strategies, the distinction between f and a value of f has to be rigorously maintained.

INDEXED SETS. The language of mathematics uses symbols (usually single letters) to denote objects. We begin by using letters for "ordinary" objects—my head, the number one, and so forth. We next use letters to denote sets of such objects and then to denote functions from one set to another. A function is quite a complicated "object," of course, so quite a lot is now being summed up by a simple letter such as "f."

Sometimes we run out of letters to denote the many objects we want to discuss. Then we may use the same letter, *subscripted* differently. For example, to denote 10 objects we might use the numbers $1, \ldots, 10$ as subscripts and write

$$t_1, t_2, \ldots, t_{10}$$

to denote our 10 objects.

A subscripted collection of objects such as this, written inside *round* brackets instead of braces, like

$$(t_1, \ldots, t_{10}),$$

is called an *indexed set*. Note that this is not just a set: for the fact that our objects are subscripted ("indexed") means that the same object may appear more than once in an indexed set—for example, we may have $t_1 = t_2$. This is not possible with an ordinary set.

The subscripted objects t_i appearing in an indexed set are called *components* of the set, and t_i is called the "ith" component.

Actually an indexed set is a function. It is a function from the set of indices (here the set $\{1, \ldots, 10\}$), called the *index set*, to the set of distinct components (here the set $\{t_i | i \in \{1, \ldots, 10\}\}$). Instead of writing "$t(i)$" for a value of this function, we write "t_i": that is all the difference. A function gets to be called an "indexed set" because of the special purpose to which we are putting it, namely, to use the elements of the domain (the "index set") as indices by which to keep track of elements of the codomain.

The set of positive integers is a favorite choice for an index set, but in general any set may be used for this purpose. Suppose we wish to denote the action of a country "going to war" by the letter g. We might use the set of countries as an index set to distinguish whether we mean, for example, *America* going to war

$g_{\text{U.S.}}$

or *Argentina* doing the same

g_{ARG}.

The indexed set $(t_1, \ldots, t_{10})$ may also be written

$(t_i | i \in \{1, \ldots, 10\})$

and in general

$(x_y | y \in z)$

denotes an indexed set with yth component x_y and index set z. We repeat that this is different from

$\{x_y | y \in z\}$,

which is an ordinary set—the set of distinct components of the indexed set.

UNION AND INTERSECTION OF INDEXED SETS. If $(S_\alpha | \alpha \in A)$ is an indexed set of sets (that is, each S_α is a set), we write

$$\bigcup_{\alpha \in A} S_\alpha$$

for the union of all its components and

$$\bigcap_{\alpha \in A} S_\alpha$$

for their intersection. Thus, for example,

$$S_1 \cup S_2 = \bigcup_{i \in \{1,2\}} S_i,$$

and

$$S_1 \cap S_2 = \bigcap_{i \in \{1,2\}} S_i.$$

CARTESIAN PRODUCTS OF SETS. If $(S_\alpha | \alpha \in A)$ is an indexed set of sets, also called an indexed *family* of sets, their *Cartesian product* is the set of all indexed sets

$$(s_\alpha | \alpha \in A)$$

such that $s_\alpha \in S_\alpha$ for all $\alpha \in A$. Thus the Cartesian product contains all combinations formed by selecting one element from each set S_α.

Cartesian products are used to describe things. We can describe something by stating a combination of properties possessed by the thing. For instance, I might describe a man by saying he is fairly tall, fat, and has brown hair. Or I might describe the position of an object on a rectangular table by saying it is 6 inches out from side A and 2 inches out from side B (side B being at right angles to side A).

In each case we have certain sets of properties such that the object must possess one and only one property out of each set. We say that the man has one and only one kind of height—the set D_h being an exclusive set of possible descriptions of his height; he has one and only one kind of fatness—the set D_f being the set of possible mutually exclusive kinds of fatness; and he has one and only one hair color—the set D_c being the set of hair colors. The description is then effected by choosing one element from each set to represent the man. Similarly we choose a distance from side A (6 inches) and one from side B (2 inches) to represent the position of the object on the table.

Such a description d is merely an element of the Cartesian product of the sets of properties—for example, if the man is fairly tall, fat, and brown-haired, his description d is

$$d = (d_h, d_f, d_c),$$

where each $d_\alpha \in D_\alpha$ and $d_h = $ fairly tall; $d_f = $ fat; $d_c = $ brown-haired. The Cartesian product itself is the set of all possible descriptions obtainable using the sets D_h, D_f, and D_c.

The Cartesian product of an indexed family $(S_\alpha | \alpha \in A)$ is written

$$\prod_{\alpha \in A} S_\alpha.$$

Sometimes we do not bother to use indices explicitly to denote an indexed set. Instead, we write the components in a certain fixed order, always the same. (This of course amounts implicitly to using the position of a component as an index.) For example, the possible locations of an object on a table 6 feet long and 3 feet wide might be described by forming two sets—the set $S = \{x \mid x$ is a real number of feet between 0 and 3$\}$ and a set $T = \{y \mid y$ is a real number of feet between 0 and 6$\}$. The Cartesian product of S and T is written

$$S \times T,$$

and an element of this Cartesian product is written

$$(x, y),$$

where it is understood that x is an element of S and y an element of T because x is written first. A corner of the table having been chosen for the position $(0, 0)$, each ordered pair (x, y) then denotes a location on the table. For example, a point 4 feet up the length of the table and 2.7 feet across its width would be denoted by the pair $(2.7, 4)$.

LOGICAL IMPLICATION. An arrow "$\Rightarrow$" is used to denote logical implication. Thus if A and B are statements,

$$A \Rightarrow B$$

is the statement

A implies B.

This is construed to mean that if A is true, B is true also. For instance, if P and Q are sets, the statement

$$x \in P \Rightarrow x \in Q$$

is construed to mean simply that $P \subseteq Q$.

Note that if the statement A is false, then the statement "$A \Rightarrow B$" is true, regardless of what the statement B may be. (Thus, "$\Rightarrow$" is used like "if ... then ..." in such sentences as "If that is so, then I'll eat my hat.") This usage of "$\Rightarrow$" corresponds to our pre-

vious remark that the empty set is a subset of every set. For we wish
"$x \in P \Rightarrow x \in Q$" to mean the same as "$P \subseteq Q$" even in the case when
P is empty.

NEGATION. We write "$\sim A$" for the *negation* of the statement A.
Thus "$\sim A$" reads "not A." For example, if A is the statement

"Penny has black hair,"

then $\sim A$ is the statement

"Penny does not have black hair."

Clearly the statement "$\sim(\sim A)$" means the same as A itself.

Using this notation, we can say that "$A \Rightarrow B$" as we have defined it
means the same as

$\sim A$ or B,

which in turn means the same as

$\sim(A$ and $\sim B)$;

that is, "$A \Rightarrow B$" simply says that we cannot have A true and B false.
Note: When we use the word "or" in mathematics, we intend the
inclusive "or," meaning "either or both," rather than the exclusive
"or," meaning "either but not both."

EQUIVALENCE. If $A \Rightarrow B$ and also $B \Rightarrow A$, then the statements A and B
are equivalent, and we write

$A \Leftrightarrow B$,

which reads "A if and only if B." For example, if P and Q are sets,

$x \in P \Leftrightarrow x \in Q$

means the same as

$P = Q$.

QUANTIFIERS. We write "$\exists$" to mean "there exists . . . such that . . . ."
For instance

$\exists x : x \in Y$

is read "there exists x such that x is an element of Y," and it means
simply that Y is a nonempty set.

The symbol "∃" is called the *existential quantifier*. It is used to assert that something exists.

Also we have the *universal quantifier*, written "∀" and read "for all." Thus the statement

$$\forall x : x \notin Y$$

is read "for all x, x is not an element of Y," and it asserts simply that Y is empty.

We can see that to negate a statement

$$\exists x : A$$

(where A is a statement), we simply negate A and change the quantifier. Thus,

$$\sim \exists x : A$$

means the same as

$$\forall x : \sim A.$$

And, of course,

$$\sim \forall x : A$$

means the same as

$$\exists x : \sim A.$$

We can compose quite a long statement using quantifiers, for instance,

$$\exists x \, \forall y \, \exists z : (x \in P) \Rightarrow [(y \in P - Q) \text{ or } z \in R].$$

Negating this, we obtain

$$\forall x \, \exists y \, \forall z : (x \in P) \text{ and } \sim [(y \in P - Q) \text{ or } z \in R],$$

which is to say

$$\forall x \, \exists y \, \forall z : (x \in P) \text{ and } (y \in P - Q) \text{ and } (z \notin R).$$

A rule concerning quantifiers is that "$\exists x \, \forall y : A$" implies "$\forall y \, \exists x : A$." But this rule is not reversible. We cannot infer from "$\forall y \, \exists x : A$" the statement "$\exists x \, \forall y : A$."

NOTE. Almost always, when we use the universal quantifier to assert something "for all x," we really mean for all x belonging to a certain set we have previously defined. The same usually applies when we assert "there exists x": we mean that there exists x belonging to a certain set. We can specify this set by writing

$\forall(s \in S): \ldots$

or

$\exists(s \in S): \ldots,$

but often instead of this we say something like "let s be a typical element of S," leaving it to be understood that thereafter "$\forall s \ldots$" means "$\forall(s \in S): \ldots$." For instance, we discussed previously the Cartesian product containing all locations (x, y) on a certain tabletop. In that example we might have said "Let x be a typical element of S" (S being the set of distances across the width of the table), allowing us therefore to write

$\forall x : x \leqslant 3.$

It may happen that the set S, of which s is supposed to be a typical element, is empty. In this case, corresponding to our previous usage for the "$\Rightarrow$" sign and to the rule that the empty set is a subset of every set, we have to say that the statement

$\forall s : A$

is true whatever the statement A may be. Hence,

$\exists s : A$

is false whatever A may be. For "$\forall s : \sim A$" is true; "$\exists s : A$" is its negation; and the negation of a true statement is always false.

PROBABILITIES IN FINITE SETS. There is considerable disagreement among philosophers and scientists as to what probabilities are. What does it mean to say "right now there is one chance in five of nuclear war?" On the other hand, there is close agreement as to how probabilities should be represented mathematically. One might say that probabilities are like electricity: we don't know what electricity is, we know only how to deal with it mathematically.

Probabilities are discussed in this book somewhat incidentally. The mathematics of probability is quantitative, whereas our aim is a nonquantitative theory. The following facts about probabilities are all that we need.

If E is a finite set of events, one and only one of which must occur, a *probability distribution* on E is a function p from the set E to the set of numbers that obeys

$$\forall(x \in E) : 0 \leqslant p(x) \leqslant 1;$$
$$\sum_{x \in E} p(x) = 1.$$

(*Note*: Here "$\Sigma_{x \in T}\, P(x)$" means the sum of all the numbers $p(x)$ such that $x \in T$. This is similar to the notations

$$\bigcup_{\alpha \in A}, \bigcap_{\alpha \in A}, \prod_{\alpha \in A}$$

used earlier for unions, intersections, and Cartesian products.)

The value $p(x)$ is interpreted as the proportionate "chance" that x will occur: for example, if $p(x) = \frac{1}{5}$, this means that there is one chance in five that x will occur. Hence zero probability represents "impossibility," and a probability of one represents "certainty."

Given the probabilities of some events, the probabilities of other events may be deduced. If x and y are two *mutually exclusive* events (that is, both cannot occur), then the probability of x *or* y occurring is $p(x) + p(y)$. Hence, if E as above is a set of events, one and only one of which must occur, then we must have $\Sigma_{x \in E} p(x) = 1$; for the events $x \in E$ are mutually exclusive, and it is certain that one of them will occur.

On the other hand, if x and y are two *independent* events (that is, the occurrence of one has no effect on the probability of the other occurring), then the probability of both x *and* y occurring is $p(x)\, p(y)$, the product of their separate probabilities. Generally, if D is a set of independent events, the probability of every event in D occurring is

$$\prod_{x \in D} p(x),$$

where "$\Pi_{x \in D} p(x)$" stands for the product of all the numbers $p(x)$ such that $x \in D$. (The same notation is thus used for a product of numbers as is used for a *Cartesian product* of sets. The context usually makes it clear which kind of product is meant.)

To illustrate these ideas, consider the throw of a die. The probability of a 3 being thrown is $\frac{1}{6}$: in fact, each of the six sides has the same probability of being thrown, so that if E is the set of six sides, the function

$$p(x) \equiv \tfrac{1}{6}$$

is a probability distribution over E and does obey $\Sigma_{x \in E} p(x) = 1$. A 3 and a 2 cannot both be thrown; so the probability of 3 *or* 2 is $\frac{1}{6} + \frac{1}{6} = \frac{1}{3}$. Finally, suppose the die is thrown twice. One throw has no effect on the probabilities at the next throw, so the probability of a 3 followed by a 2 is $\frac{1}{6} \times \frac{1}{6} = \frac{1}{36}$.

ON PROOFS IN MATHEMATICS. A mathematical development begins by laying down certain definitions, as we have done in our definitions of union, subset, and so forth. From these definitions, other properties of the objects defined may be deduced. This is a mathematical proof. An example is our earlier proof that there is only one empty set. We did not set this out formally. Had we done so, we might have written:

Theorem
There is not more than one empty set.
Proof: Suppose A and B are empty. If $A \neq B$, then by our definition of equality between sets, one of the sets A, B must contain an element not contained in the other. But this is impossible, since both are empty, that is, contain no elements. Therefore, it cannot be true that $A \neq B$; therefore, $A = B$.

This is known as an *indirect* proof. It proceeds to prove a thing by supposing the opposite is true: that we have two sets A, B, both empty, such that $A \neq B$. From this supposition it deduces a contradiction: either A or B contains an element. This shows that we cannot suppose the theorem is not true, since to do so leads to contradiction. Therefore, the theorem must be true.

Another method of proof is called *inductive*. In its simplest form, this proves a proposition about any positive integer n by proving first, that the proposition is true for $n = 1$. Then it proves that if the proposition is true for some given integer (say, $n = r$), then it must be true for the next integer ($n = r+1$). These two proofs combined give us the proof for all n. For example, to prove that the sum of the first n integers is $n(n+1)/2$, first note that the sum of the first *one* integer is $1 = 1(1+1)/2$, so that the formula is true for $n = 1$. Next, assume it is true for $n = r$. Then the sum of the first r integers is $r(r+1)/2$. Add to this $r+1$, and we obtain, by ordinary addition, $(r+1)(r+2)/2$. This is the formula for $n = r+1$, however.

Sometimes we wish to prove that something exists. For example, do equilibria exist in every game? They do not. Do they exist in every game of a certain type? Yes. To prove that something *exists* is equivalent to proving that a certain set (here the set of equilibria) is nonempty. Usually we do this by constructing (showing how to find) an element of this set.

Sometimes we wish to prove that something (for example, the empty set) is *unique*. This is equivalent to showing that a certain set (the set of empty sets) has only one member.

Sometimes we wish to show that one thing follows from another, for example, a game with such and such a property p must also have a property q. This amounts to proving q given p, that is, proving that

$$p \Rightarrow q$$

or, equivalently, to proving that the set $P = \{x \mid x \text{ has property } p\}$ is a subset of $Q = \{x \mid x \text{ has property } q\}$. This is also described by saying that p is a *sufficient condition* for q, or by saying that q is a *necessary condition* for p, both of which phrases just say that we cannot have p without q.

Sometimes we can show that p is not only necessary but also sufficient for q. This means

$$p \Leftrightarrow q$$

or

$$P = Q.$$

Such a theorem is called a *characterization theorem* for q; it characterizes the conditions for the truth of q by proving that these are precisely p. To prove such a theorem we must of course show that q follows from p *and* p from q.

Appendix B
Experimental
Results

FIRST BATCH OF EXPERIMENTS. Most of these experiments were run under single-shot, noncooperative conditions, since these seemed the conditions most likely to prove the theory false. The games used were 2×2 games. Subjects were separated physically and never saw or knew the identity of their opponent.

The hypothesis being tested was that a subject's anticipated outcome would be a metarational outcome for him. This implied that an *actually stable* outcome (one anticipated by both players) would be a general equilibrium. It was therefore a stronger hypothesis (one more likely to be falsified) than the hypothesis concerning actual stability.

The first requirement was an operational definition of an anticipated outcome. We obtained this by asking subjects what strategy they expected their opponent to choose before asking them what strategy they chose themselves. The outcome composed of the two strategies they wrote down was defined operationally to be their *anticipated outcome*.

This definition was not wholly satisfactory. It forced players to have an anticipated outcome. Theoretically, an anticipated outcome should be a strategy choice plus the assumption (concerning the other's strategy choice) upon which the strategy choice is based. There is no reason why an anticipated outcome should always exist; a subject need not base his choice on any (single) assumption concerning the other's choice. About halfway through the experiments we inserted a questionnaire asking subjects whether they had based their choice on their expressed "anticipation," but the results were not very informative.

In order that subjects should play the desired game, it was necessary to induce them to have the right preference ordering between the outcomes. They were paid different dollar amounts for each different outcome on the presumption that they would prefer more dollars to less. Nevertheless, after the subjects had studied the game and communicated (when written communication was allowed), they were asked to state their true preferences, whether these were in the straight dollar ordering or not. Again, we found this rather un-informative.

The experiments were not statistical in nature. Many different games were run under different conditions. The object was to try to falsify the theory, not to estimate any kind of "probability" that it would be true. The only statistical measure that was appropriate was related to the probability of experimental error, that is, the probability of error due to such things as clerical mistakes, confused understanding of the game, careless filling in of questionnaires, and so on. The ideal experiment is one in which this probability is zero, but the ideal can never be reached. Thus in a large number of experiments one must expect a few *apparent* falsifications. By making a crude assumption about experimental error—that it would lead to the four possible anticipated outcomes being chosen with equal probability—we could, given the number of experiments, estimate how much experimental error would have to be assumed if a given number of counterexamples were to be assigned to this cause.

This calculation was carried out as follows. Assuming the theory is true, the probability of an apparent falsification is the probability of an experimental error times the probability of an apparent falsification given an experimental error:

$$p(\text{fals.}) = p(\text{exp. error})\, p(\text{fals.}|\text{exp. error}).$$

Hence the estimate of experimental error is

$$p(\text{exp. error}) = \frac{p(\text{fals.})}{p(\text{fals.}|\text{exp. error})}.$$

In this equation the right-hand side is known. We have $p(\text{fals.}|\text{exp. error})$ = proportion of times that an experimental error will lead to a falsification.

For example, if two games are run such that in game 1 for player 1, 3 out of 4 possible anticipations would confirm the theory; in game 1 for player 2 and in game 2 for either player, 2 out of 4 possible anticipations would confirm the theory; then we have $p(\text{fals.}|\text{exp. error}) = \frac{7}{16}$.

Also we have p(fals.) = proportion of times that there has been a falsification.

For instance, if on running the above two games we obtain one falsification of the theory, p(fals.) = $\frac{1}{4}$.[1]

Hence the above experimentation must, if the theory is not to be regarded as false, be estimated to have had a probability of experimental error equal to

$$\frac{\frac{1}{4}}{\frac{1}{16}} = \frac{16}{28} = \frac{4}{7},$$

which is of course far too large—but only two games have been run. The estimate of experimental error must be taken over a fairly large number of experiments. When this is done, we regard the theory as confirmed if experimental error can be estimated at less than 5 percent.

The effect of this calculation, of course, is to multiply the proportion of failures of the theory by a factor that takes into account the weakness of the theory. Above we failed one in four times; but this was multiplied till it became four out of seven times.

In some games subjects were allowed written communication. In others no communication was allowed. Conditions of information concerning the opponent's payoffs were also varied. Sometimes subjects knew each other's dollar payoffs, sometimes they knew only the dollar ordering of the other's payoffs, at times they were told nothing about the other's payoffs (though in these games they were always allowed to communicate, or they would have had no basis on which to form an anticipation as to what the other would do), and at other times they were misinformed about the other's dollar payoffs.

A number of experiments were also run in which subjects effectively played in a complete metagame matrix—that is, in the game $12G$ or $21G$. In these experiments one subject had to state a policy to the other, who then made an ordinary basic choice. In order to allow the subjects to explore the metagame matrix, the first subject was then allowed either to accept the other's choice or to state another policy. This continued until the first subject was satisfied. We called these experiments "games with *certainty*"—the "certainty" being the

1. Each player separately can falsify the theory. Hence two games provide four tests of theory.

certainty of being able to follow a policy in the metagame matrix.

The hypothesis being tested in these experiments was that the final stated policy of the policy-choosing player would be a policy making the final outcome metarational for the other; that is, that in the end the other player would maximize along the policy-chooser's policy. Also, the final outcome would be undominated.

By way of illustration we describe what happened in three actual experiments. Then we shall discuss the results of the experiments.

The first experiment we shall describe is one of the few in which a player's anticipated outcome, though it was metarational, was not symmetric metarational for him.

EXPERIMENT NO. 8' (the numbering of the experiments is given later in the appendix). Players Blue and Red were each shown the payoff matrix in Figure B.1 (payoffs in dollars). Each had full knowledge of the other's payoffs. Before making their choices they exchanged the following written messages.

Blue (who judging by his accent and appearance was a foreign student from a Far Eastern country): If we choose 1–1, we will get the maximum total gain, what do you think!

Red (an American. Both subjects appeared to be over 25): Since I'm a selfish bastard, I naturally want to maximize *my* gain.

Blue: Sorry to hear this, my choice will be "0," what a mess!

Red: I know very well that you're going to choose "0"—except of course, you want to make some money.

Blue: (chooses not to answer).

Red: (on being told that Blue does not wish to answer): You've got to choose "0" and I've got to choose "1." So far, no risk. But now you're better off voting "1"—if you think I won't change to "0." In any case, the point at which things get hot for you is clearly indicated—right?

	$	Red 0	Red 1
Blue	0	41	22
	1	14	33

Figure B.1. Payoff Matrix in Experiment No. 8'.

Blue: In my case, the choice (if I don't trust you) will be obvious "0," since the first row add[2] up to six $(4+2 = 6)$ and second row add up only to four.

Too bad you destroy my confidence to human being's goodwill in general.

Red: You miss the point—you don't have to trust me. I repeat—I'm out to maximize *my* net gain.

Blue: Yes, I am going to maximize my "expectance," you are going to maximize yours, that means "0–1."

I think the "1–1" choice can only be achieved through mutual trust.

Red: I agree.

Having finished communication, the subjects stated their preferences between the outcomes. Neither gave his preferences in the straight dollar ordering. Blue gave the preference order "11, 00, 10, 01," with the explanation "I aim at the maximum 'total.'" Red gave the order "11, 10, 01, 00," explaining: "Obviously, the gross benefit of (10) is greater to me. But I attach a positive value—in this case 1 unit—to the ability to convince the opponent that he ought to vote (11) (he would *never* vote (10))."

Each subject then said what he expected the other to choose and what he himself chose. The (01) result turned out to be the expected outcome for both subjects (and was therefore the actual outcome). This was symmetric metarational for Red (whose min max payoff was 2) but not for Blue (whose min max was 3). If we consider, not their dollar ordering, but their stated preference ordering, the stable outcome (01) was again symmetric metarational for Red but not for Blue, who actually opted for the outcome to which he assigned least preference. However, the stable outcome was a general metarational outcome for both players if we consider their dollar payoffs.

EXPERIMENT NO. 21'. In this example the game is chicken (the "Cuba" game of Section 6.4). The subjects were shown the payoff matrix in Figure B.2. The subjects knew each other's payoffs. No communication was allowed. After studying the matrix, the subjects stated

2. Blue's messages contained several grammatical errors.

		Red	
		0	1
Blue	0	33	24
	1	42	11

Figure B.2. Experiment No. 21′.

		Red	
		0	1
Blue	0	02	35
	1	13	51

Figure B.3. Experiment No. 39.

straight dollar orderings as their preference orderings among the outcomes. They then stated their expectations and their choices. Blue's expected outcome was (10). Red's expected outcome was (00). Thus both subjects were symmetric metarational.

EXPERIMENT NO. 39. Subjects were ignorant of each other's payoffs and played under conditions of "certainty." Their actual payoffs are shown in Figure B.3. The exchange began with Blue stating a policy.

Blue: 1, 1 (that is, "I will always choose 1.")
Red: 0
Blue: 1, 0 (that is, "If you choose 0, I choose 1. If you choose 1, I choose 0.")
Red: 1
Blue: 1, 1
Red: 0
Blue: 1, 1
Red: 0
Blue: 1, 0
Red: 1

Preferences were in the straight dollar ordering.

RESULTS OF THE EXPERIMENTS. Figure B.4 shows the number of experiments run in each category.

	Communication	No Communication	Certainty	Totals
Full information about other's payoffs	26	38	6	70
Knowledge of ordering of other's payoffs	6	2	8	16
Ignorance of other's payoffs	12	0	6	18
Misinformation about other's payoffs	2	0	2	4
Totals	46	40	22	108

Figure B.4. Number of Experiments in Each Category.

No experiments were run under Ignorance/No Communication as the subjects would have had no basis on which to anticipate their opponent's choice. Nor were games run under Misinformation/No Communication, as experimentally these would not have differed from Full Information/No Communication conditions. Apart from this we concentrated on games and conditions that would test the theory most rigorously.

Each experiment without certainty provided two trials of the metagame prediction, since each player's anticipated outcome had to be metarational for him. There were therefore 172 trials of the "anticipated outcome" prediction and 22 trials of the "policy" prediction (that in games with certainty the other player would finally maximize along the policy-chooser's policy).

METAGAME PREDICTIONS. There were no counterexamples to the metagame predictions in either the 172 trials without certainty or the 22 trials with certainty.

"RATIONAL" PREDICTION. The prediction that only equilibria can be stable, translated into terms of the experiments without certainty would mean that a player's anticipated outcome should be rational for him. This prediction was falsified 34 times in 172 trials. Since random experimental error (assumed to be such that each outcome is chosen with equal probability as the anticipated outcome) would lead to this prediction being confirmed 50 percent of the time, our estimate of experimental error must be $2 \times 34/172 \approx 40$ percent if we are not to regard this prediction as false. We must believe that the experiments "went wrong" 40 percent of the time.

In the games with certainty, the "rational" prediction was the same as the metagame prediction and was not falsified in 22 trials.

"SECURITY LEVEL" PREDICTION. The metagame prediction in the games without certainty is weak. Random experimental error would lead to its being confirmed 75 percent of the time in many of the games we used. In a large majority of trials it in fact amounted to saying that a player's anticipated outcome would not be the outcome yielding him his smallest payoff. Of course, this alternative "explanation" of the results is not an explanation at all and does not account for the confirmation of the "policy" prediction in the games with certainty. It suggests, however, the "theory" that players always maximized their "security level" in the games without certainty, that is, chose the strategy not containing their smallest payoffs. This was falsified 63 times in 172 trials.

"SYMMETRIC METARATIONALITY" PREDICTIONS. An alternative interpretation of metagame theory would predict that only symmetric metarational outcomes will be anticipated. This was falsified only 5 times and could be accepted if we were willing to accept that experimental error ran at about 8.2 percent. It is not very convincing in general, however. Far more convincing on general grounds is the prediction that only symmetric metarational outcomes will be anticipated when a symmetric equilibrium exists. This was falsified 3 times. It had a 62 percent chance of being confirmed by random experimental error, and can be accepted as confirmed if we are willing to believe that about 4.5 percent of the experiments without certainty "went wrong."

In any case, we regard these results as confirming the strength of symmetric rationality, though we must recall that the experiments were not statistical and cannot be interpreted as providing estimates of "proportions" or probabilities of occurrence.

SUBSIDIARY QUESTIONNAIRES. Two subsidiary questionnaires were given to subjects in the experiments without certainty. The first asked them to state their preferences; the second asked whether their choice was based on their "anticipation" of the other's choice. No positive findings resulted from the answers: 172 subjects answered the first questionnaire, 17 of whom stated preferences different from the "straight" dollar ordering. Eight of these disobeyed the "rational" prediction out of 34 disobeying it; 9 obeyed the "rational" prediction out of 138 obeying it. This does not "save" the "rational" prediction, since there remain 26 players claiming straight dollar preferences who disobeyed the "rational" prediction; and we recall again that no conclusions regarding "proportions" or probabilities of occurrence can be drawn from these figures. Only 80 subjects were given the second questionnaire. It was biased against the subjects claiming not to have based their choice on their anticipation, but 7 subjects claimed not to have done so. All 7 of these obeyed the "rational" prediction.

To sum up: the metagame prediction that an anticipated outcome will be metarational for the player was confirmed in 172 trials; the prediction that a player will maximize along the other's policy was confirmed in 22 trials.

The prediction that an anticipated outcome will be rational for the player was falsified in 34 out of 172 trials. The prediction that a player will maximize his "security level" was falsified in 63 out of 172 trials.

The prediction that, if a symmetric equilibrium exists, a player's anticipated outcome will be symmetric metarational for him and otherwise will be metarational was falsified in only 3 out of 172 trials.

There follows a list of all the experiments and their results. They are grouped according to the conditions under which they were run. The numbers given to the experiments indicate the order in which they took place. The experiments x and x' (as, for example, 7 and 7') took place simultaneously, and except in the case of games with misinformation, consisted of the same game run under the same conditions. This was a result of the way the experiments were organized. Four subjects, *a*, *b*, *c*, and *d*, were invited on a single evening. Subject *a* met only with *b*, and *c* only with *d*. Subjects *a* and *b* first practiced playing a certain game together, while subjects *c* and *d*, in a separate room, practiced the same game; then, using this game, *a* played experiment *x* with *c* while *b* played experiment *x'* with *d*. In this way subjects had an opportunity to practice each game they played although they never met their actual opponent and never played against the same opponent twice. In the case of games with misinformation it was necessary that the game practiced should not be the same, as regards the opponents' payoffs, as the game played, although the subject had to think it was the same. This was achieved by making the practice games different from each other, although each subject had the same payoffs in his actual game as in his practice game. This had the further effect of making *x* different from *x'*.

The letters *r* and *b* inserted in cells of the payoff matrices indicate the recorded anticipated outcomes of Red and Blue when that experiment was run. From these, of course, the actual outcome can be deduced if we recall that Blue chooses from the rows and Red the columns. In the experiments with certainty, asterisks mark the final policy of the player (always row-player) that had to choose a policy, while a letter "0" marks the outcome (belonging to that policy) finally chosen by column-player. The numbers indicate payoffs in dollars.

Full Information/Communication

1	4 2 ^b|^r 1 3			1'	4 2	1 3
	3 4	2 1				3 4 ^{br}| 2 1
8	4 1	2 2			8'	4 1 |_{br} 2 2
	1 4 ^{br}| 3 3				1 4	3 3
10	4 1 _b	_r 2 3			10'	4 1 _b	_r 2 3
	1 4	3 2				1 4	3 2
12	1 3 _r| 4 2			12'	1 3	4 2
	2 4 ^b	3 1				2 4 ^{br}	3 1
28	2 1 |_b 4 2			28'	2 1	4 2
	1 3	^r 3 4				1 3 ^{br}	3 4

```
30     2 1 | 4 2            30'    2 1 | 4 2
       3 4 br| 1 3                 3 4 br| 1 3

32     2 1 |b 4 2           32'    2 1 |r 4 2
       1 3 |r 3 4                  1 3 |b 3 4

34     2 1 b|r 3 2          34'    2 1 | 3 2
       1 4 | 4 3                   1 4 r|b 4 3

36     1 1 |r 4 2           36'    1 1 | 4 2
       2 3 |b 3 4                  2 3 |br 3 4

40     3 0 | 5 2            40'    3 0 | 5 2
       4 3 br| 2 1                 4 3 br| 2 1

47     1 1 | 4 2            47'    1 1 | 4 2
       3 4 br| 2 3                 3 4 br| 2 3

3      4 2 b|r 1 4          3'     4 2 b|r 1 4
       2 3 | 3 1                   2 3 | 3 1

51     3 1 b| 2 4           51'    3 1 | 2 4
       1 3 |r 4 2                  1 3 r|b 4 2
```

Ordering/Communication

```
42     0 1 |b 5 2           42'    0 1 | 5 2
       3 3 r| 4 0                  3 3 br| 4 0

44     2 1 | 4 2            44'    2 1 |b 4 2
       1 4 |br 3 3                 1 4 r| 3 3

53     2 1 |b 3 4           53'    2 1 | 3 4
       1 2 |r 4 3                  1 2 |br 4 3
```

Ignorance/Communication

```
4      2 3 |br 3 4          4'     2 3 |b 3 4
       4 2 | 1 1                   4 2 r| 1 1

31     2 1 | 4 2            31'    2 1 |b 4 2
       1 3 |br 3 4                 1 3 |r 3 4

33     2 1 | 3 2            33'    2 1 b|r 3 2
       1 4 |br 4 3                 1 4 | 4 3
```

```
38      4  4 br| 1  2          38'     4  4 br| 1  2
       ----------------               ----------------
        2  1  | 3  3                   2  1  | 3  3

46      1  0  |br 3  3         46'     1  0  |br 3  3
       ----------------               ----------------
        2  2  | 0  1                   2  2  | 0  1

49      0  0  |b 5  1          49'     0  0  | 5  1
       ----------------               ----------------
        1  5 r| 2  2                   1  5 |br 2  2
```

Misinformation/Communication

```
        Blue's Perception       Actual              Red's Perception
14      4  1 | 1  4          4  4 | 1  2          1  4 | 2  2
       -------------        -------------        -------------
        2  2 | 3  3          2  1 |rb 3  3         4  1 | 3  3

14'     1  4 | 2  2          1  1 |r 2  4          4  1 | 1  4
       -------------        -------------        -------------
        4  1 | 3  3          4  2 |b 3  3          2  2 | 3  3
```

Full Information/No Communication

```
2       4  2  | 1  4          2'      4  2 b|r 1  4
       ----------------               ----------------
        2  3 r|b 3  1                  2  3  | 3  1

6       2  1  |br 3  2         6'      2  1  |br 3  2
       ----------------               ----------------
        4  3  | 1  4                   4  3  | 1  4

7       2  1 b| 3  2          7'      2  1  |r 3  2
       ----------------               ----------------
        1  4  |r 4  3                  1  4  |b 4  3

9       4  3 br| 1  4         9'      4  3 b| 1  4
       ----------------               ----------------
        2  2  | 3  1                   2  2 r| 3  1

15      2  1  |b 3  2         15'      2  1 b| 3  2
       ----------------               ----------------
        1  4 r| 4  3                   1  4 r| 4  3

16      4  1 b| 2  2          16'      4  1  | 2  2
       ----------------               ----------------
        1  4  |r 3  3                  1  4  |br 3  3

17      4  3 r| 1  4          17'      4  3 b|r 1  4
       ----------------               ----------------
        2  2 b| 3  1                   2  2  | 3  1

18      2  1  |b 3  3         18'      2  1  |b 3  3
       ----------------               ----------------
        1  4 r| 4  2                   1  4 r| 4  2

19      2  1  | 3  4          19'      2  1  |r 3  4
       ----------------               ----------------
        1  3 r|b 4  2                  1  3  |b 4  2
```

```
20      3  1 |br 2  2          20'     3  1 |b  2  2
        ─────────────                  ─────────────
        4  3 |   1  4                  4  3 |r  1  4

21      3  3 r|b 2  4          21'     3  3 r|  2  4
        ─────────────                  ─────────────
        4  2 |   1  1                  4  2 b|  1  1

22      4  1 |r  2  2          22'     4  1 |b  2  2
        ─────────────                  ─────────────
        3  3 b|  1  4                  3  3 |r  1  4

23      4  3 |r  2  4          23'     4  3 r|b 2  4
        ─────────────                  ─────────────
        1  1 |b  3  2                  1  1 |   3  2

24      3  1 |r  2  2          24'     3  1 |br 2  2
        ─────────────                  ─────────────
        4  3 b|  1  4                  4  3 |   1  4

25      2  1 |br 3  2          25'     2  1 |br 3  2
        ─────────────                  ─────────────
        4  3 |   1  4                  4  3 |   1  4

26      1  1 |b  4  2          26'     1  1 |b  4  2
        ─────────────                  ─────────────
        2  3 |r  3  4                  2  3 |r  3  4

29      3  1 |   2  2          29'     3  1 |   2  2
        ─────────────                  ─────────────
        1  4 |br 4  3                  1  4 |br 4  3

45      3  3 |   1  4          45'     3  3 b|  1  4
        ─────────────                  ─────────────
        4  1 |br 2  2                  4  1 |r  2  2

52      4  0 |   2  4          52'     4  0 |r  2  4
        ─────────────                  ─────────────
        1  3 |br 3  2                  1  3 |b  3  2
```

Ordering/No Communication

```
41      1  2 |br 2  4          41'     1  2 b|r 2  4
        ─────────────                  ─────────────
        0  5 |   3  3                  0  5 |  3  3
```

Full Information/Certainty

```
11      3  3 *0| 2  4          11'     3  3 *0| 2  4
        ─────────────                  ─────────────
        4  2 |*  1  1                  4  2 |*  1  1

13      4  1 *0|* 3  0         13'     4  1 *0|* 3  0
        ─────────────                  ─────────────
        1  3 |   2  5                  1  3 |   2  5

37      3  3 *0| 1  4          37'     3  3 *0| 1  4
        ─────────────                  ─────────────
        4  1 |*  2  2                  4  1 |*  2  2
```

Ordering/Certainty

```
5      4  3 *| 2  0            5'     4  3 *| 2  0
       0  2 |*○3  5                   0  2 |*○3  5

27     1  1 |* 3  2            27'    1  1 |* 3  2
       4  3*○| 2  4                   4  3*○| 2  4

48     1  0 |* 5  2            48'    1  0 |* 5  2
       3  3*○| 2  4                   3  3*○| 2  4

50     4  1 *| 2  3            50'    4  1 *| 2  3
       1  4 |*○3  2                   1  4 |*○3  2
```

Ignorance/Certainty

```
35     1  1 *|*○3  4           35'    1  1 *|*○3  4
       2  3 |  4  2                   2  3 |  4  2

39     0  2 |*○3  5            39'    0  2 |*○3  5
       1  3 *| 5  1                   1  3 *| 5  1

54     1  1 |* 4  2            54'    1  1 |* 4  2
       3  3*○| 2  4                   3  3*○| 2  4
```

Misinformation/Certainty

```
43     Blue's Perception       Actual              Red's Perception
       1  2 | 3  4             1  1 |* 3  2         3  1 | 4  2
       4  1 | 2  3             4  3*○| 2  4         1  3 | 2  4

43'    3  1 | 4  2             3  2 *|*○4  4        1  2 | 3  4
       1  3 | 2  4             1  1 | 2  3          4  1 | 2  3
```

REACTION GAME EXPERIMENTS. The experiments just described were conducted at the Management Science Center, University of Pennsylvania, during 1966. In 1967 and 1968 "reaction game" experiments, initiated by A. Ducamp, were conducted at the Management Science Center. We briefly describe some of these.

In the first reaction game experiments two players were involved. Each player was presented with a payoff matrix which, as illustrated in Figure B.5, showed his own dollar payoffs and the rank ordering

	C	D	E
R	(5) $2.50	(1) $0.50	(3) $4.50
S	(4) $3.50	(9) $1.00	(6) $2.00
T	(2) $0.75	(7) $1.50	(8) $1.25

Figure B.5. "Reaction Game" Experiment. Row-player was shown this matrix.

of his opponent's payoffs. The players were not asked to make a final choice immediately. They were told by a referee that they would begin at a certain outcome of the matrix. They were given five minutes in which to bargain by passing messages to one another via the referee, indicating that they were changing their choice of a row or column. After any such move the players were considered to be at the outcome that lay at the intersection of the new row and column, and the next move used this as a starting point. There was no restriction on the order in which the players moved; the only condition imposed was that two moves could not occur at the same time.

After five minutes the referee indicated that the first bargaining period was over, and players were asked whether they would accept or reject the outcome arrived at. If either player rejected this outcome, the bargaining process was repeated for a period of approximately three minutes, and again the players were asked whether they accepted the new outcome. If agreement was not reached, the players carried out a third and final bargaining process. If both players did not accept the resulting outcome they played a one-shot game using the same matrix (that is, as earlier, a game in which the players simultaneously and independently chose a single row or column and were paid according to the outcome). Both players knew what the total procedure would be before they started the game, and indeed a practice game was played (with a different opponent) before the experiments began.

Another series of experiments was run in which players knew nothing (not even the ordering) of their opponent's payoffs. The matrix they were given was as illustrated in Figure B.6. Due to this lack of information the length of each bargaining period was doubled.

	C	D	E
R	— $2.00	— $4.00	— $0.50
S	— $5.00	— $1.00	— $6.50
T	— $7.00	— $0.00	— $6.00

Figure B.6. Reaction Game without Knowledge of the Other's Payoffs.

In these experiments, rejection of the outcome resulting from a bargaining process was always determined by a rejection level below which every outcome was rejected. The level was not a level of dollar payoff (this was tested by varying the dollar payoffs while keeping the ordering of outcomes the same) but was an ordinal level related to the structure of the game.

These results confirmed but were stronger than the predictions of metagame theory as presently formulated. They indicated, in fact, that (1) If symmetric equilibria exist, asymmetric equilibria will never be stable. (2) Even when no symmetric equilibria exist the level below which outcomes are rejected is higher than the "max min" level deduced by metagame theory.

Glossary of
Technical Terms

Actual Stability.
Each player choosing his strategy on the assumption that the other players will choose the strategies they do choose.

α-core.
The set of outcomes that are general metarational for every coalition.

Analysis of Options.
A method of analyzing real problems in which the "experts" build and analyze their own model, guided by an analyst.

Ancestor of the Metagame $H = k_1 \ldots k_r G$.
Any metagame of the form $k_s\, k_{s+1} \ldots k_r G$, where $s \geqslant 1$.

Anticipated Outcome.
The outcome determined by a player's own choice together with his prediction of the other players' choices.

Asymmetric Metarational Outcome.
An outcome that is general but not symmetric metarational.

Basic Game.
The game that models the real-world situation.

Basic Outcome.
An outcome in the basic game.

Basic Strategy.
A strategy in the basic game.

β-Core.
The set of outcomes that are symmetric metarational for every coalition.

β-Operator.
The function that takes a metagame outcome into the corresponding outcome of the immediate ancestor.

C-Cooperative Anticipation for a Player $i \in C$.
A joint metastrategy $\bar{x}_{N-i}$ such that $\forall x_i : (x_i, \bar{x}_{N-i}) \in R_i(H) \Rightarrow (x_i, \bar{x}_{N-i}) \in R_C(H)$.

Chance.
A fictitious player whose decision is determined by a probability distribution.

Coalition.
A nonempty subset of players.

Complete Metagame.
A metagame in which every player is named in the title at least once.

Conflict Point.
An outcome at which each player is holding out for an undominated equilibrium that suits him better.

Continuous Game.
A game in which each player chooses a number in a closed interval of the real line as his strategy choice.

Cooperative Game.
A game in which players can make binding agreements.

Credible Sanction.
A sanction that a player believes would be carried out against him if he made a particular choice of options.

Decision Node. A point in the game tree where players make decisions.

Descendant of a Metagame $H = k_1 \ldots k_r G$. Any metagame of the form $j_1 \ldots j_s k_1 \ldots k_r G$ where $s > 0$.

Determinate Game. A game in which every metarational outcome is symmetric metarational.

Dominates. An outcome s dominates t if s is preferred by every player.

Equilibrium. An outcome that is rational for every player.

Existentialist Axiom. An axiom that says that if certain factors affect a subject's choice behavior, and he is conscious of this, he may choose to make his behavior obey any function from the set of possible values of those factors to the set of his alternative choices.

Follows. A player k follows a player j in a metagame if $j \neq k$ and some occurrence of k's name follows (is further to the right of) some occurrence of j's name in the title of the metagame.

Follows Last. A player k follows a player j last in a metagame if k follows j in the prime representative of the metagame or if k but not j is named in the title of the metagame.

Fully Deteriorated Game. A game in which no further preference deterioration is possible.

Game of Coordination. A game in which an outcome rational for one player is rational for all players.

General Equilibrium. An outcome that is general metarational for every player.

General Metarational Outcome. A basic outcome that is metarational for a player from some metagame.

Induced Outcome. The outcomes induced by a strategy are those that are contained in the strategy and are rational for the other player.

Inducement. Action taken by a player that, if the others react rationally, will lead to a preferred outcome for himself.

Inducement Equilibrium. An outcome that is inducement rational for both players (in a two-person mutually ordinal game).

Inducement Metaequilibrium. A basic outcome that is yielded by an inducement equilibrium in some metagame.

Inducement Metarational Outcome.	A basic outcome that is yielded by an inducement rational outcome of some metagame.
Inducement Rational Outcome.	An outcome that is rational for a player and induces as much as any rational outcome open to him.
Inducement Value of a Strategy.	In a two-person mutually ordinal game, the value obtained if the other player reacts rationally.
Inescapable Improvement.	A unilateral move by a player that gives him a preferred outcome no matter what the other players do.
Inessential Coalition.	A coalition from which, if the coalition were formed, the members of that coalition would not gain.
Lexicographic Payoff Functions.	A sequence of payoff numbers modeling the fact that though a player's own payoffs may have greatest priority for him, nevertheless he will be influenced, lexicographically, by the others' payoffs whenever his own payoffs would reveal indifference.
Metaequilibrium.	An outcome of the basic game yielded by an equilibrium of some metagame.
Metagame.	A game derived from a given game by allowing one of the players to choose his strategy (in the given game) after the others in knowledge of their choices.
Metagame Equilibrium.	An outcome that is metarational for every player from some one single metagame.
Metaoptimal Outcome.	A basic outcome yielded by an outcome that is optimal in some metagame.
Metaoptimum.	A basic outcome yielded by an optimum of a metagame.
Metarational Outcome.	A basic outcome yielded by an outcome that is rational in some metagame.
Mixed Strategy.	A method of play whereby, instead of necessarily choosing a determinate strategy, a player chooses any probability distribution over his determinate strategies and allows his actual strategy choice to be determined from the probability distribution.
Mutually Ordinal Game.	A game in which a player is never indifferent between two outcomes unless all players are indifferent.
Noncooperative Game.	A game in which players cannot make binding agreements.

Numerical Utility.	A real number that is assumed to express the "degree of preference" a player feels for an outcome.
Objective Rationality.	Rationality in circumstances when all relevant information is known.
Ω-Set.	In the analysis of options, the set of options appearing at every stage of the analysis with the property that some assumption must be made about every combination of these options before that stage of the analysis can be called "complete."
One-Shot Game.	An experimental game in which players make their strategy choices simultaneously and independently.
Optimal Outcome.	An outcome that is rational for a player and also such that the player cannot induce more than he is getting.
Optimum.	An outcome that is optimal for both players.
Option.	A yes/no alternative open to a player. A strategy may be represented by a number of options that are either taken or not taken.
Ordinal Game.	A game in which all players have ordinal preferences.
Ordinal Preferences.	To say that a game has ordinal preferences means roughly that outcomes can be ranked in a certain order reflecting their preferences. There may be "ties" so that two or more outcomes occupy the same position in the preference ordering. Formally, a game has ordinal preferences if the not-preferred relation is reflexive, the preferred relation is transitive, and if when two outcomes are not preferred to each other, they bipartition the outcomes into "preferred" and "not preferred" in precisely the same way.
Outcome.	An n-tuple of strategies. A cell in the game matrix determined when each player chooses a strategy.
Particular Outcome.	In the analysis of options, the outcome that is being analyzed for its potential stability
Particular Player.	In the analysis of options, the player from whose point of view the given situation is being analyzed.
Partly Ordinal Game.	A game in which the not-preferred relation is reflexive and the preferred relation is transitive. This implies that there are no cycles in the preference graph—where a cycle is a path traced by preference arrows, that returns into itself.
Perfect Game.	A game that has an undominated equilibrium and in which for each player his sure-thing policy is maximally inducing.

Perfectly Optimal Outcome.	A basic outcome that is metaoptimal for a player from every metagame.
Perfect Optimum.	An outcome that is perfectly optimal for both players.
Player.	A conscious decision-maker.
Play of the Game.	A path through the game tree.
Policy.	A metagame strategy that is not a basic strategy.
Preference Deterioration.	A change in preferences brought about by the structure of the game itself or by the way in which it is played.
Preference Function.	A function from the set of all outcomes to the set of all subsets of outcomes. Let M_k stand for player k's preference function. Then $M_k s$ is interpreted as the set of all outcomes not preferred to s by k.
Prime Metagame.	A metagame in which any player is named (i.e., his name appears in the title of the metagame) at most once.
Prime Representative.	The prime metagame obtained by striking out all but the last occurrence (the one furthest to the right) of each player's name in the title of metagame.
Quasi Equilibrium	An outcome that is metarational for every player, but such that there is no single metagame from which it is metarational for all players.
Rational Decision-Maker.	A decision-maker that chooses the decision that yields him the most preferred result.
Rational Game.	A game G in which the inducement value of each player k's sure-thing metastrategy in kG is maximal.
Rational Outcome.	An outcome is rational for a player when, given the the strategy choices of the other players, he cannot obtain a preferred outcome.
Reaction Game.	A game used in experiments in which a player can change his strategy choice, thus allowing him to "react" to the strategy choices of the other players.
Saddle Point.	An outcome at which a player is doing the best he can for himself while the other players are doing the worst they can for him.
Sanction.	A joint strategy of the other players such that, should they carry it out, the player cannot in any way reach an outcome preferred to the particular outcome. If a sanction exists, the particular outcome is symmetric metarational for the particular player.

Strategy.	A complete plan of action covering all contingencies.
Subjective Game.	The game or metagame a player sees himself as playing in.
Subjective Rationality.	Rationality that is relative to a player's beliefs about the situation.
Sure-thing Strategy.	A strategy of a player such that no matter what the opponents choose, the outcome will be a rational one for the player.
Symmetric Equilibrium.	An outcome that is symmetric metarational for all players.
Symmetric Metarational Outcome.	An outcome that is metarational for a player from some descendant of any metagame.
Two-Person Zero-Sum Game.	A two-person game in which one player's preference function is the inverse of the other's. It is a game in which each player's motivation is solely to "harm" the other player.
Undominated Outcome.	An outcome such that no outcome is preferred to it by all players.
Unilateral Improvement.	A strategy by which if the other players' strategies remain fixed, a player improves his position.
Value of an Outcome.	In an ordinal game, the set of outcomes not preferred to the outcome by a player.
Value-outcome.	A list of values for all the players obtained from an outcome.
Well-behaved Game.	A game obeying certain general rules regarded as normal and typical.

References

Ackoff, R. L., and M. W. Sasieni 1968. *Fundamentals of Operations Research*, John Wiley & Sons, New York.

Arrow, K. J. 1963. *Social Choice and Individual Values*, 2nd ed., Cowles Commission Monograph 12, John Wiley & Sons, New York.

Aumann, R. J. 1959. "Acceptable Points in General Cooperative n-Person Games," in Tucker and Luce 1959, pp. 287–324.

——— **1961.** "The Core of a Cooperative Game without Side Payments," *Transactions of the American Mathematical Society* 98, 539–552.

Aumann, R. J., and M. Maschler 1964. "The Bargaining Set for Cooperative Games," in Dresher, Shapley, and Tucker 1964.

Aumann, R. J., and B. Peleg 1960. "von Neumann–Morgenstern Solutions to Cooperative Games without Side Payments," *Bulletin of the American Mathematical Society* 66, 173–179.

Borel, E. 1953. "The theory of play and integral equations with skew symmetrical kernels"; "On games that involve chance and skill of the players"; and "On systems of linear forms of skew symmetric determinants and the general theory of play," translated by L. J. Savage, *Econometrica* 21, 97–117.

Dresher, M., A. W. Tucker, and P. Wolfe, eds., 1957. *Contributions to the Theory of Games*, vol. 3, Annals of Mathematics Studies, 39, Princeton University Press, Princeton.

Dresher, M., L. S. Shapley, and A. W. Tucker, eds., 1964. *Advances in Game Theory*, Annals of Mathematics Studies, 52, Princeton University Press, Princeton.

Festinger, L. 1957. *Theory of Cognitive Dissonance*, Stanford University Press, Stanford, Calif.

Fraenkel, A. A. 1953. *Abstract Set Theory*, North-Holland Publishing Co., Amsterdam.

Harsanyi, J. C. 1959. "A Bargaining Model for the Cooperative n-Person Game," in Tucker and Luce 1959, pp. 325–355.

——— **1963.** "A Simplified Bargaining Model for the n-Person Cooperative Game," *International Economic Review* 4, 194–220.

——— **1964.** "A General Solution for Finite Non-Cooperative Games, Based on Risk-Dominance," in Dresher, Shapley, and Tucker 1964, pp. 651–679.

—— 1966. "A General Theory of Rational Behavior in Game Situations," *Econometrica* 34, 613–634.

—— 1967– 1968. "Games with Incomplete Information Played by 'Bayesian' Players," Part I, Part II, *Management Science* 14, 159–182, 320–334.

Howard, N. 1966a. "The Theory of Metagames," *General Systems*, Yearbook of the Society for General Systems Research, 11, 167–186.

—— 1966b. "The Mathematics of Metagames," *General Systems*, Yearbook of the Society for General Systems Research, 11, 187–200.

—— 1968a. "A Method for Metagame Analysis of Political Problems," *Papers*, vol. 9, Peace Research Society (International).

—— 1968b. "Metagame Analysis of Vietnam Policy," *Papers*, vol. 10, Peace Research Society (International); also in W. Isard, *Vietnam: Some Issues and Alternatives*, Schenkman Publishing Co., Cambridge, Mass., 1969.

—— 1968c. "The Theory of Metagames," Ph.D. Thesis, University of London.

—— 1969. "Comments on Harris' 'Comments on Rapoport's Comments,' " *Psychological Reports* 25, 826.

—— 1970a. "Note on the Harris-Rapoport Controversy," *Psychological Reports* 26, 316.

—— 1970b. "Some Developments in the Theory and Applications of Metagames," *General Systems*, Yearbook of the Society for General System Research, 15, 205–231.

Kuhn, H. W., and A. W. Tucker, eds., 1950. *Contributions to the Theory of Games*, vol. 1, Annals of Mathematics Studies, 24, Princeton University Press, Princeton.

—— 1953. *Contributions to the Theory of Games*, vol. 2, Annals of Mathematics Studies, 28, Princeton University Press, Princeton.

Luce, R. D., and H. Raiffa 1957. *Games and Decisions*, John Wiley & Sons, New York.

Management Science Center, University of Pennsylvania 1967. "A Model Study of the Escalation and De-Escalation of Conflict," mimeographed report ACDA ST-96, U.S. Arms Control and Disarmament Agency, Washington, D.C.

—— 1968.   "Toward a Quantitative Theory of the Dynamics of Conflict," mimeographed report ACDA ST-127, U.S. Arms Control and Disarmament Agency, Washington, D.C.

—— 1969a.   "Conflicts and Their Escalation: Metagame Analysis," mimeographed report ACDA ST-149, vol. 1, U.S. Arms Control and Disarmament Agency, Washington, D.C.

—— 1969b.   "The Analysis of Options: A Computer Aided Method for Analyzing Political Problems," mimeographed report ACDA ST-149, vol. 2, U.S. Arms Control and Disarmament Agency, Washington, D.C.

Maschler, M., and B. Peleg 1966.   "A Characterization, Existence Proof, and Dimension Bounds for the Kernel of a Game," *Pacific J. Math.* 18, 289–328.

Nash, J. F. 1950.   "The Bargaining Problem," *Econometrica* 18, 155–162.

—— 1951.   "Non-cooperative Games," *Annals of Mathematics* 54, 286–295.

—— 1953.   "Two-Person Cooperative Games," *Econometrica* 21, 128–140.

Peleg, B. 1966.   "The Independence of Game Theory of Utility Theory," *Bulletin of the American Mathematical Society* 72, 995–999.

Rapoport, A. 1967.   "Escape from Paradox," *Scientific American*, July 1967, 50–56.

Rapoport, A., and A. M. Chammah 1965.   *Prisoner's Dilemma*, University of Michigan Press, Ann Arbor.

Rapoport, A., and M. Guyer 1966.   "A Taxonomy of 2×2 Games," *General Systems*, Yearbook of the Society for General Systems Research, 11, 203–214.

Saaty, T. L. 1964.   "A Model for the Control of Arms," *Operations Research* 12:4, 586–609.

—— 1968.   *Mathematical Models of Arms Control and Disarmament*, John Wiley & Sons, New York.

Scarf, H. E. 1967.   "The Core of an n-Person Game," *Econometrica* 35, 50–69.

Shapley, L. S. 1953.   "A Value for n-Person Games," in Kuhn and Tucker 1953.

Stearns, R. E. 1964.   "Three-Person Cooperative Games Without Side Payments," in Dresher, Shapley, and Tucker 1964.

Thrall, R. M., and W. F. Lucas 1963. "N-person Games in Partition Function Form," *Naval Research Logistics Quarterly* 10, 281–298.

Tucker, A. W., and R. D. Luce, eds., 1959. *Contributions to the Theory of Games*, vol. 4, Annals of Mathematics Studies, 40, Princeton University Press, Princeton.

von Neumann, J. 1959. "On the Theory of Games of Strategy," in Tucker and Luce 1959, pp. 13–42; translated from "Zur Theorie der Gesellschaftsspiele," *Mathematische Annalen* 100, 295–320, 1928.

von Neumann, J., and O. Morgenstern 1953. *Theory of Games and Economic Behavior*, 3rd ed., Princeton University Press, Princeton. 1st ed. 1944.

Index